D0094880

Religion, Politics, and Diversity

The Church-State Theme in New York History

Religion, Politics, and Diversity

THE CHURCH-STATE THEME IN NEW YORK HISTORY

By John Webb Pratt

Cornell University Press

ITHACA, NEW YORK

CORNELL UNIVERSITY PRESS

First published 1967

Library of Congress Catalog Card Number: 67–12094

PRINTED IN THE UNITED STATES OF AMERICA
BY KINGSPORT PRESS, INC.

To GGP *and* EWP
Who Know Why

Preface

NEW YORK STATE, with its colonial origins, its great diversity, and its political complexities, provides one convenient starting point for a study of the main issues and forces that have helped to shape the relations of church and state not only in New York but in the nation at large.

The people of the United States have been unusually fortunate in avoiding many of the great evils of church-state contention that have shaken other lands. This has been due in large measure to their willingness and ability to settle church-state issues in ways that respect the vital interests on each side.

Because the framers of our Constitution saw no reason to disturb the conduct of religious affairs in the states, differences between religious groups and civil government have been regarded as state and local problems throughout much of our history. This is why it is important to understand how the states in our federal system have dealt with these differences. Only when we know something of this story can we deal meaningfully with the church-state question as it enters a new phase of national concern. I regard this survey as an invitation to others to begin the quest for such understanding.

Part One of this book, as a necessary prelude to what follows, discusses the roots of religious conviction and conduct, and their relation to government during the century and a half of New York's colonial existence. Part Two examines the church-state settlement worked out during the Revolutionary period by the framers of the state's first constitution. In the years following, as new problems unanticipated by the people of the eighteenth century have appeared, the Revolutionary settlement has undergone significant modifications. It is to these problems and to the efforts to deal with them that Parts Three and Four of this study are devoted.

Before proceeding, certain qualifications need to be made perfectly clear. This book is not meant to be a history of religion, or of the various denominations, or even of the politics of religion as such in New York. Neither is it intended as a survey of organized bigotry or nativism in the Empire State. My concern has been with those points in time where significant church-state problems have arisen and with the means employed to deal with these problems.

My obligations are many. I am deeply indebted to Professor Frederick Merk of Harvard University, now retired, both for introducing me to the rich materials of my subject and, unknowing as it was on his part, for his influence as one of the really fine gentlemen of my profession. I have benefited from the expert supervision of Professor Frank Freidel at Harvard while writing the portions of this study which later became my dissertation. Other portions of the book grew out of researches carried on under the direction of Professor Arthur E. Sutherland, Jr., during an exciting year at the Harvard Law School. My work, which is mainly one of synthesis, was a good deal less arduous because of the kindnesses of many librarians and archivists. A final revision and rewriting were made possible by grants from the Research Foundation of the State University of New York. Miss Barbara Ripel has been a great help to me with the last-minute chores of checking proof and preparing the index. Of course, none of these is responsible for the final result.

To my wife and children I can only apologize for the upset this book has all too often meant for them.

A portion of Chapter 7 originally appeared, in different form, in *New York History* and is reprinted by permission of the New York Historical Association, Cooperstown, New York. Other portions of the book, dealing with Boss Tweed, were originally published in the *New-York Historical Society Quarterly*.

J. W. Pratt

State University of New York at Stony Brook
May 1966

Contents

PART ONE

The Colonial Background

THE ideas of religious freedom and a separation of church and state, which received legal recognition at last in New York's first state constitution of 1777, were not the invention of that small group of patriots who framed this document. Neither were they the sole possession of the generation which fought the War for Independence. Like other compelling ideas which come to be accepted as fundamental truths, their roots ran far back into New York's colonial past. It is possible to see in retrospect that for a century and a half these principles had been slowly evolving toward their formulation in the new state's frame of government of 1777.

Almost from the beginning, under the Dutch flag, men and women had contested with their rulers for the right to worship freely according to the dictates of their consciences. Later, under English rule, after winning a *de facto* freedom of worship, New Yorkers began to move toward a sense of the usefulness of having church matters separated from matters of state. It was through their frequently bitter experience with an unbending and unpopular Anglican establishment, never supported by more than a small minority, that dissenters came to see that their worship could never be completely free until religion was independent of the whims and favoritisms of civil officials.

The framers of New York's first constitution merely gave legal force to convictions firmly implanted by time and experience in the minds of their fellow citizens.

I

The Dutch Trading Colony, 1624–1664

NEW YORK, called New Netherland during Dutch rule, was intended by the founding Dutch West India Company to be first and foremost a profit-making venture. Furs were its major commodity. In 1624 the first permanent settlement was located at Fort Orange, on the present site of Albany, where it could open up a fur trade with the Indians of the interior. New Amsterdam, the village raised in 1626 on the lower tip of Manhattan Island, was to be the shipping center and headquarters of the colony, linked with Fort Orange by the water route of the Hudson.[1]

New Amsterdam, laid out to resemble a native Dutch village, embodied the company's intentions to recreate the life of the homeland in the wilderness of the New World. At its center a stone fort sheltered the first buildings erected in the town: a governor's residence, barracks, offices, a jail with its gallows, and the inevitable gabled church with its squat tower barely rising above the other structures. Around the fort were house and farm lots, intended for sturdy Dutch farmers, arti-

[1] I have followed Charles M. Andrews, *The Colonial Period of American History* (New Haven, 1934–38), III, 71–96; and David M. Ellis and others, *A Short History of New York State* (Ithaca, N.Y., 1957), ch. ii, for general background material in the opening pages of this chapter.

sans, tradespeople, and company officials who would administer the colony and manage its commercial affairs.

But New Netherland did not attract the numbers of Dutch settlers anticipated by the company. With never more than a tenuous hold upon the shores of New York Bay and the banks of the Hudson, the colony usually was on the verge of disaster. In 1664, when the English took over, there were only about eight thousand people in the entire colony, most of them residing in New Amsterdam or clustered in a few tiny villages in the surrounding countryside. The stable, prosperous life of the Netherlands was too attractive to Dutch burghers and farmers for them to venture on the uncertain and harsh existence offered to newcomers by the colony.

Other nationalities, however, took more kindly to the relative freedom and the generous land grants held out by the Dutch West India Company to lure settlers. Dissatisfied Englishmen crossed Long Island Sound from Puritan Connecticut to Long Island; French Protestants, Germans, and Scandinavians arrived in small numbers; Jewish refugees were grudgingly admitted. A visitor in 1643, the French Jesuit missionary Father Isaac Jogues, observed that "on this island of Manhate and in its environs there may well be four or five hundred men of different sects and nations."[2] The colony's governor, the director general, had told him that no less than eighteen languages were spoken there. These people, who came to live and work, brought their religions with them. Father Jogues reported that there were, "besides Calvinists, in the Colony Catholics, English Puritans, Lutherans, Anabaptists, here called Mnistes &c."[3]

In the lusty materialism, the always precarious situation of the company, the transplanted Dutch practices, and the polyglot population lay the conditions that were to shape the

[2] E. B. O'Callaghan, ed., *Documentary History of the State of New York* (Albany, 1849–51), IV, 21.

[3] *Ibid.*, p. 22.

relationships between New Netherland's government and its people, frequently in ways unintended by the parent company. Centrifugal economic, political, and religious pressures were loosed which the colony's administration, alternating between a ruthless quest for profits and efforts to build a stable community life, never was quite able to cope with.

In the Netherlands, the Dutch had an established church as closely bound to the government as the establishments of the other European states. The Dutch branch of the Calvinist faith, the Reformed church, was alone entitled by law to worship publicly. Its pastors, appointed by the church's governing bodies, were inducted into their clerical offices by Dutch magistrates. Local Reformed churches were supported by public funds derived from taxes levied on all the people. The state permitted liberty of conscience to other sects, but the law allowed no expression of this liberty in the form of public worship.

In practice, however, the Netherlands afforded a degree of religious tolerance unusual for that age. The country was the refuge of countless religionists driven from their homelands by the hounding zeal of religious conformity. It will be recalled that the Pilgrims, after they had fled England, dwelled for a time in Holland before coming to the New World. There were many such refugee sects. Their members were not persecuted, and even managed to worship together with the connivance of the Dutch authorities. In the major Dutch cities and towns a large and prosperous body of Lutherans had their own churches and ruling bodies all virtually unmolested by their neighbors of the Reformed faith.[4]

It was expedient for the government, called the States-General, and the merchant classes to avoid divisive internal conflicts over religion like those sweeping other European nations

[4] H. J. Kreider, *Lutheranism in Colonial New York* (New York, 1942), pp. 3–5.

in that century of cruel religious wars. A major objective of the Dutch nation at that time was to win commercial supremacy both in Europe and overseas. Religious disturbances could only have an unsettling effect upon trade and business. This material motive supported and justified the remarkably free and tolerant religious settlement of the seventeenth-century Netherlands.

The religious system of the Netherlands was among the institutional forms carried over to New Netherland by the Dutch. The colony, like the Netherlands, had its established Reformed church. Yet those practices favorable to dissenters, observed in the home country though lacking legal authorization, were not always so freely allowed in New Netherland. Because the colony was intended to be an efficient, disciplined trading center in a strange and unaccommodating wilderness, its leaders thought it essential to enforce existing social controls in a rigorous manner. The combination of a zealous Reformed clergy and a professional soldier-governor, Peter Stuyvesant, operated time and again to compel obedience to the letter of the laws governing religion at the expense of the liberal spirit of toleration that had diluted the force of these laws in the Netherlands. To these leaders the grim alternative was departure from familiar ways and dissolution of the colony.

Faced by conditions encouraging worldliness at the sacrifice of piety among their flock, and by an especially trying array of dissenters, the Dutch pastors of New Netherland were determined that the laws establishing their faith had to be strictly applied or else all was lost. Dominie Megapolensis, Reformed minister at New Amsterdam, wrote in 1655 defending his opposition to the admission of Jews:

We have here Papists, Mennonites and Lutherans among the Dutch; also many Puritans or Independents, and many Atheists and various other servants of Baal among the English under this Government, who conceal themselves under the name of Christians; it would create still further confusion, if the obstinate and immovable Jews came to settle here.[5]

Stuyvesant, whose army career had trained him to appreciate the importance of discipline and to obey his instructions to the letter, arrived in the colony in 1647 to find it near collapse. A horrible Indian uprising had been put down by the preceding governor, Willem Kieft, only after great loss of life and property. To the east, the English from Connecticut were continually encroaching on the colony. Internally, discipline and morality had fallen before the assaults of a rampant secularism encouraged by a succession of lax governors. There could be little respect for authority when former Governor Wouter Van Twiller chased the Dutch pastor with a drawn sword during his drunken rages, and Kieft sought amusement in discharging cannon on the green during church services. The new governor was astounded by the degree of alcoholic consumption, brawling, and Sabbath desecration that he found. In 1650 every fourth house in New Amsterdam was said to be either a tavern or grogshop.[6] Confronted with this grave threat to organized community life, Stuyvesant felt obliged to use every power at his command to save the tested instruments for maintaining order, including the Reformed church. A man of his times, he not unnaturally reacted as if orthodoxy, enforced morality, and suppression of dissent were the only alternatives to complete and utter political, economic, and moral dissolution.

The responsibilities of the secular and ecclesiastical authorities for religion in New Netherland were formidable and far-reaching. The States-General of the Netherlands, while retaining ultimate powers, was usually content to leave routine matters to the company, but it reserved authority to lay down

[5] E. T. Corwin, ed., *Ecclesiastical Records of the State of New York* (Albany, 1901–16), I, 335–36; hereafter cited as *Eccles. Recs.*

[6] A. V. Goodman, *American Overture: Jewish Rights in Colonial Times* (Philadelphia, 1947), p. 69.

general rules for the government of the colony if deemed necessary. As proprietor of New Netherland, the Dutch West India Company claimed the same civil powers over religion in the colony as did the States-General at home. These powers were exercised by a board of nineteen directors, located in Amsterdam, where a commanding group of shareholders exerted considerable influence over policy. This board supervised the administration of New Netherland and appointed its director general. Among their many powers, the directors possessed a full power of patronage over the church in the colony.[7]

In return for having given up the privilege of appointing church officers, the Dutch Reformed church demanded and received extensive ecclesiastical powers in New Netherland. The administration of these powers fell to the Amsterdam Classis, the governing body of the church residing in the city where the headquarters of the Dutch West India Company was located. Before they could go to New Netherland, Reformed ministers had to pass the inspection of the Classis as to their personal and ministerial qualifications. They were then presented to the directors of the company for the required approval and appointment by secular authority.[8]

The key figure in this system of control was the director general resident in New Netherland. It was to his attention that most religious matters came in the first instance. He usually decided these questions after consulting the colony's Dutch Reformed clergy, who were the local agents of the ecclesiastical authority residing with the church in the mother country. Often the clergy proposed, and the director general simply disposed. However, as an officer responsible directly to his company, the director general could, and sometimes did, oppose the suggestions of the Reformed ministers. This

[7] F. J. Zwierlein, *Religion in New Netherland* (Rochester, N.Y., 1910), pp. 38, 43–44.

[8] *Ibid.*, pp. 38–42; *Eccles. Recs.*, I, 38–39 and n.

tended to be the case when the demands of orthodoxy conflicted with the company's considerations of economic interest.

In any event, the director general made the day-to-day decisions with the help of an advisory council of company officials. These decisions were, in turn, subject to review by the directors. Much depended upon the personality of the particular governor and the conception of self-interest prevailing at any time among a majority of directors in Amsterdam. In the administration of Director General Stuyvesant, the tendency was for close co-operation with the church in New Netherland. But frequently the company in Amsterdam found it necessary to intervene to veto or ameliorate the stern religious measures resulting from the alliance of church and state in the colony.

An enumeration of the powers of the governor and his council reveals the pervasive nature of the church-state relation in New Netherland. Ministers and teachers appointed by the Amsterdam directors and commissioned by the Classis could not take up their offices until the director general had legally inducted them. When, as sometimes happened, the director general chose a Dutch Reformed minister directly, the action had to be approved by the appropriate civil and ecclesiastical authorities in the Netherlands.[9]

The people of the colony, with one major exception,[10] were obliged to support the ministers and teachers of the Dutch church through the payment of tithes. The tithes were a tax on land and the produce of the fields. They were difficult to collect and even when paid often did not measure up to anticipations; because of the attractions of the Indian trade

[9] Zwierlein, pp. 44–45; E. B. O'Callaghan and B. Fernow, eds., *Documents Relating to the Colonial History of the State of New York* (Albany, 1853–87), XIV, 395; hereafter cited as *Col. Docs.*

[10] The English branches of the Reformed religion; see below, pp. 12–14.

and the scarcity of labor much land remained uncultivated. The government of the colony sometimes dipped into its own treasury to pay church and ministerial expenses, or it could lay new taxes if the tenths proved insufficient.[11]

Tithes were administered by the magistrates of each town. Where townspeople were tardy in paying, the law provided for collection of the tax by distraint if necessary. To remain in arrears for church taxes ultimately subjected the offending party to arrest and fines.[12]

The director general and his Council "confirmed, approved, and commanded" the construction and maintenance of churches and their satellite schools.[13] Such institutions were considered important adjuncts of civil government in the task of inculcating sound rules of public morality. A set of instructions in 1661 to the magistrates of one town specifically directed them to make provisions "relative to the building of churches . . . and other similar public works." [14]

As in all Christian countries of that age, government controls extended to public morals which were closely and minutely supervised in the administration of Stuyvesant. Detailed laws regulating Sabbath observance were repeatedly enacted by the director general and Council. Blasphemy was a serious criminal offense, and those accused of it were brought directly before the governor and Council sitting as a court of original jurisdiction.[15] Minor church officials, such as deacons and overseers of the poor in the Dutch church, were ultimately responsible to the director general. Local magistrates could be required to produce proof of their adherence to the

[11] Zwierlein, p. 47; E. B. O'Callaghan, ed., *Laws and Ordinances of New Netherland, 1638–1674* (Albany, 1868), pp. 180–81.

[12] *Ibid.*, pp. 304–07; *Col. Docs.*, XIV, 395, 414.

[13] Zwierlein, p. 44. [14] *Col. Docs.*, XIII, 198.

[15] Zwierlein, pp. 44, 47–60; O'Callaghan, *Laws and Ord. New Neth.*, pp. 258, 328, 448; E. B. O'Callaghan, ed., *Calendar of Historical Manuscripts in the Office of the Secretary of State, Albany, N.Y.* (Albany, 1865–66), I, 198; *Col. Docs.*, XIII, 198.

Reformed faith and to swear to exercise and uphold it "and no other." It is to be noted, however, that this extreme degree of control over religion was more formidable in conception than in practice. Stuyvesant employed it more often than his predecessors, but usually only when local officials had been especially neglectful of the laws prohibiting dissenting religious services.[16]

The special position accorded the Reformed church in New Netherland from the beginning was formally confirmed in a charter negotiated by the States-General and the company in 1640. The relevant section of the charter reads:

> no other Religion shall be publicly admitted in New Netherland except the Reformed, as it is at present preached and practiced by public authority in the United Netherlands; and for this purpose the Company shall provide and maintain good and suitable preachers, schoolmasters, and comforters of the sick.[17]

This provision was broad enough to include English Calvinists, recognized by the Dutch church as fellow believers of the Reformed faith, and was intended to attract settlers from among the English Puritans.

But beyond this inducement, Stuyvesant was to draw a line short of allowing non-Reformed dissenters similar privileges of public worship. Organized dissenting worship was consistently opposed during Stuyvesant's tenure in the absence of express instructions from home. Dissenting sects in New Netherland, relying on Dutch practice rather than Dutch law, anticipated otherwise.

With church-state matters settled to the satisfaction of both the States-General and the company by the 1640 charter, a stable religious life for New Netherland was hopefully expected. But this reckoned without the strong dissenting im-

[16] Zwierlein, pp. 45–46, 101–02; O'Callaghan, *Calendar Hist. Mss.*, I, 146; O'Callaghan, *Laws and Ord. New Neth.*, p. 396; *Col. Docs.*, XIII, 196–97. [17] *Col. Docs.*, I, 123.

pulse in the colony fed by a growing influx of non-Dutch peoples. These people were attracted by the economic opportunities held out to them after the 1640 charter and by the seeming promise of a freer religious existence than Europe or New England offered.[18]

A chief purpose behind the charter of 1640 had been to strengthen the colony by encouraging population growth. The States-General feared that unless the population of New Netherland was increased, the colony would soon fall victim to growing English power on all sides. But numbers could not be built up until the West India Company relaxed its strict and exclusive controls over trade and the conditions of settlement. The effect of the policy delineated in the 1640 charter eventually was to open the internal trade of the colony to the competition of local inhabitants and to other friendly peoples who might be persuaded to emigrate there. As part of this policy, religious dissenters began to be admitted to New Netherland on the sufferance of the local authorities.[19]

The charter of 1640 coincided with the expansion of Puritan New England. Already Englishmen were moving into the area disputed by the Dutch and English along the New Netherland–Connecticut border and even into present-day Westchester and western Long Island, which were under Dutch

[18] Even communicants of the Dutch Reformed church, encouraged by the weakening of Old World restraints, developed New World expectations that clashed with the preconceptions and practices of the colony's government. In 1649, largely through the initiative of the Dutch element, a remonstrance was sent off to the States-General. Included in the list of grievances were abuses of religion attributed both to Kieft and Stuyvesant. See *ibid.*, pp. 271–318, 332–46; Zwierlein, pp. 78–81.

[19] Zwierlein, p. 70, 136–37, 141–42; E. B. O'Callaghan, *History of New Netherland* (New York, 1845–48), I, 208; O'Callaghan, *Calendar Hist. Mss.*, I, 68–69. Zwierlein, pp. 136–37, and his authority, O'Callaghan, *History New Neth.*, I, 200–03, err in dating the opening of trade in 1638. Liberalization of trade followed from the Charter of 1640; see *Col. Docs.*, I, 113–15, 119–23.

control. The English came into these last areas either with or without Dutch permission. Challenged by the Dutch, many of the new settlers applied for permission to remain and submitted to Dutch authority. After 1640, the Dutch actively encouraged these migrations by admitting the newcomers on equal terms with the older inhabitants.[20]

Among the English who took advantage of the liberalized terms for settlement in New Netherland were Calvinists of both the Presbyterian and Congregational persuasions, dissenters affiliated with no particular denomination, and some with no religion at all. They had left New England for many reasons. Some were on the losing side in doctrinal disputes within their former congregations; some with views too radical for the Puritan commonwealths were forced to leave; others came in search of material betterment. Many of the Presbyterians and Congregationalists arrived in organized groups with their own ministers and settled in towns of one or the other persuasion bordering on areas under English control. These groups were particularly welcomed by the Dutch, for it was believed that their settlements would act as buffers against further English expansion.

The Presbyterian and Congregational towns were allowed the free public exercise of their religion since the Dutch officials and clergy considered them to be of kindred belief. As recognized adherents of the Reformed religion, they came within the terms of the charter of 1640 permitting public worship. In addition, these towns were allowed to select their own magistrates and levy town rates for the support of their ministers and churches.[21]

The towns of Maspeth and Hempstead on Long Island were typical of those founded as a result of this policy. Maspeth was settled by a group of Presbyterians from Cohan-

[20] Zwierlein, pp. 143–44; *Col. Docs.*, I, 181, and XIII, 8.

[21] Zwierlein, pp. 144–46; *Col. Docs.*, II, 150–51, III, 37–39, XIII, 8; *Eccles. Recs.*, I, 192.

net (now Taunton), Massachusetts, led by their minister, Rev. Francis Doughty. Director General Kieft, in 1642, granted them a town patent that included the right "to exercise the Reformed Christian Religion and church discipline, which they profess." [22] The Revs. Richard Denton and Robert Fordham brought their Presbyterian flock from Stamford, Connecticut, to Long Island in early 1644 to establish the town of Hempstead. They received a patent very similar to Maspeth's by which church and state were closely linked. The town government in 1650 passed a Sabbath law requiring mandatory attendance of all inhabitants at the town's established English church; those who failed to appear were subject to fine. Seven years later Director General Stuyvesant gave this law the formal approval of the colony's government.[23]

English immigrants not of the Reformed religion received lesser privileges than their countrymen of the Reformed persuasion. They were permitted a liberty of conscience and allowed to conduct family worship in the privacy of their homes, but they could not keep a church or call a minister, and they were cautioned against disturbing the public peace. The communities of Flushing and Gravesend on Long Island typify the towns settled by this class of Englishmen. They received charters from the Dutch which granted their inhabitants a liberty of conscience, meaning that families might worship privately. But public worship was prohibited on the grounds that these dissenters did not conform in their beliefs to the Reformed religion.[24]

Non-Reformed sects, encouraged by the more relaxed reli-

[22] O'Callaghan, *History New Neth.*, I, 425; *Col. Docs.*, I, 426–27.

[23] B. F. Thompson, *History of Long Island*, 3d ed. (New York, 1918), II, 469–72; B. D. Hicks, ed., *Records of the Towns of North and South Hempstead, Long Island, New York* (Jamaica, N.Y., 1896–1904), I, 56–58.

[24] O'Callaghan, *Doc. Hist.*, I, 629–32; B. F. Thompson, III, 6–10; Zwierlein, pp. 161–62.

gious atmosphere in New Netherland after 1640, soon became dissatisfied with the mere grant of a liberty of conscience. Some began to press for broader privileges which, in effect, would have amounted to a complete freedom of worship for their own coreligionists. It was as if a little freedom had created expectations that could in turn be satisfied only by more freedom. Animating these dissenters was the conclusion that the freedom they were given to believe as they chose, in the privacy of their innermost thoughts, was small comfort when what their faith demanded of them was openly to proclaim the true way. At first, it is clear, this feeling took form as demands from particular dissenting sects for freedom for themselves. These claims for the most part evince little awareness that a sect can never feel secure so long as the state claims any broad power to distinguish between approved and disapproved forms of worship. But such awareness presupposes a frame of mind receptive to sectarian diversity, and to that age such a frame was alien to both established and dissenting sects alike.

The first formal dissenting requests for public worship in New Netherland came from the Lutherans, who had been among the earliest settlers in the colony. Some were native Dutch; others were of German and Scandinavian stock who had originally sought refuge in the Netherlands. Through the early years in the colony, the members of this sect had of necessity either to attend the Dutch churches or else stay away from services altogether. Fearing the loss of their religious identity, the Lutherans yearned for a church and pastor of their own. Understandably, they assumed that because the Lutheran church of the Netherlands functioned openly, they would be permitted to do the same in New Netherland.[25]

[25] Kreider, pp. 3–5; *The Lutheran Church in New York, 1649–1772: Records in the Lutheran Church Archives at Amsterdam, Holland* (New York, 1946), p. 36; Zwierlein, p. 187.

Between 1649 and 1653, Lutherans petitioned the governing body of their church in Amsterdam, the directors of the West India Company, and the States-General, pleading for permission to worship in public. But their hopes were in time dashed by a powerful opposition raised in the colony and communicated to the authorities in the mother country.[26] The Dutch clergy of New Netherland protested to their Amsterdam Classis against the Lutheran request. The Classis approached the company and received assurances that the Lutheran petitions would be rejected. The Classis and the directors agreed that any concession to the Lutherans might inspire other dissenters in the colony to demand the same privilege. As a result of these developments, all that the Amsterdam Lutherans could advise, solicitous as they were of their own ill-defined position, was that further petitions would be futile; it might be better if the Lutherans in the colony quietly called a minister without public sanction.[27]

The New Netherland Lutherans now organized private worship services under lay leadership. The local Dutch ministers again complained to the authorities. In early 1656, the governor and Council passed a strict ordinance against dissenting conventicles. It was clear that Stuyvesant and the Dutch clergy would have no such deviation from the religious statutes as was tolerated in the Netherlands. The Lutherans protested the harsh ordinance, which seemingly contradicted even the tacit policy of allowing private services, to the Lutheran Consistory in Amsterdam. It in turn sounded out friends among the company directors. These hinted, apparently more to avoid controversy than to clear up the issue, that there were grounds to expect authorization for public worship soon.[28] This intimation was given credence by an

[26] Kreider, pp. 14–15; *Lutheran Church in N.Y.*, pp. 16, 29.

[27] Kreider, pp. 15–16; *Eccles. Recs.*, I, 322, 324.

[28] Kreider, pp. 16–17.

official action of the directors. They wrote to Stuyvesant rebuking him for the 1656 ordinance and informing him that "hereafter you will not publish such a similar placat without our knowledge, but you must pass it over quietly and let them have free religious exercises in their homes." [29] But what the Lutherans interpreted as an allowance of formal worship in New Netherland actually was only a restatement of the old policy of overlooking unobtrusive private family worship.

Emboldened by the happy news from their Amsterdam Consistory, New Netherland Lutherans once more petitioned Stuyvesant in the fall of 1656. They asked him to be allowed to hold public services until a pastor arrived in the spring with the requisite formal permission from home. The director general ignored the petition. The Lutherans also sent an agent to Amsterdam, confidently expecting him to obtain the needed authorization as well as a minister. A pastor, Johannes Ernestus Gutwasser, was obtained by the Consistory to go to the colony, but he was destined to depart without the letters of approval that Stuyvesant insisted on seeing. The Amsterdam Lutherans continued to act, however, in the belief that their brethren would get by connivance what they could not get by law.[30]

Gutwasser's arrival at New Amsterdam in the summer of 1657 led directly to outcries from the Dutch clergy. The minister was called before the town officials, interrogated, and expressly forbidden to preach. On petition of the Dutch ministers, Stuyvesant and the Council went further and "requested" Gutwasser to return to Holland. When the Lutherans appealed for time,[31] Stuyvesant's reply was a new order commanding Gutwasser to leave on the next ship, "the more so as the Director General and Council consider this necessary

[29] *Col. Docs.*, XIV, 351.

[30] *Lutheran Church in N.Y.*, pp. 254–55; Kreider, pp. 17–19.

[31] *Ibid.*, pp. 19–20; *Eccles. Recs.*, I, 386–90, 393–94, 405–08.

for the glory of God, for the promotion of the Reformed religion, and the mutual tranquility, peace and harmony of this province."[32]

Rather than see their pastor banished before he had even preached to them, the Lutherans hid Gutwasser in the country, where for almost a year he conducted furtive services in the woods and fields. Meantime, another attempt to obtain relief in Amsterdam had failed. Illness forced Gutwasser back to New Amsterdam, where, on his recovery, the order for his deportation was executed.[33]

Despite this setback, the Lutherans once more pressed their claim. A last petition was forwarded to the company, but the directors had already written a letter to Stuyvesant upholding him. The letter also impressed upon him the wisdom of being less aggressive and more conciliatory, though this came as advice rather than an order. With this final blow, the Lutheran agitation collapsed. Writing privately to the Amsterdam Consistory in 1663, Henrick Bosch, a Lutheran, lamented that "although hope among us has not lessened . . . that someday we may be rightly helped, the fact is, alas, that many of the congregation begin to stray like sheep and that they dare not come together here to offer any sign of devotion, much less trust themselves jointly to sign a petition to your honors, for fear of being betrayed."[34]

During the last three years of the skirmish with the Lutherans, other assaults upon the ramparts of orthodoxy were being launched from entirely different directions. It is important to keep in mind that these struggles of church and state in New Netherland arose and flourished concurrently in the decade of the 1650's as a relaxed immigration policy and the inflexible rule of Stuyvesant repeatedly collided. While the authorities

[32] *Lutheran Church in N.Y.*, p. 31. [33] Kreider, p. 20.

[34] *Lutheran Church in N.Y.*, pp. 47–48; see also Kreider, p. 20, and *Col. Docs.*, XIV, 418, 421.

were stamping out the Lutheran threat, they were confronted by a grave Quaker heresy sweeping the English towns of Dutch Long Island. And all this time the defenders of the faith were fighting a rear-guard action with a despised and hated new element, the Jews.

Stuyvesant and the Dutch dominies were agreed that strict enforcement of the laws regulating religious practice was essential. Social stability depended upon it. But peace was not to be. Economic expediency, the Dutch reputation for tolerance, and an infusion of peoples to whom Dutch ways were alien militated against peace. Moreover, Stuyvesant and many of those under him were unfitted both by temperament and their situation to deal with the problem in moderation. The harassed Dutch authorities in New Netherland could see no alternative but to fall back upon the seeming certainties of force and suppression to counter the growing demands for a broader toleration of dissenting practices.

The first Quakers mentioned in the records appeared in the colony in 1657. They came ashore secretly at New Amsterdam in the month of August. This itself suggests a certain wariness of the reception they could expect if discovered.[35] As Bolsheviks were feared after the Russian Revolution of the twentieth century, so the very thought of Quakers frightened people in the seventeenth. Their refusal to swear to oaths was considered subversive; their passive resistance to civil authority was infuriating. To an age where few questioned the tie between religious orthodoxy and an orderly polity, such unorthodoxy was regarded with the same abhorrence directed in a later age against political subversion.

Two Quakers from the landing party, both women, had the misfortune to be moved by the Spirit in the streets of New Amsterdam and were collared and banished. Three male

[35] Zwierlein, pp. 213–14; *Eccles. Recs.*, I, 399–400; B. Fernow, ed., *The Records of New Amsterdam, from 1653 to 1674* (New York, 1897), II, 346–47.

members of the same party crossed over into Long Island. Two kept moving eastward, but the third, Robert Hodgson, sought a haven at Hempstead. For preaching in public, Hodgson was soon arrested for illegal acts in that Presbyterian community. Bound with ropes, and taken under guard to New Amsterdam, Hodgson was examined by the director general, convicted of "insolence" and unauthorized preaching, and heavily fined. Unable as well as unwilling to pay, the hapless Quaker was imprisoned and later beaten for failure to work. In time he was released, but only to be banished immediately from the colony.[36]

Hempstead as well as neighboring Gravesend, Jamaica, and Flushing were so stirred up by the Quaker enthusiasm that the director general and Council were impelled to take strong corrective measures. An ordinance was passed making any vessel bringing Quakers to the colony liable to confiscation; persons receiving Quakers in their homes were to be fined. The people of the dissenting hamlet of Flushing protested this, claiming an infringement of their charter and patent guarantees of a liberty of conscience after the custom of the Netherlands. The famous Flushing Remonstrance embodied their formal protests.[37]

The Remonstrance attacked the premises of the law against harboring Quakers. God alone, it said, is the rightful judge of matters of conscience, and should presumptuous men judge wrongly, "it is a feareful to fall into the handes of the liveing God[.] wee desire therefore in this case not to iudge lest wee be iudged neither to Condem least wee bee Condemed but rather to let every man stand and fall to his own." [38] Explaining that Flushing would not obey the anti-Quaker ordinance,

[36] Zwierlein, pp. 214–19.

[37] *Ibid.*, p. 219; J. R. Brodhead, *History of the State of New York* (New York, 1853–71), I, 637; *Col. Docs.*, XIV, 402–03.

[38] *Ibid.*, p. 402.

the petition pointed out that the State could properly enforce laws against religion only when religious acts directly threatened its perpetuation. In all else the "Lord hath taught . . . the Civill power to giue an outward libertie." The remonstrance then pointed to "the law of loue peace and libertie . . . extending to *Jewes Turkes* and *Egiptians* as they are Considered the sonnes of Adam which is the glory of the outward State of Holland." [39]

The Flushing Remonstrance is the first recorded plea in the history of New York that men of diverse faiths be permitted freedom to worship as they choose. But these broad views were premature where excitable officials balked at allowing even the degree of toleration countenanced in the Netherlands. Contrary to later tradition, the Remonstrance came to nothing.

Elsewhere, persons were fined in Gravesend and Jamaica for harboring Quakers and encouraging the citizens of Flushing to sign the Remonstrance.[40] In Flushing itself, town officials who prepared the petition were arrested and frightened into silence. The town charter was altered to give the Dutch a deciding voice in town affairs, and the dissenting townspeople were assessed quotas for the support of a Dutch Reformed minister.[41]

When these measures did not succeed entirely, and when Quakers reappeared in the towns in 1661, arrests, fines, and deportations followed. Soldiers were quartered on Jamaica, the center of the new outbreak, to harry dissenting leaders out of the colony and to assist newly appointed magistrates in extracting an anti-Quaker oath from the inhabitants. The next year, following further deportations, a sweeping new ordinance was passed against Quaker and other forbidden conven-

[39] *Ibid.*, p. 403. [40] *Ibid.*, pp. 405–08; Zwierlein, pp. 225–27.

[41] *Col. Docs.*, XIV, 403–09, 413; O'Callaghan, *Laws and Ord. New Neth.*, pp. 338–42.

ticles. Citizens were warned against assisting heretics or introducing their "seditious" writings into the colony.[42]

When Stuyvesant reported his actions to the Amsterdam directors, the latter once more felt compelled to intervene. Such stern measures would only frighten off potential immigrants and further impede the already faltering drive for profits. In a letter to the director general of April, 1663, he was advised to overlook the laws in cases of religious dissent, or at least not try to force people's consciences so long as they conducted themselves quietly. Stuyvesant was told that the custom of old Amsterdam, meaning the permitting of dissenting worship in private, was the wisest course to follow. After this, the governor relaxed his strenuous efforts to enforce orthodoxy and the religious controversy subsided, although the grievances that had produced it remained largely unremedied.[43]

The problem of the Jews was somewhat different from that of the Lutherans and Quakers. It reveals, as the other instances do not, the problems created by the clash of interests between the officials on the scene and company officers at home, as well as how these incompatibilities could work to the advantage of a religious minority when the latter possessed strategically placed spokesmen in the Netherlands.

Twenty-three Jews landed at New Amsterdam in September of 1654. They were refugees from the former Dutch holdings in Brazil recently seized by the Portuguese. Most of the possessions they brought with them had to be sold to pay their passage. With winter coming on, they found themselves alone and virtually penniless in a strange and hostile community.[44] The Reformed deacons of New Amsterdam, dispensers

[42] Zwierlein, pp. 230–42; *Col. Docs.*, XIV, 489–93; B. F. Thompson, I, 446–47; O'Callaghan, *History New Neth.*, II, 453–56, *Calendar Hist. Mss.*, I, 240, and *Laws and Ord. New Neth.*, pp. 428–30.

[43] Zwierlein, pp. 241–43; *Col. Docs.*, XIV, 526.

[44] Goodman, pp. 76–77.

of public charity, objected to allowing the Jews to stay for fear they would become public charges, which in fact they did become. Director General Stuyvesant, who thought of the Jews as usurers and dishonest businessmen, also wished to exclude them. But before acting, he wrote off to the Company for instructions. He advised that "the deceitful race—such hateful enemies and blasphemers of the name of Christ—be not allowed further to infect and trouble this new colony." [45]

The directors' reply was to deny the request. In their letter of April, 1655, there is a carefully phrased passage which reports their reasoning:

> We would have liked to effectuate and fulfill your wishes and request that the new territories should no more be allowed to be infected by people of the Jewish nation, . . . but having further weighed and considered the matter, we observe that this would be somewhat unreasonable and unfair, especially because of the considerable loss sustained by this nation, with others, in the taking of Brazil, as also because of the large amount of capital which they still have invested in the shares of this company.

The directors concluded that, after much deliberation, they would allow the Jews to "travel and trade to and in New Netherland and live and remain there." [46]

Nothing was said in these instructions about what should be done if the Jews asked for permission to hold worship. When Stuyvesant asked specifically for advice on this point, he was told that Jewish privileges did not extend to synagogue worship. But the next year, in a letter rebuking the director general for interfering with Jewish trading activities contrary to company orders, it was casually put to him that private worship for the Jews would be facilitated if they were encouraged to settle in their own quarter in New Amsterdam. In this fashion, Stuyvesant was informed that the Jews were to

[45] S. Oppenheim, *The Early History of the Jews in New York, 1654–1664* (n.p., 1909), pp. 4–5; see also Zwierlein, pp. 255–56.

[46] Quoted by Oppenheim, p. 8 n.

have their own community and the privilege of group worship in their homes. Though Jews in the colony were not to have a synagogue until after the English came, they had won important concessions.[47]

It must be conceded that Dutch New Netherland permitted a latitude in religion much broader than was the case in many other early American colonies. But Dutch toleration and the struggle for economic survival brought many people to the colony whose religious aspirations placed them at odds with this comparatively light regime. The source of these difficulties lay in the efforts of the civil authorities to prevent public dissenting worship. Dissenters, however, wished something more than liberty to hold family devotions in the privacy of their homes after the custom of the Netherlands. Their convictions impelled them to public worship, to the building of churches and the calling of ministers to lead them in the way of truth. These were the expressions of men whose enjoyment of some of the attributes of freedom led them to ask for more.

To have expected the colonial authorities to surrender completely to these pressures would have been to expect the impossible from men who were the creatures of their times and circumstances. If, as it was to Stuyvesant, religion was an important instrument of social control, and governments were justified in closely regulating it, to allow religion to go unsupervised was not only a derogation of duty but an invitation to an anarchy of contesting beliefs. In New Netherland, moreover, the old rules were complicated by new factors. Under the wilderness conditions of the New World, environmental as well as social conditions tended toward a loosening

[47] *Ibid.*, pp. 19–21, 33 n.; Zwierlein, pp. 258–61; *Col. Docs.*, XIV, 351. Also, see David and Tamar de Sola Pool, *An Old Faith in the New World: Portrait of Shearith Israel, 1654–1954* (New York, 1955), pp. 22–23.

of community ties. Given the frame of mind of a Stuyvesant, such loosening could only mean a weakening of community. And for this, duty as well as experience obliged officialdom to apply the religious statutes in an even stricter fashion than was true of the home government.

The directors of the West India Company, when they were required to take time from other pressing duties to deal with this problem, were able to view it somewhat more clearly from the vantage point of distance and a larger perspective. What checks there were on the heavy hand of the director general were those ordered by company directors obliged by their positions to make less rigid assessments of the conditions necessary for the success of their venture. But if distance lent insight, it also impeded communication. The directors simply were not in close enough touch with events in the colony to exert a continuing and consistent oversight.

Because of what now appears to be the unwise inflexibility of those in command locally, an inflexibility often untempered by higher authority until serious complications had arisen, religious policy in New Netherland was inconsistent. It alternated between harsh suppression and periods of inaction or retreat that usually followed the latest dispatches from Amsterdam. Given the fluid conditions of life in the colony and the inability of the government to exert constant and unbending force, suppression bred resentment and weakened allegiance to Dutch rule. On the other hand, inaction or concessions only heightened dissenting expectations while fortifying the governor in his certainty that relaxation would destroy order. The failure of the Dutch regime in New Netherland was that the contradictions inherent in its position were never clearly realized.

II

The English Province, 1664–1701: The Roots of Religious Liberty

IN 1664 King Charles II of England granted New Netherland to his brother James, duke of York and Albany, as one of a series of steps to remove the Dutch as competitors for the trade of the empire. In the late summer of the same year, a fleet of four English warships, supported by troops from New England, dropped anchor off New Amsterdam and trained their guns on the crumbling town fort. Doughty old Peter Stuyvesant readied himself to make a fight of it. But Dutch townsmen and the English on Long Island, at long last able to vent their extreme dislike of the governor, refused to answer Stuyvesant's call to arms. The director general stamped about angrily on his peg leg, fumed at the disloyalty of his people, and then surrendered to the superior force of the English.

In one swoop the duke of York, the future James II, had won a prize that stretched from the Kennebec in Maine, down through western Connecticut, New York, and New Jersey, to Delaware Bay, and out into the Atlantic beyond Long Island to Nantucket and Martha's Vineyard. His possession of New Netherland, the heart of his new domain, was quite unlike the other English colonies in North America. The majority of its people were alien Dutch. Liberally mixed in with them was a confused array of nationalities and religions. There were Englishmen from New England, Swedes,

Finns, French-speaking Walloons, Germans, Sephardic Jews by way of Brazil, and Negro slaves. Virtually every religion was represented but the Anglican, the established church of James' England. Dutch Calvinists, New England Presbyterians and Congregationalists, Dutch, German, and Swedish Lutherans, English Quakers and Baptists, Hebrews, and a few Catholics made their homes in the colony. And then there were many for whom religion was only something to be avoided. It was this diverse population which the duke had to govern and somehow turn a profit from.

This strange and complex colony cried out for moderate policies if it was to be pacified and made prosperous. The duke and his agents frequently proved to be models of wise flexibility in this respect. This was especially true for religion. The picture of James that emerges from his twenty years as proprietor of New York is an interesting contrast to that of the highhanded monarch whose arbitrary acts were to bring on the Glorious Revolution and cost him the throne of England.

Charles II's charter for the new proprietary colony granted James near absolute powers over his subjects. The only qualification imposed was that the laws and rules made in the duke's name should not run counter to the laws of England, but should be as "conveniently" agreeable to them as possible. This presented no great impediment, and in effect allowed the duke of York to do about as he pleased.[1]

The duke and his deputies, despite the temptations of such broad powers, determined upon a conciliatory policy for the colony, presently renamed New York. A major reason for this policy was to create stable conditions in order to promote opportunities for profit in the form of taxes and customs duties. This led the new ruler to make a very liberal grant of religious toleration, a recognition of the religious diversity of

[1] A. E. McKinley, "The Transition from Dutch to English Rule in New York," *American Historical Review*, VI (1900–01), 694.

the colony. Undoubtedly, the duke also wished to afford a haven for Roman Catholics who were being hounded in Protestant England and in most of the overseas English possessions. James was always sympathetic to members of the faith of which he was soon to become a communicant.[2]

The first step in implementing the policy of moderation was the signing of Articles of Capitulation by the leaders of the Dutch inhabitants. The eighth article of the agreement signed at New Amsterdam, now called New York, specified that the "Dutch here shall enjoy the liberty of their consciences in Divine Worship and church discipline."[3] The Dutch themselves had never dared to give such a concession to dissenting sects when they had ruled the colony. Later, similar articles drawn up for the town of Albany, formerly Fort Orange, contained the same guarantee. Thus, while the Dutch Reformed establishment was necessarily ended by the English conquest, the Dutch were permitted to retain many of their former church privileges.[4]

The Articles of Capitulation served the predominantly Dutch areas, the town of New York and the Hudson Valley, as a temporary basis of government for several years.[5] The areas where the English were concentrated, as on Long Island, were treated separately. Colonel Richard Nicolls, first of the English governors, formed Long Island, Staten Island, and the Bronx peninsula into the great county of York. In early 1665 Nicolls sent out a call for an assembly of delegates from the towns of Yorkshire.

The delegates convened at Hempstead shortly afterward. In return for a declaration of submission to the crown and to

[2] C. M. Andrews, *The Colonial Period of American History* (New Haven, 1934–38), III, 96 ff.; T. F. O'Connor, "Religious Toleration in New York, 1664–1700," *New York History*, XVII (1936), 391.

[3] E. B. O'Callaghan and B. Fernow, eds., *Documents Relating to the Colonial History of the State of New York* (Albany, 1853–87), II, 251; hereafter cited as *Col. Docs.*

[4] *Ibid.*, XIV, 559; McKinley, pp. 694–95. [5] *Ibid.*, p. 695.

the laws passed in the name of the duke and his successors, the assembly was presented with a set of fundamental laws which was to serve as the foundation of their government. This code, which Nicolls appears to have authored, came to be known as the Duke's Laws. It was partly based upon English experience in their other American colonies, most specifically Massachusetts and New Haven, but Dutch customs were not forgotten.[6]

The code avoided many of the narrow religious ways of Puritan New England, while showing evidence of tolerant Dutch influence. There was no religious qualification for officeholders; heresy, which figured so prominently in New England practice, was not even mentioned; and religious toleration was provided for. No doubt Nicolls' instructions, which implied the need to respect religion as it was practiced in New Netherland, guided him closely in the formulation of these provisions. Moreover, he had already conceded freedom of worship and church discipline to the defeated Dutch; he could not very well deny the same to the English community without running the risk of trouble. Finally, the diversity of religious belief on Long Island itself would have made difficult any attempt at a uniform religious establishment.[7]

However, while Nicolls' position was a modification of the seventeenth century's commitment to establishments and the desirability of close co-operation between church and state, he did not give it up. Nicolls' solution was what has been called a multiple establishment.[8] Each town, being designated a parish, was ordered to build a public church. The important question of control over these churches was resolved in the following manner:

For the making and proportioning the Levies and Assessments for building and repairing the Churches, Provision for the poor,

[6] *Ibid.*, pp. 696, 704. [7] *Ibid.*, pp. 704–07, 709 and n., 711–12.

[8] Leo Pfeffer, *Church, State, and Freedom* (Boston, 1953), pp. 70–71.

maintenance for the Minister; as well as for the more orderly managing of all Parochiall affairs . . . Eight of the most able Men of each Parish be by the Major part of the Householders of the said Parish Chosen to be Overseers out of which Number the Constable and the . . . Eight Overseers shall yearly make choice of two of the said number, to be Church wardens.[9]

This would sanction the formal establishment of the denomination claimed by the majority of the voters in any town. The town constable and magistrates were empowered to see that all inhabitants paid rates for the support of the town church whether they belonged to it or not. This arrangement represented an advance over the former Dutch establishment, for it allowed a greater degree of local control over religion than had the Dutch. From these local situations the germ of the idea of church-state separation would later arise.[10]

Not only were the constables to supervise the collection of church rates, but the regulation of public morals was now to be centered in the towns. Sabbath-breaking and blasphemy were to come under town scrutiny. Ministers within the jurisdiction of the Duke's Laws had to show proof of ordination either from a Protestant English authority or from a competent one within the domain of any foreign prince of the Reformed religion, this last meant to encompass Dutch clergymen. To the governor was reserved the power to induct qualified ministers into their offices. These regulations indicate the English determination to have a continuing close relationship between church and state in New York. The chief difference was that now much of the initiative was transferred down from the central administration to the localities.[11]

An important qualification was inserted in the code, doubtless to make the new establishments more acceptable to sects that could not claim a majority vote in any town. It stated

[9] New York [State], *The Colonial Laws of New York* (Albany, 1894–96), I, 24.
[10] *Ibid.*, p. 59. [11] *Ibid.*, pp. 20, 25, 26.

that "no Congregations shall be disturbed in their private meetings in the time of prayer preaching or other divine Service Nor shall any person be molested fined or Imprisoned for differing in Judgment in matters of Religion who profess Christianity."[12] Minorities were thus free not only to profess, as was the case under the Dutch, but also to worship openly in their own churches. Moreover, by specifying Christianity as the criterion, this privilege was broad enough to include Roman Catholics as well as Protestants.

Nicolls had acted wisely and tolerantly in giving to non-Reformed groups the privilege of public worship long denied to them by the Dutch and in preserving the religious *status quo* of the English towns. The result was to underwrite the diversity of permissible religious practice, though this diversity was not founded upon any conceded right but rather upon the gift of the duke. At this point, however, any thought of separating church and state would have been absurd if not highly dangerous to the great majority of worshipers whose churches were to receive public support in the several towns.

Colonel Nicolls and Colonel Francis Lovelace, successor to Nicolls as governor in 1668, hewed closely to the duke's instruction that the people of New York be treated "with humanity and gentleness."[13] The various churches were left to their own devices as long as they kept the public peace. There was also a notable lack of official concern for moral and religious behavior in the province, contrasting with Stuyvesant's vigorous efforts in that direction.

Official oversight of religion extended only to upholding the relevant provisions of the Duke's Laws and the Articles of Capitulation. The provincial authorities backed up the towns with established churches when these had to resort to the law to collect church rates. They also obligingly supported non-

[12] *Ibid.*, pp. 25–26.

[13] Quoted in D. M. Ellis and others, *A Short History of New York State* (Ithaca, N.Y., 1957), p. 29.

established denominations in their exercise of the privilege of public worship. Soon after the English conquest, Colonel Nicolls granted the long-refused request of New York Lutherans for permission to practice their religion openly. In 1666 the governor published a broadside informing the populace that their proprietor, the duke, "doth approve of ye Tolleration given to the Lutheran Church in theise partes." Nicolls cautioned the other sects to "live freindly & peaceably with those of that profession giving them no disturbance in ye Exercise of their Religion." [14]

Where overzealous Presbyterians of Southold on Long Island not only levied taxes on the minority but also tried to compel it to attend the town-supported church, the governor intervened to protect the liberty of conscience and worship provided by law. In July 1671, Lovelace addressed a stinging rebuke to the town pastor and others of Southold:

> When that extraordinary Indulgence was afforded you by my predecessor of ye Exercise of your Religion after your own manner; It was not thereby Intended that such Severity should be extended to those of a different perswasion to your discipline; noe more than you would accompt it hard for any of you that lived under another Church, in Conformity to his Majesty's Establisht Lawes should be soe rigorously dealt withall for your dissenting Opinion.[15]

Generally the several sects were content with the English religious settlement. The records of the time are remarkably free of complaints save for those from the Dutch Reformed clergy. Dutch ministers no longer received their salaries from the state, but from contributions by their congregations. Letters sent to the Amsterdam Classis bemoaned that the pastors now had to humble themselves by going from door to door to

[14] *Col. Docs.*, XIV, 626; see also *The Lutheran Church in New York, 1649–1772* (New York, 1946), pp. 48–49.

[15] E. T. Corwin, ed., *Ecclesiastical Records of the State of New York* (Albany, 1901–16), I, 618; hereafter cited as *Eccles. Recs.*

collect their money.[16] Not only did they have to beg for their salaries, but their people also expected them to preach regularly if they wished to be paid at all. As one Dutch dominie wrote, "under this English government the case is thus: when the labor ceases, the salary also ceases." [17]

Dutch pastors, whose memories of their former privileges died slowly, blamed their difficulties on the ungodly English. They often appealed to Lovelace, but his customary reply was that if the Dutch wanted to worship in their own way they should be willing to support their ministers without any outside assistance. In 1670 Lovelace relented to the extent of agreeing to a tax raised by the government of predominantly Dutch New York City for the support of the city's Dutch church, but beyond this he would not go.[18]

In 1673, with the Netherlands again at war with the English, the Dutch temporarily recaptured New York and held it until 1674, when a treaty of peace returned it to England. During their brief stay the Dutch swept away the English religious settlement, returning to the old Reformed establishment. But when rule passed back to the English, this was undone with little difficulty.[19]

After the restoration of English rule, the duke of York not only continued his tolerant religious policy but even enlarged it. His instructions to the new governor, Major Edmund Andros, ordered him to "permitt all persons of what Religion soever, quietly to inhabitt wthin ye precincts of yor jurisdiccôn, wthout giveing ym any disturbance or disquiet whatsoever, for or by reason of their differring opinions in matter of Religion." [20] The only proviso was that the peace be maintained and that no sect interfere with the equal privilege of

[16] *Ibid.*, pp. 587, 595. [17] *Ibid.*, p. 596.

[18] *Ibid.*, p. 602; *Col. Docs.*, XIII, 423, and III, 189.

[19] E. B. O'Callaghan, ed., *Laws and Ordinances of New Netherland, 1638–1674* (Albany, 1868), pp. 467, 492–94, 496, 512; *Col. Laws N.Y.*, I, 102, 104; *Eccles. Recs.*, I, 634. [20] *Col. Docs.*, III, 218.

others to the free enjoyment of religion. By and large Andros faithfully carried out this order during his tenure as governor.[21]

Andros, despite the religious calm, encountered strong opposition from the colonists over the duke's refusal to convene an elective assembly and the steep duties imposed on imports. To quiet this opposition, in 1683 the duke sent over a new governor, Colonel Thomas Dongan, with orders to call a general assembly to pass laws for the common welfare of the colony.[22]

As its first order of business, the newly elected Assembly passed a Charter of Liberties and Privileges setting forth the principles by which the government of the colony was to be guided. Its religious provisions, far from containing any innovations, demonstrated popular approval for the essentials of the existing system:

> Noe person or persons which professe ffaith in God by Jesus Christ Shall at any time be any wayes molested punished disquieted or called in Question for any Difference in opinion or Matter of Religious Concernment . . . But that all and Every such person or persons may from time to time and at all times freely have and fully enjoy his or their Judgments or Consciencyes in matters of Religion throughout all the province.[23]

This amounted to a full grant of religious freedom to Christians, the only reservation being a general injunction on outward behavior threatening to the public peace and welfare, a reservation no government in New York has ever forgone. Of interest is that this grant was not cast as a privilege conceded by the state and subject to recall; it was a "Liberty" that all "persons may . . . at all times freely have and fully enjoy." The only significant departure from the duke's instructions of

[21] *Ibid.*, p. 225; S. H. Cobb, *The Rise of Religious Liberty in America* (New York, 1902), pp. 330–31; *Eccles. Recs.*, I, 699 and *passim.*

[22] *Ibid.*, II, 867; *Col. Docs.*, III, 331.

[23] *Col. Laws N.Y.*, I, 115.

1674 was the restriction of this liberty to Christians, while the Duke had extended his protection to all religions.

The charter also stated that the guarantee of religious liberty was in no way intended to revoke the privileges of the established town churches provided for under the earlier Duke's Laws. The support of the state, however, was held out to all other Christian churches by defining them as "privileged churches." As such, contracts or salary agreements between their congregations and ministers were enforceable at law. Where a member of a church refused to pay his agreed-upon share of the pastor's salary, he could be ordered to do so by the local constable on warrant issuing from any justice of the peace.[24] Thus the assembly of 1683 affirmed its belief both in freedom of worship and in the usefulness of state assistance for the maintenance of churches. This was not an unnatural reaction of people who had come from European societies with their religious establishments and whose churches in New York were often in economic difficulty. They chose the best of two possible worlds, apparently with little fear that the state would ever try to enlarge its share of the partnership.

The Charter of 1683 was destined for a short life. The duke of York mounted the throne of England in 1685 as James II on the death of his brother Charles. Soon after, the Charter of Liberties and Privileges was disallowed by the King in Council. James was turning to the idea of combining the northern colonies in America into one large province that could be more easily and cheaply managed and defended. Particularistic local assemblies would only obstruct such a design. In the spring of 1686 new instructions were issued to Governor Dongan ordering him to end the life of the New York Assembly and reconcentrate all authority in his own hands.[25] Yet in spite of this change of direction, Dongan's instructions indicated that James intended to follow the same liberal religious policy in New York from the throne as he had as proprietor.

[24] *Ibid.*, pp. 115–16. [25] *Col. Docs.*, III, 357–59, 369–75.

The new instructions carried a direct copy of provisions in former instructions commanding a full liberty of conscience and worship for all peaceable inhabitants of the province.[26]

James II in the meantime was pursuing his ambitious political plans. To tighten his rule in America, in 1688 he combined New York and New Jersey with the New England colonies as part of the Dominion of New England. Andros, now knighted as Sir Edmund, was set over it as governor. Following his instructions, Andros began to undermine the primacy of the Puritan churches in Massachusetts by introducing Anglicanism and fostering its growth. But not a hand was laid on the churches of New York. In fact, Andros' instructions of April 1688 contained the very same grant of a liberty of conscience as had appeared in Dongan's orders of 1686.[27] When the Dominion of New England collapsed in the wake of the Glorious Revolution in England and the abdication of James II, the short and turbulent reign of that monarch had affected the proprietary religious settlement in New York not at all.

But the revolution in England had released the pent-up animosities of many New Yorkers against those who had received special favors from the colonial government in the reign of James II. A rising, known as Leisler's Rebellion, overturned the Dominion government in New York behind the cries of "No Popery" and "No Arbitrary Government." But while of great significance for New York politics in the years to come, Leisler's Rebellion had no more immediate effect upon the provincial religious settlement than had the rule of James II.[28]

After the great excitements of the years 1688–1689 had subsided, and Jacob Leisler had been undone by agents of the new English monarchs, William and Mary, the religious set-

[26] *Ibid.*, p. 373.

[27] C. P. Nettels, *The Roots of American Civilization* (New York, 1938), pp. 296–99; *Col. Docs.*, III, 546.

[28] *Eccles. Recs.*, II, 962–1011.

tlement of James was one of the few remaining features of his rule in New York. One result of the Glorious Revolution, the Act of Toleration of 1689, permitting toleration of Protestant dissenting worship in England, suggested a postrevolution attitude toward religion on the part of the government at home not incompatible with the main lines of the religious settlement in New York. But the Toleration Act could not possibly better New York's religious condition, even if it was extended to apply to the American colonies. During the twenty-five years preceding the Glorious Revolution the colony had enjoyed a liberty of conscience and of worship unusual for that time. The religious settlement of the duke of York was firmly planted in the popular mind. Virtually unfettered freedom of worship had become a living reality, while under the Toleration Act English dissenting worship would still be subjected to confining restrictions.[29]

Actually, the Glorious Revolution settlement in England was to bring something of a step backward in the religious condition of New York. The liberty of conscience so long enjoyed by New Yorkers was allowed to stand, but a series of governors, dedicated to planting the English establishment in the province, wrought changes of great peril for the tradition of free worship. Between 1693 and 1708 the Church of England, though it had little support among the populace, was established in New York. For the first time under English rule a religious test was prescribed for holders of public office. Roman Catholicism was declared an illegal form of worship. Increasingly religious affiliation became the measure of a citizen's privileges and standing in the colony, with the Anglican establishment providing the standard.[30]

[29] The Toleration Act appears at 1 William and Mary, cap. 18 (1689); 6 *Statutes of Realm*, 74–76.

[30] C. Z. Lincoln, *The Constitutional History of New York* (Rochester, N.Y., 1906), I, 451–52. On the American and English setting for what follows in this chapter and in Chapter 3, see Carl Bridenbaugh, *Mitre and Sceptre: Transatlantic Faiths, Ideas, Personalities, and Politics, 1689–1775* (New York, 1962).

The new Anglican policy collided with the colony's religious habits. Many New Yorkers had come to see the necessity of leaving religion to each man's conscience in the interests of getting on. They were willing to accept state assistance to religion, but would not with similar equanimity accept any interference in the government of their churches. To these people the Anglican establishment was a dangerous and unwonted innovation threatening to their rights. The English dissenting element in New York province never ceased to oppose the Church of England at every convenient opportunity.

After 1689, elective assemblies became a regular fixture in New York, and in time a forum for opponents of the Anglican church. The first Assembly elected in the reign of William and Mary quickly registered its preference for the liberal religious settlement instituted under the duke of York. In May of 1691 the Assembly adopted "An Act declareing what are the Rights and Priviledges of their Majesties Subjects inhabiting within their Province of New York" which was essentially a re-enactment of the Charter of Liberties and Privileges of 1683. The passage guaranteeing freedom of conscience, with the exception of two new additions, was copied directly from the guarantee in the section on religion of the eariler charter.[31]

Of the additions, the first actually strengthened the rights of worshipers. It stated that all persons could "freely meet at Convenient places within this Province, and there worshipp according to their respective perswasions without being hindered or molested."[32] But the second, tacked on at the insistence of the governor, probably as a condition for the passage of the entire article, read: "Allwayes provided that noething herein mentioned or Contained shall extend to give Liberty for any persons of the Romish Religion to exercise their

[31] *Col. Laws N.Y.*, I, 248. [32] *Ibid.*

worship Contrary to the Laws and Statutes of their Majesties Kingdom of England."[33] Strangely, the Act of 1691 carried no detailed provision for the maintenance of ministers as the Charter of 1683 had, suggesting that the support arrangements in the Duke's Laws and other similar acts were no longer to be recognized. This was a portentous omission.

Though the Assembly had its own settled views on the proper religious arrangement for New York, the governors had their instructions from the crown and orders to carry them out. Henry Sloughter, first governor after the Glorious Revolution, arrived carrying detailed instructions to establish the Church of England. Included was the authority to collate, or appoint, to pastoral office.[34] Similar terms had appeared in the royal instructions as early as 1686. But Sloughter and his successors, unlike the royal governors under James II, were now fully expected to enforce these provisions. The only concession made to local expectations in the orders to the governors following the Glorious Revolution was a clause "to permit a liberty of Conscience to all Persons (except Papists) so they be contented with a qu[i]et and Peaceable enjoyment of it, not giving offence or scandall to the Government."[35]

To compare this last provision with the religious clauses in the 1683 Charter of Liberties and Privileges and in the Act of 1691 is to see the great gap in understanding between the colonists and the English government. The people of New York had long since passed beyond a mere liberty of conscience and were determined to worship freely as they were long accustomed to. The crown and its representatives were as equally determined to see the Church of England established in New York. This was achieved, but in a form never entirely satisfactory to the Anglican church. The colonists, on the other hand, retained their freedom of conscience and of public worship, though the English authorities always refused

[33] *Ibid.* [34] *Col. Docs.*, III, 625, 685–91. [35] *Ibid.*, p. 689.

to recognize these as rights and reserved broad powers to intervene in their exercise.

Sloughter died after a brief administration, having had little time for the affairs of the church. His successor, Benjamin Fletcher, proved a good deal more vigorous on behalf of the Church of England. Fletcher, a proud and overbearing man, was convinced of the superiority of the dogmas and organization of the English state church. He was not one to trifle with the Assembly over an institution so fundamental to England's greatness and virtue as the church.

But the New York Assembly was not as docile on this matter as Fletcher expected. When he recommended to his first Assembly that "provision be made for the support and Encouragement of an able Ministry," [36] the Assembly did nothing, apparently convinced that the existing ministry was able enough. Fletcher pressed the issue at the next Assembly session in a manner implying that God's judgment of the colony waited upon an act establishing the Anglican religion. When the Assembly again failed to heed his prophetic call, Fletcher became annoyed. At the close of the session he reminded the representatives of his request and said—his words tinged with irony—that he hoped they would take it up as the first order of business at their next meeting. "There are none of you but what are bigg with the priviledge of Englishmen, and Magna Charta, which is yor right," he told them, "And the same Law doth provide for the religion of the Church of England." [37]

At the session convened in the fall of 1693, and after considerable pressure had been applied, the Assembly finally passed a law for the support of ministers of religion. Fletcher, though failing to get it amended to include his collating power, assented to the law. Entitled "An Act for Settling a Ministry & Raising a Maintenance for them," it was a strange

[36] New York [State], *Journal of the Legislative Council of the Colony of New York* (Albany, 1861), I, 25. [37] *Ibid.*, pp. 35, 39.

piece of legislation in view of Fletcher's demands.[38] There was not one mention of the Church of England in it. It referred only to "good sufficient Protestant" ministers. Neither did the act apply to the entire colony but only to the city and county of New York and the counties of Richmond, Queens, and Westchester.

In all, six parishes were created with provision that in each parish the local justices would call together the freeholders to elect ten vestrymen and two church wardens. These officers, acting with the justices of the peace, were to levy assessments against all ratepayers sufficient to meet the salaries set by the act. In the event a vestry failed to act, its members could be fined, while the justices would make the required assessments themselves. Local constables were to collect the tax money and turn it over to the wardens, who would pay the ministers. The act as it stood was similar to the terms of the Duke's Laws of 1665, which had permitted a majority in a town to elect church officials who would call a pastor, the understanding having been that where one denomination had a majority it would settle its own church upon the town. The key clause of the Ministry Act of 1693 stated that the ministers settled under it "shall be called to officiate . . . by the respective Vestry men and church wardens aforesaid." It was following this that Fletcher had wanted an amendment inserted: "And presented to the Governor to be approved and collated." [39]

Under the Act of 1693, the establishment of Anglican parishes would turn on whether the vestries or the governor would make the choice of a minister. If the former, then the Ministry Act was simply a re-enactment of the Duke's Laws. There were not enough Anglican votes in the whole province to decide a vestry election in even the smallest of the new parishes. If the governor prevailed, however, there was no

[38] *Col. Laws N.Y.*, I, 328–31; see also *Eccles. Recs.*, II, 1074, and *Jour. Leg. Council*, I, 47–48. [39] *Eccles. Recs.*, II, 1079.

question but that Fletcher would use the collating power to approve only Anglican clergymen for the new places.

The governor called the Assembly before him prior to prorogation and made it quite clear that he alone would approve or disapprove the choice of ministers under the act:

> If you seem to understand by these words (calling the Minister) that none can serve without your collation or Establishment, you are far mistaken; for I have the power of collating or suspending any Minister in my Government . . . ; and whilst I stay in the Government, I will take care that neither heresy, sedition, schism, nor rebellion be preached amongst you, nor vice and profanity encouraged.[40]

In other words, dissenting views would not be permitted in any of the pulpits created by the new law. These offices would be filled with men of the true religion, that is to say, Anglicans. Fletcher was as good as his word. When parishes in New York City and Westchester later tried to call dissenting ministers, he refused to collate them, saying he would approve only Anglicans for these places.[41]

Fletcher had devised a means to establish the Church of England, but it was still only a partial triumph. He now had to find Anglican clergymen to fill the new places. In 1693 there was an Anglican chaplain at the fort in New York City, but none anywhere else in the province. The vestries in the three counties outside the city were slow to form as local dissenting majorities dragged their heels. Dissenters often agreed to serve on a vestry only to escape prosecution for failure to execute the election provisions of the Ministry Act. They would then delay raising taxes or calling Anglican pastors. Fletcher never did manage to fill the pulpits in these counties during his administration.[42]

[40] *Jour. Leg. Council*, I, 48.

[41] R. T. Henshaw, "The New York Ministry Act of 1693," *Historical Magazine of the Protestant Episcopal Church*, II (1933), 203–04.

[42] R. T. Henshaw, "The Ministry Act of 1693," *Quarterly Bulletin of the Westchester County Historical Society*, X (1934), 1, 6.

The governor's main effort was the founding of an Anglican church in New York City. Here most of the small band of Anglicans in the colony were gathered. And most of them were soldiers on garrison or members of Fletcher's official family. Though a minority, they were a powerful one.

A Ministry Act vestry was first elected in the city in January of 1694. It included only three Anglicans, a measure of their strength in the town. By majority vote, the vestry called a dissenting minister despite Fletcher's known opposition. The governor, as expected, refused to approve, suggesting that his chaplain fill the office. The vestry balked and let it be known that they would raise no tax until the minister was chosen. It was obvious that if Fletcher got his hands on the money before a choice had been made, he would act with no regard for the vestry's wishes.

The stalemate dragged on. A second vestry was elected in January 1695, containing but one Anglican. Fletcher roared and threatened legal action; the vestry decided it was the better part of wisdom to make a call. William Vesey, an Anglican lay worker on Long Island, was asked to fill the office. Since the governor was still insisting on the appointment of his chaplain, perhaps he would object to Vesey and further delay could be had.

In the meantime the vestry petitioned the Assembly for an interpretation of the Ministry Act's terms. This was becoming a standard political tactic in the colonies. If you could not obtain favorable access to one of the two centers of power in a colony, the governor or the assembly, you turned to the other. If both were hostile to your appeals, you hung on and hoped that a change of governors or an assembly election would bring your friends into power. The other alternative was to approach friends in England. Religious groups in time would become as adept at these tactics as other groups in colonial politics. The New York Assembly, in this instance, decided that the act allowed the vestry to call a "Dissenting Protestant Minister." Fletcher upbraided the Assembly for presuming to interpret a statute, which was the function of the courts, and then he prorogued the body indefinitely.

The controversy continued until the third annual vestry election in early 1696. This time the Anglican party appears to have taken steps to break the deadlock. The new vestry had a majority of Anglicans and Dutch friends of Fletcher. In short order the vestry laid the tax for the minister's salary, called Vesey to be their pastor, received Fletcher's approval, and sent Vesey off to England for ordination by the bishop of London.[43]

Fletcher then moved to incorporate the Anglican congregation in New York City as Trinity Church. He undoubtedly realized that if the fortunes of the Anglicans depended solely upon the management of the elected vestry, it would be possible for a dissenting majority to elect unfriendly vestries in the future. Incorporation would create a parish vestry of Anglican laymen that would have direct charge of the church. The elected vestry would then become a civil or town vestry whose only function was to collect the ministerial support money, with penalties provided by law for failure to perform. The civil vestry could not otherwise interfere. By his own patent, Fletcher granted the corporate charter in 1697, designating Trinity as the legally established church of New York City.[44]

The year before, Fletcher had also chartered the Dutch Reformed church in the city. While its members were still subject to tax for the support of Trinity's minister, their charter enabled them to hold and convey money and property, to be exempted from the governor's collating power, and

[43] The contest between the New York City vestry and Fletcher can be followed in *Eccles. Recs.*, II, 1092, 1095, 1097, 1112, 1114; Morgan Dix, *A History of the Parish of Trinity Church in the City of New York* (New York, 1898–1906), I, 83–90 and nn.; *Jour. Leg. Council*, I, 76.

[44] E. B. O'Callaghan, ed., *Documentary History of the State of New York* (Albany, 1849–51), I, 407–08; Dix, I, 91, 92, 94.

to have recourse to compulsory legal process for raising funds from among the congregation to pay its pastor. This charter was the forerunner of several others incorporating Dutch churches in the colony.[45]

Coming one after the other, with the election of Vesey intervening, the two charters had all the earmarks of an accommodation between the Anglicans and the Dutch. The members of the Dutch church saw fit to give Fletcher a gift of silver plate worth seventy-five to eighty pounds;[46] they may have also given their votes at the 1696 vestry election in return for the inestimable grant of a church charter of incorporation.

For the future, the grant to the Dutch had even greater significance. Through incorporation, Dutch churches gained privileges placing them apart from the dissenters. To throw in with the latter to oppose the English establishment might have led the authorities to withdraw their concessions. Conservative, Old World–oriented Dutch clergymen and merchants were too content with their favored position, the next best thing to an establishment of their own, to chance losing it by supporting dissenters in a cause with which they were in disagreement anyway. In this manner, the large Dutch community became wedded to the Anglican settlement in religion.

The Anglicans, having the greatest stake in preserving this settlement, benefited from the acquiescence of the Dutch. They sensed that their church would take root in the colony only if they could depend upon the support, or at least the neutrality, of the sizable Dutch group. Otherwise, hopelessly outnumbered in the Assembly and among the electorate, they would be continually harassed by the dissenters. The Dutch were most co-operative. Grateful for their church privileges, they obligingly accepted the Anglican establishment. So long as the Dutch community approved its leaders' attachments to

[45] *Eccles. Recs.*, II, 1136–65; Dix, I, 95 n.

[46] *Ibid.*, pp. 94–96; *Eccles. Recs.*, II, 1168–69.

conditions as they were, dissenters lacked both the numbers and influence to drive home any attack on the Anglican church.

For a generation after Leisler's Rebellion, New York politics were influenced by a division between those who had favored and those who had opposed the Leisler movement. Where Fletcher had been allied with the anti-Leislerians, his successor, Richard Coote, earl of Bellomont, turned to the Leislerian faction, with which dissenting elements in the colony were also associated. This being the case, Lord Bellomont had little incentive for continuing Fletcher's policy of promoting the Anglican church. The years of Bellomont's governorship, 1698–1701, were years of marking time in the settling of the Church of England upon the province.

Lord Bellomont believed that Fletcher's efforts on behalf of his church had been unwise, for they had opened up a serious religious rift.[47] He was prepared to use his influence to redress the balance and appease angry dissenters. Following this policy, Bellomont obtained a law from the Assembly, where Leislerians were in the ascendent, revoking a land grant that Fletcher had made to Trinity Church. The Assembly attached an amendment stripping the Dutch minister at Albany, another recipient of Fletcher's favors, of his pastoral office.[48] The governor also intervened on the side of the Leislerian minority in the Dutch church of New York City; the minority was striving to prevent the calling of a conservative, anti-Leislerian assistant pastor.[49] The conservative majority in the Dutch congregation, of course, complained bitterly over this interference, their complaints pointing up an increasingly evident phenomenon. Religious groups were coming around to the idea that when in political disfavor it was useful to

[47] *Col. Docs.*, IV, 325–26.

[48] *Ibid.*, p. 510; *Eccles. Recs.*, II, 1296–97, 1311–12, 1320–26; *Col. Laws N.Y.*, I, 412–17.

[49] *Eccles. Recs.*, II, 1246–61, 1264–66.

appeal to a concept of non-intervention by the state in ecclesiastical affairs. As yet, this was a defensive political tactic and not a question of principle. Once more back in the good graces of the governor or Assembly, the appeals were conveniently forgotten. However, the lesson suggested does not seem to have been wasted on dissenting sects that had been legislated by the Ministry Act of 1693 into a permanently subordinate position.

The Assembly wished to go much farther than Bellomont was willing or able to. When it adopted a bill in 1699 to support ministers in the province, an unconcealed attempt to reinvoke the ministerial maintenance provisions of the Duke's Laws, the governor had it defeated in the Council. His instructions clearly prevented him from accepting a measure that would have destroyed the special standing of the Church of England.[50]

Dissenters did obtain one concession from this. A bill was passed allowing towns to raise money by general taxation for building and repairing meeting houses and other public buildings. This, in effect, would permit the construction of dissenting churches at public expense.[51] Obviously, the main ground for dissenting objections to church establishments was not so much the settling of one church, the Anglican, as it was the denial of similar privileges to other sects. The concept of multiple establishments remained the dissenters' solution to the question of proper church-state relations as the seventeenth century drew to a close in New York. By this time, dissenters enjoyed a full liberty of conscience so firmly planted in their experience that it would have been unthinkable for them to contemplate its loss. In addition they had the privilege of public worship in churches and with ministers

[50] New York [Colony], *Journal of the General Assembly of the Colony of New York, 1691–1765* (New York, 1764–66), I, 101, 102; *Jour. Leg. Council*, I, 136, 137, 138–139; *Col. Docs.*, IV, 536.

[51] *Jour. Leg. Council*, I, 140, 141, 143; *Col. Laws N.Y.*, I, 427–28.

of their own choice. This was somewhat restricted by the Anglican establishment in the four lower counties with its requirement that dissenters pay taxes for its support. But the dangers to the religious liberties of dissenters that might arise from too great a dependence on the assistance of the state were not yet clearly seen.

III

The English Province, 1702–1776: Trials of Church and State

THE history of church-state relations over the seventy-five years before the American Revolution falls into three distinct phases. First, there was a period of great excitement as the Anglican church was forcibly planted in the counties of Richmond, Queens, and Westchester. Then came forty years of comparative calm during which the Anglicans gradually lost much of their earlier militancy, and dissent continued to grow in numbers and influence. Finally, another time of tensions and religious animosities occurred, merging with the general movement for independence. Partly in reaction to the unhappy experiences with the Anglican establishment and to the continually unsettling involvement of religion with politics there developed a widespread belief in the expediency of a separation of church and state.

The first phase covered the administration of Edward Hyde, Lord Cornbury, Bellomont's successor. Arriving in 1702, that infamous man soon won the hatred of his dissenting subjects. Vain, irascible, corrupt, Cornbury so aroused the province that ever after his name was associated with all that was bad in English rule. His profligate appropriation of public moneys for his personal pleasures forced the Assembly to take protective measures that permanently altered the political balance between governor and legislature in its favor. His interference in religion strengthened beyond recall the hostility of dissenters to the Anglican settlement. William Smith, Jr., the historian of New York province, writing a half-century later, accurately characterized Cornbury: "His talents were perhaps not superior to the most inconsiderable of his predecessors; but in his zeal for the church he was surpassed by none."[1]

This zeal for the church, from an otherwise unscrupulous and immoral man, boded ill for those who were not Anglicans.[2] Cornbury's ambition to carry forward the work of the Anglican church led him to interpret his instructions in a broad and dictatorial manner never before seen in the colony. Cornbury meant to place the privileges of Trinity Church in New York City beyond the reach of its enemies. He intended to carry out the Ministry Act in the parishes beyond the city, breaking resistance as he went and compelling dissenters to accept and maintain Anglican clerics. He used his collating powers to control the growth of dissent, teach its proud leaders some respect for authority, and place the worship of all the sects within his oversight.

Cornbury aligned himself politically with the anti-Leislerians.[3] He employed his influence to force the Leislerian faction in the Assembly from power. Having helped return the Assembly to anti-Leislerian control, he was able to steer important religious legislation through that body with little difficulty. One of his first acts was to restore the land grant to

[1] William Smith, *The History of the Late Province of New York from Its Discovery to the Appointment of Governor Colden in 1762*, I, in New-York Historical Society, *Collections*, 1st ser., IV (New York, 1829), 146–47.

[2] Morgan Dix, *A History of the Parish of Trinity Church in the City of New York* (New York, 1898–1906), I, 137–40.

[3] Smith, in N.Y. Hist. Soc., *Coll.*, IV, 147; E. B. O'Callaghan and B. Fernow, eds., *Documents Relating to the Colonial History of the State of New York* (Albany, 1853–87), IV, 1010–17; hereafter cited as *Col. Docs.*

Trinity Church that Bellomont had rescinded, so safeguarding the title that future attempts to rescind the grant would be forestalled.[4] In 1703 he obtained a law raising the salary of the Anglican pastor in New York City from the hundred pounds specified in the Ministry Act of 1693 to one hundred sixty pounds, the latter significantly increasing the general levy on all taxpayers.[5] The following year Cornbury induced the Assembly to recognize Fletcher's corporate charter for Trinity Church. What had rested on the favor of an earlier governor now stood on a legislative enactment. Since the Trinity charter proclaimed it the sole established church of New York City, Cornbury in effect had obtained Assembly assent to what it had previously refused to accept, namely, that the Ministry Act encompassed only the Church of England.[6]

Governor Fletcher had been prevented from carrying out the Ministry Act by a lack of Anglican clergymen. Cornbury succeeded where Fletcher had failed through the assistance of the English Society for the Propagation of the Gospel in Foreign Parts, the SPG. The SPG was chartered by King William in 1701 for the specific purpose of invigorating the church in the American colonies. It was a product of a philanthropic spirit and missionary zeal appearing in the English church after the Restoration, reaching a peak of intensity in the reign of Anne, and then giving way to a latitudinarianism and rejection of enthusiasm characteristic of the Anglican church during the eighteenth-century Whig supremacy in England. The Ministry Act itself and the religious activism of

[4] New York [State], *The Colonial Laws of New York* (Albany, 1894–96), I, 524, and *Journal of the Legislative Council of the Colony of New York* (Albany, 1861), I, 226; E. T. Corwin, ed., *Ecclesiastical Records of the State of New York* (Albany, 1901–16), III, 1597–98, hereafter cited as *Eccles. Recs.*

[5] New York [Colony], *Journal of the General Assembly of the Colony of New York, 1691–1765* (New York, 1764–66), I, 162, 164; *Jour. Leg. Council*, I, 195, 196, 199, 204.

[6] *Ibid.*, pp. 212, 213, 220; *Col. Laws N.Y.*, I, 564–69.

Cornbury were manifestations of this same missionary vigor.

In New York, as in other colonies, the activities of the SPG were inspired by the fear that colonists were backsliding into atheism and infidelity from which only Anglicanism could rescue them. It was this attitude of superiority that was to be so infuriating to dissenting sects which had been active in New York long before the Church of England.[7]

Immediately upon its formation, the SPG began soliciting contributions in England from the wealthy and from Anglican congregations to supplement the often inadequate salaries of Anglican ministers in the colonies and to recruit clergymen for America. In return the society expected the colonial governors to foster and protect the church and to provide suitable livings for its missionaries.[8] Through the efforts of Rev. William Vesey and Lord Cornbury, six of the first missionaries sent over by the SPG came to New York. In all, the SPG sent fifty-eight ministers to New York, virtually the only Anglicans who ever served there. Of these, thirty-three officiated at various times in the six parishes constituted by the Ministry Act; thirteen ministered to the Iroquois. During seventy-five years of activity, only eleven ever served in settled areas of New York outside the parishes created by the Ministry Act, attesting to the weakness of the Church of England everywhere save in the four established counties.[9]

[7] For the SPG generally, see H. P. Thompson, *Into All Lands: The History of the Society for the Propagation of the Gospel in Foreign Parts, 1701–1950* (London, 1951), pp. 3–17; the SPG charter is in *Classified Digest of the Records of the S.P.G., 1701–1892* (London, 1893), pp. 925–28.

[8] H. P. Thompson, pp. 19–34.

[9] *Ibid.*, p. 71; for listings of SPG clergy in New York see E. T. Corwin, "The Ecclesiastical Condition of New York at the Opening of the Eighteenth Century," *Papers of the American Society of Church History*, 2d ser., III (1910–11), 81–115; John Clement, "Anglican Clergymen Licensed to the American Colonies, 1710–1744," *Historical Magazine of the Protestant Episcopal Church*, XVII (1948), 207–50; and *Digest S.P.G. Recs.*, pp. 825–26.

Most of this last group could not have remained without the support of SPG money which generally was their only income.[10]

Supplied with Anglican ministers, Cornbury proceeded to fill the parishes settled on the Church of England by the Ministry Act. It was seldom that he did not encounter resistance and have to resort to force to overcome it. In 1702 an SPG missionary arrived in one of the two Westchester parishes. Colonel Caleb Heathcote, wealthy landowner, governor's councilor, militia commander, and ardent Anglican, had prepared the way by obliging the local Presbyterian minister to leave. But it was still necessary to appeal all the way to the Privy Council before the Anglican clergyman was given land to live on. Over the years the movement of Anglicans from the city to Westchester County secured the Anglican hold upon the parish.[11] Rye parish, the other Westchester parish, received an Anglican minister in 1704. The town of Bedford, lying within the parish, had a strong dissenting church opposed to settling the newcomer. Cornbury had to arrest and jail the justice of the peace and the pastor of the Bedford church before the local people would submit.[12] The parish on Staten Island had an SPG missionary in 1705. A few years after Cornbury left New York, it was necessary to turn the Richmond magistrates out of office, replacing them with friends of the establishment, to assure success there.[13] The Hempstead parish of Queens County, which also served Oyster Bay, was settled by an SPG appointee in 1704. With the backing of "Cornbury's most favorable countenance" and the pressure of several influential residents, the minister was able to hang on, though he was never very popular. The large

[10] H. P. Thompson, pp. 45–46.

[11] D. R. Fox, *Caleb Heathcote, Gentleman Colonist* (New York, 1926), pp. 201–09.

[12] *Eccles. Recs.*, III, 1554, 1611, 1612; E. B. O'Callaghan, *Documentary History of the State of New York* (Albany, 1849–51), III, 932–35.

[13] *Eccles. Recs.*, III, 1610, 1900.

Presbyterian element and a smaller Quaker body paid their yearly support to the Anglicans only after much grumbling.[14]

Jamaica parish in Queens County offered the greatest resistance to Cornbury. Its people were Presbyterians who had been in the habit of maintaining their minister at town expense since the time of the Duke's Laws. They had recently completed building a new town church. Jamaica's resistance to the Anglicans continued throughout the remainder of the colonial period. It became the most notorious example of the persecutions suffered by dissenters in the cause of religious freedom.

The contest began in 1703 when an Anglican minister and his friends took possession of the new town church under the ruse of borrowing it far a church service. Dissenters then rioted and forcibly regained the church. Cornbury hailed the Presbyterian pastor and his chief supporters before him, forbade the former ever to preach from his own pulpit again because it was now occupied by the Church of England, and extracted apologies from the other rioters under the threat of jailing them. In July of 1704, Cornbury commanded the Presbyterian minister to turn his parsonage over to his Anglican rival, ordering the high sheriff of the county to throw him out bodily if he refused. The next month the governor completed the takeover by compelling the church wardens to begin paying salary to the Anglican cleric as provided by the Ministry Act. Bowing to superior force, the people of Jamaica held back their anger and complied for the remainder of Cornbury's term.[15]

By 1705 Cornbury was forced to admit that he was encountering difficulties in the vestries elected to support his appointees. He asked the Assembly for a law compelling the payment of salaries within a stated time limit, coupling this

[14] *Ibid.*, 1610; B. F. Thompson, *History of Long Island*, 3d ed. (New York, 1918), II, 505–13.

[15] O'Callaghan, *Doc. Hist.*, III, 114, 205–09, 211–12.

with a recommendation that the Ministry Act be extended to include the dissenting towns of Suffolk County in eastern Long Island. Perhaps he meant to frighten dissenters in the Assembly into accepting an amendment to the Ministry Act by threatening far worse things in the form of an enlarged establishment.[16] The Assembly complied by passing an act setting the time limit, and Suffolk County was forgotten. Included in the act was a recognition of the governor's power of induction, something which the Assembly had refused to give Fletcher in 1693 since it amounted to accepting the exclusive authority of the governor to approve ministers called to the established parishes. The addition significantly enhanced the position of the Church of England under the Ministry Act.[17]

Cornbury acted within his powers when he settled the Anglican church on the country parishes, though his means were impolitic. His instructions and the official interpretation of the Ministry Act were his authorities. Of course, dissenters never accepted the Anglican construction of that law, but they lacked means for effective protest. But not content with securing the appointments to the Church of England, Cornbury tried to bring all ministerial appointments within his control. His commission specified collation of ministers by the governor. Cornbury claimed that by construction he had the authority to license pastors called to dissenting and Dutch pulpits as well as to the Anglican. Since licenses were valid only during his pleasure, Cornbury conceivably could use this power both to appoint and to dismiss from clerical office. In the hands of Cornbury, this might destroy the independence of the non-Anglican churches. Cornbury proceeded to remove all doubts by employing licensing to gain just such ends.

It had become the custom of some non-Anglican sects to inform the governors when they called new ministers. This

[16] *Jour. Leg. Council*, I, 225. [17] *Col. Laws N.Y.*, I, 576–79.

was done out of courtesy and had not been required of them. In the past, executive approval had been given as a matter of course. But in 1702 when the elders of the Dutch churches in Kings County, not without objection by members who insisted it was legally unnecessary, notified Cornbury of their call to the Dutch pastor in Schenectady, the governor refused his permission. He maintained that this pastor had been involved with an opposing political faction and did not merit the call. Therefore, he would use his power to prevent it.[18]

Again, when the Dutch minister at Kingston in Ulster County returned to Holland, Cornbury arbitrarily named an Anglican cleric to the vacant post. He replied to Dutch protests by informing them that their minister had merely been "tolerated" by the provincial government, while his choice was of the "Establisht Church of England" and was to be provided at once with a suitable residence. The Dutch were amazed and angered. The Kingston church applied directly to the mother church in the Netherlands for a replacement. When he arrived, Cornbury would not allow him to preach at Kingston without a license. The Dutch argued that this was contrary to the practice of their church and of the English colonial government running all the way back to the Articles of Capitulation of 1664. The new minister was advised by lawyers not to apply for a license as it would violate the Reformed church's liberty of church discipline and create a dangerous dependence on the will of the governor. Spokesmen for the church at Kingston pleaded with Cornbury that none of his predecessors had ever required a license of non-Anglicans and that the licensing clause of his instructions was widely interpreted in the colony as applying only to Anglican clergy. The governor lost his temper, swore at the emissaries, and abruptly ended the meeting. Only after the intercession of some of the most influential figures in the Dutch community, whom it may be assumed discussed the political facts of

[18] *Eccles. Recs.*, III, 1503–07.

life with him, would Cornbury give in and permit ministers to preach at the Reformed churches in Kingston and Kings County without his license.[19]

In 1707 Cornbury's will was pitted against the Presbyterians, whose outspoken antagonism to the Anglican establishment was especially hateful to him. Two Presbyterian ministers, Francis Makemie and John Hampton, had come from Virginia and Maryland to help build up their church in New York. Cornbury had them arrested for violating his private instructions by preaching without a license. When these men appealed to the English Act of Toleration, they were told that English ecclesiastical law did not extend to New York. Subsequently the charge was altered to a breach of the nonconformist preaching regulations in the Toleration Act, the governor having received legal advice that the applicable clause of his instructions was not valid in the absence of supporting legislation. A grand jury, hand-picked by Cornbury, returned an indictment to the charge against Makemie. At his trial, which attracted much interest in the colony, Makemie's lawyers argued that preaching was an offense unknown to the common law, the only law relevant to the case, since the Toleration Act, the Act of Uniformity, and Cornbury's instructions had no force in New York. The reason advanced was that the provincial legislature had never recognized these by any act of positive law. The trial jury, despite directions to return a verdict of guilty from the colony's chief justice, accepted this defense argument and acquitted Makemie of the charge.[20]

Presbyterian and Dutch leaders, incensed by Cornbury's

[19] *Ibid.*, pp. 1574, 1577, 1615–19, 1652, 1653, 1659, 1667–68.

[20] "A Narrative of a New and Unusual American Imprisonment of Two Presbyterian Ministers . . . ," in Peter Force, ed., *Tracts and Other Papers, Relating Principally to . . . the Colonies in North America* (Washington, 1836–47), IV, no. 4. Also see Smith, in N.Y. Hist. Soc., *Coll.*, IV, 160–64; *Col. Docs.*, IV, 1186–87; and Carl Bridenbaugh, *Mitre and Sceptre: Transatlantic Faiths, Ideas, Personalities, and Politics, 1689–1775* (New York, 1962), pp. 121–23.

latest and most flagrant act of interference, helped the Leisler faction to regain control of the Assembly in 1708. Remonstrances were sent to powerful friends in England, and Lord Cornbury was driven from office. He was held in debtors prison until his succession to the earldom of Clarendon on the death of his father brought his release and return to England.[21]

In seven short years this one man had managed to stir up a great religious controversy in New York, to fortify dissenting opposition to the Anglican establishment, and to strengthen the colonists' attachment to their freedom of conscience and of worship. New Yorkers were led to ponder their religious condition, to see that religious observance could not be forced into any uniform mold without impairing the liberties of the dissenting sects, and to recognize that the whim of individual governors was a shaky foundation on which to base these liberties. As one defense attorney at the Makemie trial had said:

> This Province . . . is made up chiefly of Foreigners and Dissenters; and Persecution would not only tend to the disuniting us all, in interest and affection, but depopulate and weaken our Strength, and discourage all such Adventurers for the future. Therefore as this Prosecution is the first of this nature or sort, ever was in this Province, so I hope it will be the last.[22]

For many years memories of Cornbury's humbling of the Presbyterians at Jamaica, the Makemie trial, and the other crude tamperings with dissenters and their religion were called up to stoke the fires of opposition to the Church of England. From the Cornbury period it is possible to date the dawning of an awareness that religious liberty could be confidently enjoyed only when religious practice was secure from intervention by the state.

During the time from 1709 to the mid-1750's the religious

[21] Smith, in N.Y. Hist. Soc., *Coll.*, IV, 163–64; *Eccles. Recs.*, III, 1672; Bridenbaugh, pp. 123–24.

[22] "A Narrative," in Force, *Tracts*, IV, no. 4, 35.

situation can best be described by the adage "let sleeping dogs lie." The Anglican church lost some of its old fire as new leaders came to the fore and militant zeal gave way to a greater forbearance. A series of governors ruled over the province who were less eager to push the claims of the Church of England. They were influenced by the accession of the Hanoverian line and the rise of Robert Walpole. In these years crown and ministry looked more kindly on dissenters and were not inclined to promote the extreme claims of the Anglican church in the colonies.[23] Such changes were also attributable to a growing tolerance and secularism in the English church. But the increasing dependence of the crown's representatives upon the good will of the Assembly for their salaries and other appropriations was basic.[24] The advancement of the Church of England was no longer vital if it meant alienating the non-Anglican majority in the Assembly and upsetting the working relations of governor and legislature.

This did not mean that official backing was withdrawn from the Anglican establishment in the four lower counties. The governors could not evade the explicit commands of their instructions on this point, but they no longer displayed the driving force of a Fletcher or a Cornbury. They would act when the Anglican clergy complained of some infringement of their privileges, but the governors seldom initiated actions themselves or went out of their way to stir up trouble. A law was obtained in 1721 to tighten the taxing provisions of the Ministry Act, setting stiffer penalties for vestries which failed to carry out their duties promptly.[25] But this was a rare measure for the period. Increasingly governors turned away from direct pressures toward reliance on the courts to uphold the Anglican establishment.

[23] Bridenbaugh, pp. 27–28, 36.

[24] For political developments see D. M. Ellis and others, *A Short History of New York State* (Ithaca, N.Y., 1957), ch. iv.

[25] *Col. Laws N.Y.*, II, 62–63.

Official assistance was not withheld, however, when an Anglican church found local support for its services. By 1743 sufficient numbers of Anglicans had moved to the neighborhood of Newburgh in Orange County to elect English trustees in that former Palatine German town. The trustees took possession of the town glebe previously occupied by a Lutheran pastor when the Germans had controlled the town, reopened the local Lutheran church closed after many of the original settlers moved on, and called an SPG missionary. The remaining Lutherans, a minority, were unable to prevail on the governor and council to recover the properties for them. By 1770 the minister and trustees of the Anglican congregation had become incorporated as St. George's Church of Newburgh parish.[26] This was one of the few places outside the four established counties where the Anglican church ever found a secure home, and then only because Anglicans were in an obvious majority.

Where they were in a hopeless minority, the government took quite a different approach. In 1719 two Anglican petitioners complained to the governor and Council that Brookhaven in Suffolk County was applying its public taxing powers to "private uses" contrary to what was permitted in areas not subject to the Ministry Act. Brookhaven was supporting a dissenting minister as it had since the time of the Duke's Laws. The town trustees and sixty-seven other citizens of Brookhaven replied that they were using town funds to secure the "publick peace," a necessary condition for which was the promotion of morality through religion. The Council informed the two complainants that there was nothing it could do, since the town was peaceful and acting as its majority desired. If the petitioners felt themselves to be injured they could bring a common law suit for damages.[27] This decision typifies the official refusal to meddle in the religious affairs of

[26] E. M. Ruttenber, *History of the County of Orange* (Newburgh, N.Y., 1875), pp. 113–30.

[27] O'Callaghan, *Doc. Hist.*, III, 384–89; B. F. Thompson, II, 319–20.

towns controlled by dissenters and where the Anglican church was not established.

The town of Jamaica was the true test of English forbearance. In 1710 it refused to pay any salary to a new Anglican minister, its church wardens believing that Mr. Thomas Poyer was "not Quallifyed according to the act of assembly of this Province as minister or Incumbent of Jamaica to demand the whole or any part of the said Sallary." [28] Still insisting on the dissenting view of the Ministry Act of 1693, the town assigned the salary to a Presbyterian minister. That same year Jamaica also repossessed its parsonage and church which it had been deprived of by Cornbury.

The governor, Robert Hunter, despite the remonstrances of the Anglican clergy, would not intervene. He was sympathetic, but advised the Anglican minister at Jamaica that this was a question of property rights which should properly be decided by the courts.[29] Anglican militants, led by Rev. William Vesey of New York City, then appealed to the bishop of London, who had ecclesiastical jurisdiction over the American colonies. If their church was left to the mercy of local courts dominated by dissenters, they claimed, Anglicans would face the loss of all their privileges. The outcome of the dispute at Jamaica might not only determine the fate of the church in New York, but in other colonies as well. Hunter had to be made to intervene on their behalf.[30]

The controversy dragged on, punctuated by exchanges of recriminations between the clergymen and Hunter supported by other Anglicans, who agreed with him that the issue should be kept out of politics.[31] There were more appeals and

[28] *Eccles. Recs.*, III, 1871; also see O'Callaghan, *Doc. Hist.*, III, 214–23.

[29] *Eccles. Recs.*, III, 1900–01; O'Callaghan, *Doc. Hist.*, III, 233–36.

[30] *Ibid.*, pp. 224–33.

[31] *Eccles. Recs.*, III, 1901–24, 1926–27, 1950–53; see especially the letters of Lewis Morris and Governor Hunter to the SPG that the Anglican church in New York might be better off with less zeal and less intermixing of politics and religion (*ibid.*, pp. 1909–15).

then counterappeals to England. The Anglican ministers of New York, aided by the SPG and the earl of Clarendon, formerly Lord Cornbury, obtained an order from Queen Anne in 1712 permitting direct appeals to the Privy Council in cases to which the church in America was a party.[32]

Encouraged by this development, Poyer brought suit against the vestry at Jamaica in 1716. He was still without salary, but was back in possession of the church, the Presbyterians having constructed a new meeting house. The case was not settled until 1719, when Poyer won the right to receive his salary from the town, although the people of Jamaica rioted and refused to pay until their leaders had been arrested and fined. Throughout these proceedings Governor Hunter continued to maintain his detached and impartial attitude.[33]

In Governor William Burnet's administration, 1720–1728, the Jamaica dissenters commenced a suit of their own to repossess their church building. The provincial Supreme Court finally decided in their favor shortly before Poyer, a broken and defeated man, died in early 1732.[34] Some years later, in 1768, Jamaica's Presbyterians once more tried to withhold payment of salary to a newly arrived Anglican clergyman. After a long contest in the courts, they were defeated again, but not before the attending publicity had reminded the other dissenting sects of the grossly unfair burdens imposed by the Anglican establishment.[35]

A changed attitude on the part of the governors of New York province was not the only development contributing to the religious calm after Cornbury. The Jamaica affair in Hunter's administration had revealed a division within the Anglican following over the best methods of promoting their

[32] *Ibid.*, pp. 1963–64; *Col. Docs.*, V, 352–53.

[33] O'Callaghan, *Doc. Hist.*, III, 275–76, 283–303.

[34] *Ibid.*, pp. 309–11.

[35] D. R. Dillon, *The New York Triumvirate* (New York, 1949), pp. 49–52.

church. On one side were the zealots who had been to the fore during Cornbury's governorship. They advocated advance no matter the cost to the dissenters; they would rivet the establishment on the province by force if necessary. There was no room for concession in their theology. Opposing them was a more tolerant group advising caution and conciliation. They believed that peaceful, persuasive means, in view of their minority status and the uncertainties of colonial politics, were the best means to spread their religion. Colonel Caleb Heathcote embodied this approach:

> I should never [allow] the Government . . . to make use of an arbitrary and illegal power to serve either Church or State, which would not only leave the matter still doubtful, but instead of serving bring a scandal upon the Church; for that the warrant which my Lord Cornbury was pleased to direct . . . to dispossess the dissenting Minister of the Parsonage house [in Jamaica] without any form or due course of law did the Church more hurt than can easily be imagined.[36]

This group believed that "men of exemplary lives, sound learning, and a mild disposition"[37] would better serve the church in New York, men like Rev. Thomas Colgan, Anglican minister at Jamaica from 1732 to 1756. Moderate, going out of his way to bring peace to contending sects, Poyer's successor had a kind word for all beliefs. He had a church built for the Anglicans using funds solicited from prominent Anglicans in the colony. With a separate Anglican church, one of the major causes of the trouble at Jamaica was removed.[38] The views of men like Colgan and Heathcote came to prevail among the Anglicans and found favor with the church's chief source of protection in the colony, the royal governors.

The calm that followed Cornbury, rather than being a

[36] Fox, p. 228. [37] O'Callaghan, *Doc. Hist.*, III, 436.

[38] *Ibid.*, pp. 313–14.

permanent peace, was merely a truce. In the 1750's a chain of events reaching back to the previous decade profoundly altered the relations of church and state in New York. The Great Awakening, a wave of evangelical enthusiasm that swept through the dissenting churches of the colonies in the early 1740's, was to have a decisive bearing on the rise of religious freedom and the separation of church and state in New York. The revivalism of the Great Awakening, of great preachers such as George Whitefield, encouraged a closer personal relationship between the worshiper and his God and less emphasis on church formalism and clerical authority. As more people were led to rely upon their own thinking rather than on the teaching of their ministers, schisms and separations from the older sects occurred. One result was an increase in the variety of religious groups in New York. This further contributed to the colony's diversity of religious persuasions, a factor that had always worked for religious freedom in New York out of the sheer necessity of permitting people of many competing beliefs to live together in peace. These new sects came to see that "they had to demolish established churches along with intricate theological structures in order to have the track cleared for their own program of spiritual regeneration and impassioned zeal," thereby contributing to the spread of separation ideas.[39] A Dutch minister at New York City, writing in 1741, unsympathetically but accurately described the impact of the Great Awakening:

[39] Perry Miller, "The Contribution of the Protestant Churches to the Religious Liberty in Colonial America," *Church History*, IV (1935), 57–66, reprinted in the *Harvard Review*, II (1963–64), 60–69; for the quote see *ibid.*, p. 68. Miller goes on to suggest: "I do not think it has ever been sufficiently emphasized, or that it can be too much stressed, that there is a subtle and close connection between the shift of vital religious interest from elaborate intellectual systems of theology to the simplified emotional fervor of the new revivalism and the turning of Protestant Americans from a concern with ecclesiastical exclusiveness to the demand for liberty to all churches."

Because there is here perfect freedom of conscience for all, except Papists, a spirit of confusion is ever blazing up more and more. Everybody may do what seems right in his own eyes, so long as he does not disturb the public peace. Hence so many conventicles exist. Hence so many are perplexed and misled; while others neglect or scoff at the divine service not to speak of those who, on various wrong pretexts, entirely abstain from the Lord's Supper.[40]

As the Dutch dominie suggested, the Great Awakening, in some cases, contributed to a declining zeal.[41] The inevitable emotional letdown after the fever pitch of a revival often led those, who could never again be satisfied with their former staid church affiliations, to religious indifference or to ideas that were essentially nonsectarian rather than antireligious. A young member of the Dutch Reformed church, writing to a troubled friend, could say that religion was really very "plain and simple, and to the meanest capacity intelligible. Every man has a right to think for himself, as he shall answer for himself, and it is unreasonable for me to be angry with any one for being of different principles, as he has the same pretence to quarrel with me." Because truth was finite while error was limitless, he continued, people should "not be so positive and dogmatical, to set up for infallibility, and anathematize those of a contrary opinion." [42]

The significance of denominationalism began to be discounted; the reasonableness of claims to orthodoxy or exclusiveness of views was being questioned. If each man was free to read the Bible and decide for himself, it was difficult to

[40] *Eccles. Recs.*, IV, 2756. For other expressions of conservative Dutch and Anglican opinion on this see *ibid.*, pp. 2798–99, and O'Callaghan, *Doc. Hist.*, III, 316–18.

[41] Samuel Seabury, Anglican minister at Jamaica, also comments to the SPG on the rise of religious indifference, *ibid.*, pp. 327–28.

[42] William Livingston to Rev. James Sprout, Sept. 22, 1744, quoted in T. Sedgwick, Jr., *A Memoir of the Life of William Livingston* (New York, 1833), p. 54.

justify the establishment of any one view by the state. To force people to support a church or a minister with their taxes, when they did not believe in the dogmas of either, raised growing doubts about the premises on which the Anglican establishment in New York was founded. It was to become no longer a mere question of expediency that this church did not deserve support at the expense of others, but a matter of principle. And if it was right that Anglican ties with the state should be sundered, then the same applied to all churches. Short of this there could be no true religious freedom for those who held to no formal belief and belonged to no formal congregation.

To similar conclusions the older, well-established sects were also coming, if from a somewhat different direction. At one time most of these would have been satisfied to return to the multiple-establishment policy of the duke of York. But for many years the greater number of the dissenting churches of New York had been obliged to maintain themselves without public assistance; now they had come to prize the freedom from interference that went with this financial independence. A Dutch Reformed pastor could exclaim in 1738:

> Praise God, we enjoy the free exercise of our religious services in every respect, although there is not the least provision made for our Church by the Civil Authorities. Hence, mutual affection, and unity in faith and piety, under God's blessing and in conformity with His Word, are the only means of preserving our Christian churches, and of making them flourishing and prosperous.[43]

By no means all non-Anglican ministers and worshipers were so ecstatic about this state of self-reliance, but the newer point of view was steadily winning adherents.

From all these sources—an official English policy of leaving religion increasingly to its own devices, the impact of the

[43] *Eccles. Recs.*, IV, 2715.

Great Awakening, and a growing pride of independence among the older sects—a new concept of a separation between church and state resulted. In time it came to be linked inextricably to the religious freedom already so deeply rooted in the colony. The unreasonableness of subordinating the dissenting sects to an Anglican church, perhaps outnumbered by as much as fifteen to one, was a contradiction of the freedom of religion otherwise allowed by the English. As the historian William Smith, Jr., observed in 1756: "Hence partly arises the general discontent on account of the ministry acts; not so much that the provision made by them is engrossed by the minor sect, as because the body of the people are for an equal, universal, toleration of protestants, and utterly averse to any kind of ecclesiastical establishment." [44] By the 1750's, however, there was little hope for an end to the establishment so long as it had the backing of English law and of English authority.[45]

In the 1750's the contentions between dissenters and Anglicans were reopened on a grand scale after the many years of relative calm. Initiative came not from the English government or its representatives in the governor's office, but from the exigencies of provincial religion and politics. The dissenters soon passed over to the offensive, and the twenty years before the Revolution became a time of repeated sallies against the ramparts of the Anglican establishment. The opponents of ecclesiastical privilege waged their war with a new sense of confidence and purpose springing from the effective and appealing ideas of religious equality and separation that were the outgrowth of the formative years immediately preceding.

The occasion for the renewal of sectarian conflict was a movement to establish a college in New York City. Between 1746 and 1754 the New York legislature, caught up in a

[44] Smith, in N.Y. Hist. Soc., *Coll.*, IV, 284–85. [45] *Ibid.*

college-building enthusiasm that soared in the colonies after 1740, voted several lotteries to raise money. In 1753 the legislature appropriated a portion of the liquor excise to help pay teachers in the college. The year before, the rector and vestry had generously offered a piece of Trinity Church's sizable real estate holdings in the city as a site for the projected college. Behind this offer lay a long-standing desire to create an Episcopal seminary to supply Anglican ministers and advance the fortunes of the church in America.[46]

With Chief Justice James De Lancey presiding over the province as acting governor, Trinity renewed its offer in 1754, but this time conditions were openly attached. In return for the gift of land, the college president was to be a practicing Anglican and religious services at the college were to follow the rites of the Church of England. The ten trustees of the college fund, appointed earlier by the legislature and including a majority of Anglicans, agreed to accept Trinity's gift, conditions and all. De Lancey and his Council, on the recommendation of the trustees, later ordered the attorney general to draw up a college charter to be issued on the prerogative of the acting governor. At no time was the Assembly, a center of antichurch sentiment as well as controller of the college funds, consulted. After these developments the dispute, until then largely a war of words, took a decided political turn before its denouement in 1756.[47]

The affair of King's College, viewed in retrospect, becomes very involved and complex.[48] At one level, it was a contest

[46] William Livingston and others, *The Independent Reflector*, M. M. Klein, ed. (Cambridge, Mass., 1963), pp. 32–35; *Eccles. Recs.*, V, 3220, 3384, 3394–95; *Col. Docs.*, VI, 777.

[47] *Eccles. Recs.*, V, 3478–80; *Independent Reflector*, pp. 34, 37, 43–45.

[48] The fullest account is Milton M. Klein, "The American Whig: William Livingston of New York" (unpub. dissertation, Columbia University, 1954), chs. ix–x. In print, there is Klein's introduction to *Independent Reflector*, pp. 32–46; and Bridenbaugh, ch. vi. The latter is not entirely adequate and is inferior to Klein's dissertation.

between the De Lancey and Livingston families for primacy in New York's tangled politics. At another, it was bound up with the perpetual competition of governor and Assembly for power. But it was also a contest over whether a college, partly financed by public money, was to be controlled by the Anglican minority. The rivalry between De Lanceys and Livingstons assumed religious dimensions so that the former found themselves associated with the interest of the Church of England and the latter with the dissenting or antichurch elements.[49] It is difficult not to suspect that the differences over religion, which set off the dispute, became in time merely ammunition for the political battle. But the fact that the affair was fought out to a large extent on the issues of religious equality and the privileges of the Anglican establishment suggests the wide appeal and importance of these questions to those for whom the politicians were performing.

Objections to an Anglican charter for the college touched on several crucial points dividing church and dissenting groups. It was contended that since a majority in the colony was not Anglican and would not send its sons to be exposed to an Anglican education, the use of public funds to support the college infringed on the majority's rights. The proposed charter would bar dissenters from college offices, while the requirement of Anglican chapel services would be "inconsistent with religious liberty." But such objections were dismissed by De Lancey, who proceeded with the chartering arrangements. King's College was officially incorporated in the autumn of 1754 for all practical purposes as an Anglican institution. It mattered little to dissenters that the college charter specified that no one would be denied admission because of his religious beliefs; the important fact to them was that the hated Anglican minority would be in control of the institution.[50]

In the Assembly, where the Livingston faction had picked up the issue and begun to oppose the Anglican college, at-

[49] Dillon, p. 33. [50] *Eccles. Recs.*, V, 3480–83, 3506–14.

tempts to prevent issuance of the charter by the acting governor proved ineffective.[51] Next, the opposition introduced an act of incorporation to supersede the charter. The Livingston party presented a bill prepared by William Livingston, William Smith, Jr., and John Morin Scott. These three, nicknamed the "Triumvirate," had carried the brunt of the anti-Anglican attack in the opening phase of the college controversy before it had been taken up in the Assembly. The bill was introduced by Robert Livingston, brother of William and a leader of the Livingston group. The proposal excluded religion from the college curriculum and even the teaching of comparative theology, and would have made domination of the college less meaningful to the Anglicans.[52]

The incorporation bill favorable to the dissenting interest was killed by the De Lanceyites, who tabled it for the remainder of the session.[53] But if the Livingstons had failed to obtain legislative incorporation of a nonsectarian public college, the Anglican-De Lancey faction was unable to secure Assembly confirmation of the Anglican college charter or the release of the lottery moneys to the new college. As the Assembly session of 1754 drew to a close, the college issue was stalemated.[54] In an effort to break this deadlock, supporters of the Anglican college sought to win the votes of Dutch Reformed legislators by offering their church a divinity professorship in King's College. A supplement was added to the charter to this effect in 1755 through the efforts of the Anglican clergy and Dominie Ritzema, a pro-Anglican leader of the Dutch church in New York City. Ritzema, however, was unable to persuade Dutch Reformed members of the Assembly to vote to release the lottery fund to King's College. For his labors he was excoriated by most of the Dutch congrega-

[51] Dillon, p. 37.

[52] *Ibid.*, p. 38; Klein, "American Whig," p. 413; *Independent Reflector*, p. 205 n. 2; *Jour. General Assembly, 1691–1765*, II, 413–19.

[53] *Eccles. Recs.*, V, 3525–26.

[54] Klein, "American Whig," pp. 415–16.

tions in the province and formally rebuked by the consistory of his own church.[55]

The impasse was broken only after Sir Charles Hardy arrived from England to become the new permanent governor. Hardy soon aligned himself with the De Lanceys. Since there was now little prospect of the governor's calling an election that might unseat the De Lanceyites in the Assembly, the college issue lost some of its attractiveness to the opposition. James De Lancey himself, tarnished by the controversy, was also inclined toward a less aggressive role. In late 1756, with the developing French and Indian War demanding action from an Assembly divided by the college issue, a compromise was reached. An act was passed apportioning the lottery fund equally between King's College and the city of New York, the latter to use its share to establish a contagion ward for diseased seamen. Thus both sides settled for less than their original demands in order to remove the college question from the political arena.[56]

But during all this time the dispute had kept religious differences boiling. It afforded dissenters an opportunity to launch their strongest attack upon the Anglican establishment since the time of Cornbury. Over the intervening years the growing acceptance of a separation between church and state had altered many of the former grounds of opposition to the establishment. The college controversy came at a time when separation ideas were being formulated as a hard-hitting ideological weapon; the dispute gave a currency to these ideas that attracted great support among New York dissenters.

The major burden for giving form to the sometimes vague

[55] *Ibid.*, pp. 424–25; letters, Henry Barclay to Samuel Johnson, Nov. 4, 1754, Johnson to William Samuel Johnson and William Johnson, Nov. 25, 1754, and Johnson to William Samuel Johnson, May 14, 1755, in Herbert and Carol Schneider, eds., *Samuel Johnson, President of King's College* (New York, 1929), IV, 25, 26, 35; *Eccles. Recs.*, V, 3542–45, 3554–55.

[56] Klein, "American Whig," pp. 427–30, 434–35; *Col. Laws N.Y.*, IV, 160–62.

aspirations to a more perfect religious liberty, through a separation of religion from politics, fell to the brilliant young trio of Presbyterians, William Livingston, John Morin Scott, and William Smith, Jr. All well-educated, prominent lawyers and active in public affairs, they embodied the harvest of prestige and talents which had come to the Presbyterian church in New York from the years of growth and experience since Cornbury's time. Each of this trio believed deeply in religious freedom and was bitterly opposed to establishments in any form. In a series of influential essays, appearing in New York City between 1752 and 1755 under the titles *Independent Reflector* and "The Watch Tower," the "Triumvirate" used the college question as a focal point for a general discussion of church-state principles.[57]

They described the college as heralding a campaign of Anglican persecution to fasten the church on the entire province. The college evidenced the hold which an unpopular minority sect was acquiring over the public life of the province through its connections with the English government. The essayists took great pains, however, to demonstrate the old dissenting contention that the Church of England had never been rightfully established in New York. Its unlawful aggrandizements had been the chief source of discord in a colony where religious diversity properly required a free competition in ideas.[58]

The Triumvirate founded their charges upon a broad conception of religious liberty and a conviction that religious zeal and persecution should give way to an enlightened tolerance of contrary views. In an early number of the *Independent Reflector*, Livingston proposed

> to defend every Sect, of whatever Denomination, in the undisturbed Enjoyment of their civil and religious Liberties, and to repress every persecuting Spirit that offers them Violence;—to

[57] Dillon, ch. ii; and Klein's character sketches, *Independent Reflector*, pp. 5–18. [58] *Independent Reflector*, nos. xvii–xxii, xliv.

expose that barbarous Zeal, which would even injure their Persons, was it not restrained by the milder Law of the Land;—to promote universal Benevolence amongst Christians of different Professions;—and to beat down all savage Wrath about Opinions where the Conduct is irreproachable with Immorality.[59]

On the subject of church-state relations, Livingston was certain that the history of mankind under establishments was one long unbroken chronicle of persecution, hypocrisy, and folly: "Among the many Instances of the Abuse of Government," he wrote, "there is none more immediately destructive of the natural Rights of Mankind, than the Interposition of the secular Arm in Matters purely religious." Such intervention by civil government "may compel the Man to act in Opposition to his Judgment, but can never gain the Mind's Assent to the Fitness of an Action, which is contradictory to the Dictates of its own Judgment, be it wrongly or rightly informed." "The Absurdity of a Religion, supported and inforced by the Terrors of the Law," Livingston concluded, "is too apparent to need much farther Display." [60]

Woven into these essays is an element not present before in the attacks of dissenters upon the Anglicans. It is the logic of natural rights philosophy, the idea that governments are limited in their actions by mankind's self-evident rights to life, liberty, and property. Religion was part of that untouchable realm that lay beyond the legal reach of secular authority. Natural rights theory in time would elevate the religious freedoms of Americans to the lofty plane of indisputable principle.

The Kings College affair had displayed the new-found resources of the Presbyterians as advocates of the dissenting cause. In the 1760's, long-smouldering differences within the Dutch church over English-language services and relations with the Netherlands church broke into the open, dividing

[59] *Ibid.*, no. vi, 89.

[60] *Ibid.*, no. xxxvii, 312, 313–14; see also no. xxxvi.

congregations and ending its leadership of the non-Anglican denominations.[61] Presbyterians now moved to the fore. Where the Old World–directed Dutch leaders had for years been a major source of support for a *status quo* favorable to the Church of England, the Presbyterians represented the newer currents of protest against Anglican privileges. Devoted to their religious liberty, Presbyterians were outspoken in attacking the establishment, recognizing the confining influence it had for their own freedom of worship.

One continuing effect of the establishment on Presbyterian worship was the inability to secure corporate charters to safeguard church property. In 1766 the New York City Presbyterian church petitioned the Privy Council for a corporate grant. Following adverse recommendations of the New York governor's Council and of the Board of Trade and Plantations, the Privy Council denied the request the next year, claiming that a charter would conflict with the king's obligation to uphold the exclusive rights of the Church of England. Particularly aggravating to Presbyterians was the implication of the New York Council's report that no dissenting church denying the legality of the provincial establishment should be favored with incorporation. It would create a petty jurisdiction to fly in the face of that establishment. This refusal came after similar refusals of incorporation for the city's Lutheran and French Protestant churches. It was but additional proof to dissenters of an English design to curb their rights of free worship.[62]

In 1767, the English bishop of Llandaff savagely attacked the religious sincerity of Americans and called for an Angli-

[61] A. J. Wall, "The Controversy in the Dutch Church in New York Concerning Preaching in English, 1754–1768," New-York Historical Society, *Quarterly Bulletin*, XII (1928), 39–58; E. T. Corwin and others, *A History of the Reformed Church, Dutch* . . . (New York, 1885), pp. 140–41, 150–58.

[62] *Eccles. Recs.*, VI, 4046–48, 4067, 4083–84, 4095–96, 4098–99; Bridenbaugh, pp. 260–61.

can episcopate in the colonies. To his voice were added those of Anglican clergymen in the middle and northern colonies. Such demands for a colonial bishop were not new. The colonial Anglican clergy, the Church of England's hierarchy, and the SPG had long maintained that a bishop with powers of ordination was needed to bolster the church's weak hold on the colonies. At this particular juncture the home government seems to have had no intention of entertaining these appeals. Because the church was so unpopular in the colonies, a bishop would only stir up American dissenters and add one more source of friction to what was already, in the late 1760's, a tense relationship between colonies and mother country. But coming when it did, following the Kings College affair and refusals of charters to dissenting churches, New Yorkers feared that the demands for a bishopric would shortly be taken up by the government at home.[63]

William Livingston once more took pen in hand to attack the idea of an episcopate in a series of newspaper pieces entitled the "American Whig."[64] In New York City, Presbyterians and Baptists joined in early 1769 to form a Society of Dissenters to "protect and to enlarge their rights" and to repel the insidious conspiracy they now saw under way. Livingston, John Morin Scott, and Alexander McDougall, a leader of the New York "Sons of Liberty," all Presbyterians, were among the society's first officers.[65]

In the same year New York City dissenters published and

[63] The leading monograph on the episcopate question is still A. L. Cross, *The Anglican Episcopate and the American Colonies* (New York, 1902); see particularly ch. iv, and pp. 164–65, 199, 256–58. The letters of Rev. Samuel Johnson, first president of Kings College, are also helpful on this question; see H. and C. Schneider, I, 71–484 *passim.* These are supplemented by Bridenbaugh, chs. vii–xi.

[64] Klein, "American Whig," pp. 597–98, 603, 605; Cross, p. 197; Sedgwick, pp. 136–40.

[65] H. L. Osgood, "The Society of Dissenters Founded at New York in 1769," *American Historical Review*, VI (1900–01), 498–507.

distributed a broadside detailing their grievances against the Anglican party. The Ministry Act of 1693, Cornbury's seizure of Presbyterian property at Jamaica, the persecution of the Presbyterian Makemie in 1707, the refusal to incorporate dissenting churches, Anglican monopolization of provincial politics by unfair means, and the threatened episcopate were the by now familiar charges leveled in this long bill of indictment. The concluding advice of the broadside was to elect only tried and true dissenters to the Assembly.[66]

During the 1769 and 1770 Assembly sessions there was a concerted effort to repeal or emasculate the laws establishing the Anglican church. A combination of dissenters and Dutch representatives from the Albany area, who had broken away from conservative leadership after the schism in the Dutch church, provided the votes for this campaign of attrition. An Assembly bill of 1769, to exempt all Protestants in the four lower counties from ministerial support taxes, was passed and sent to the Anglican-controlled Council, where it was defeated.[67] In 1770 a bill, drawn up in answer to a dissenting petition from Albany County praying for outright repeal of the Ministry Act, was passed in the Assembly only to be killed in the Council.[68] The exemption bill defeated the previous year was repassed in the lower house before being beaten down again in the upper house.[69] Acting Governor Cadwallader Colden reported to England in 1770 that these attacks on the Church of England came from an unruly faction

[66] *Reasons for the present glorious combination of the dissenters in this city, against the farther encroachments and stratagems of the episcopalians* [New York, 1769], rare book division, New York Public Library.

[67] New York [State], *Journal of the General Assembly of the Colony of New York, 1766–1776* (Albany, 1820), May 13, 15, 1769; *Jour. Leg. Council*, II, 1702, 1704, 1706; Bridenbaugh, pp. 262–63.

[68] *Jour. General Assembly, 1766–76*, Jan. 8, 25, 26, 1770; *Jour. Leg. Council*, II, 1746, 1750, 1751–55.

[69] *Jour. General Assembly, 1766–76*, Jan. 12, 13, 25, 1770.

made up "chiefly of Dissenters" who were of "Republican principles." [70]

Colden's description was essentially correct. By 1770 the campaign against the detested establishment had merged with the general political attack upon English policies in the colony. The religious grievances of New Yorkers became rooted in the protest movement leading on ultimately to hostilities and independence. Reporting on the "State of the Anglo-American Church" in October of 1776, Charles Inglis, Anglican clergyman of New York City, was well aware of the role assumed by religious influences in the separation from England; he had recently been routed in the night and forced to flee by a mob bent on collaring him. "It is now past all doubt," wrote Inglis, "that an abolition of the Church of England was one of the principal springs of the dissenting leaders' conduct; and hence the unanimity of dissenters in this business." [71] Independence was a signal for dissenters to sweep away all reminders of the hated Anglican establishment. A report from Staten Island in the summer of 1776 contained what many New Yorkers would have considered a fitting epitaph for the Anglican settlement in the province: "The Episcopal Churches in New York are all shut up, the prayer books burned, and the Ministers scattered abroad, in this and neighboring provinces. It is now the Puritan's high holiday season and they enjoy it with rapture." [72]

As New Yorkers stood in 1776 on the verge of new beginnings, they had pronounced convictions about the values of religious liberty and a separation of church and state. For many years the people of New York had enjoyed a rather wide freedom of worship. That freedom had come from a recognition by their rulers that the great diversity of religious belief made it impossible as well as inexpedient to impress any

[70] *Col. Docs.*, VIII, 208. [71] O'Callaghan, *Doc. Hist.*, III, 1050.

[72] Quoted in New-York Historical Society, *Collections, 1870* (New York, 1871), p. 270.

one mode of belief on the province. Ingrained habits and expectations arising from long usage, steeled in defending against attempts to invade their liberty in the name of a state church, had developed into the incontrovertible certainty that freedom of religion was a natural right of men. This certainty was fortified by the experience of the Great Awakening and further elaborated as secular and rationalist modes of thought came forward in the eighteenth century. Dissenters were fortunate, too, that the Anglican church had been weak and unappealing to the great mass of New York's people. Its close identification with the policies and practices of the English crown had discredited not only the Anglican church but also the very idea of extensive church dependence upon the support of government.

PART TWO

The Constitutional Basis of Church-State Relations

ONE of the great objects of the Revolutionary generation, shaped by its English heritage, was to secure order, continuity, and certainty through law. The history of church and state in colonial New York offers numerous instances of this attachment to due process and generally accepted rules of public conduct.

Opposed to this legalistic outlook was the power of the English regime to act contrary to what the people or their representatives felt to be the true interests of their colony. Governor Fletcher's unpopular construction of the Ministry Act of 1693, the persecutions of Lord Cornbury, the refusal to incorporate dissenting churches in the face of popular demands, and the granting of an Anglican charter for Kings College were all remembered as abuses of the assumed compact between the people and their rulers. Often, however, what the colonists viewed as legally binding was no more than precedent based upon usage which was not recognized as law by the English authorities. Because the crown's representatives, acting in the interests of the home government, could override these customs popularly viewed as law, by the mid-eighteenth century there was a growing element of uncertainty and insecurity present in colonial life.

This insecurity undermined the colonial faith in a government of laws and not of men. The religion of the people, such a vital part of their existence, was as much threatened by this contradiction between law and custom as was politics. To correct this unsettling imbalance, to bring the law into closer conformity with accepted practice, the Revolutionary government of New York took early action to place religious observance beyond the reach of political expediency. The palladium of the people's rights was to be a written set of fundamental laws, the state's first constitution, in 1777. It was in this document that New York's founding fathers enshrined the principles of religious liberty and separation of church and state as they understood them.

IV

The Constitution of 1777

THE Fourth Provincial Congress, the assembly of elected representatives convened at White Plains on July 9, 1776, to vote New York's acceptance of the Declaration of Independence, met at a time of great peril. The English had landed on Staten Island in force and were preparing to seize New York City. During the lifetime of the congress the British army captured the city and forced the Continentals to retreat into New Jersey and up the Hudson. Long Island and the other lower counties were lost to the enemy. Only with great difficulty and luck was Sir Guy Carleton's invasion from Canada along the Champlain route in the fall of 1776 turned back. Undaunted by the grim prospects, the congress, on July 10, 1776, changed its title to the Convention of the Representatives of the State of New York, and prepared to draw up a new republican plan of government.[1]

Shortly after, on August 2, 1776, the convention issued a proclamation calling for a day of fasting and prayer:

Resolved unanimously, That the twenty-seventh day of August instant, be kept throughout this State as a day of fasting, humilia-

[1] Of the several general and quite adequate accounts of the Revolution in New York, I have used the most recent, D. M. Ellis and others, *A Short History of New York State* (Ithaca, N.Y., 1957), pp. 100–01, and ch. x.

tion and prayer to Almighty God, for the imploring of his divine assistance in the organization and establishment of a form of government for the security and perpetuation of the civil and religious rights and liberties of mankind, and to supplicate his farther protection in the war which now rages throughout America.[2]

It was from a conviction such as this, that religion lay at the heart of the struggle for liberty, that the New York Convention proceeded to its task.

The convention of 1776–1777 was virtually a government on horseback, operating from its saddlebags. Forced to keep on the move to remain out of reach of the British, it met variously at White Plains, Poughkeepsie, Fishkill, and Kingston. Beset by an impossible array of tasks, the members were obliged to divide their attentions, to improvise, and on occasion some of them even to take the field to assume military command. The convention had to raise troops, find reliable officers to put over them, procure supplies and munitions, inspirit those of little faith, and maintain a vigilant check on the many Loyalists who remained within the Continental lines. One of the most nagging and wearisome problems was to find money to pay for these operations.[3] That they found time to prepare a new form of government and implement it, let alone adopt a constitution that would withstand the rigors of forty years of New York politics, is a source of wonder, "for the builders, every one had his sword girded by his side, and so builded" (Neh. 4:18).

The work of the convention was carried on largely through a system of special committees. As new problems

[2] New York [State], *Journals of the Provincial Congress, Provincial Convention, Committee of Safety and Council of Safety of the State of New York* (Albany, 1842), I, 554; hereafter cited as *Jour. Prov. Cong.*

[3] On the work of the convention generally, see its journal in *ibid.*, I, *passim.*

arose, new committees were selected to deal with them. The task of preparing a plan of government was assigned, on August 1, 1776, to a committee of thirteen, to which a fourteenth was added later. The members represented a fairly accurate cross-section of the abilities and interests in the convention: John Jay, Gouverneur Morris, and Robert R. Livingston would later figure prominently in the affairs of the new nation; John Sloss Hobart, John Morin Scott, and Abraham and Robert Yates were to perform able services for their state. The committee also reflected the religious diversity of New York with the Episcopal, Presbyterian, Dutch Reformed, Lutheran, and Quaker persuasions represented among the membership.[4]

Little is known of the deliberations of this committee. Members were continually being called off on other pressing matters. Its report had to be postponed several times.[5] The committee apparently did not begin serious work on a draft constitution until late in the year 1776.[6] Existing evidence indicates that John Jay authored the first draft of the constitution. But the presence of a second draft serving as the basis for debates in the full convention, and Jay's efforts to secure major amendments to this draft from the floor strongly suggest that the original Jay draft was thoroughly scrutinized and underwent extensive revision in committee.[7]

The committee finally presented its plan of government on March 12, 1777. For over a month the delegates debated the

[4] Committee members, in addition to those listed in the text, were: John Broome, Charles De Witt, William Duer, William Smith, Samuel Townshend, Henry Wisner, Sr., and James Duane, who was added later (*ibid.*, p. 552). [5] *Ibid.*, pp. 527, 649, 737, 749, 823.

[6] *Ibid.*, pp. 749; and letter, R. R. Livingston, Fishkill, to Edward Rutledge, Nov. 13, 1776, Robert R. Livingston Papers, Bancroft Transcripts, I, 277, New York Public Library.

[7] Compare Jay's floor amendments, *Jour. Prov. Cong.*, I, *passim*, with the drafts in C. Z. Lincoln, *Constitutional History of New York* (Rochester, N.Y., 1906), I, 498–99, 515. The Jay Papers at Columbia University are of no help on the question of authorship.

new constitution with frequent diversions to consider urgent war matters. Several important amendments were made at this stage. On Sunday, April 20, 1777, the first constitution of the state of New York was formally adopted by the convention with only one dissenting vote from among those present and voting.[8]

Debate on the religious provisions of the draft constitution was led by John Jay and Gouverneur Morris, frequently joined by Robert R. Livingston. While differences arose on the floor, most often between Jay and Morris, at no time was there any open resistance to the ideas of guaranteeing religious liberty and separating church and state through the constitution. These seem to have been accepted from the start as being naturally entitled to inclusion; no one ever questioned their intrinsic merit or their relevance to the document under discussion. Clashes of opinion that did occur were over subsidiary questions of scope or degree. For the Western world of that day, this amounted to a rather remarkable consensus upon fundamental religious principles.

Of the differences that did arise in the convention, one of the most vigorous and protracted concerned the religious freedom article of the proposed constitution. Again, the question at issue was not its inclusion, but whether Roman Catholics had an unqualified right to an equal enjoyment of its terms. Back of this loomed the much more important consideration of the reach of this principle. Was it to be freedom merely for thoughts acceptable to the people of that day, or freedom for all religious beliefs regardless of their compatibility with those of a current majority in the community?

John Jay, spare framed, strait-laced, severely intense in speech and gesture, spoke for those who insisted that Catholics should not be permitted the full rights accorded to others because of their supposed temporal allegiance to the pope.

[8] *Jour. Prov. Cong.*, I, 833, 891–92.

Gouverneur Morris, his ample dimensions a haven for more generous thoughts, advocated an unrestricted grant of religious freedom. Jay, consumed by the old antipopery traditions abroad in colonial America, believed that Catholicism was at root a conspiracy against Protestantism, and as such was politically dangerous if not subversive. Fortifying this view were bitter Jay family memories of the persecution and banishment of their Huguenot ancestors from France by a Catholic king. These memories were so vividly compelling that Jay, unswayed by the moderating religious influences of his day, was bent on making it impossible for Catholics to settle in New York.[9]

Morris, while no less convinced than Jay of religion's importance as a regulator of morality, and hence stability, was influenced by the increasingly secular and latitudinarian spirit of his day. He could be tolerant of alien doctrines because sectarian differences simply did not bulk as large in his thinking as in Jay's. Men of good will may differ on matters of faith, but that should not affect their rights in this world. Who can say which faith is correct? [10] It has been written of Morris that "he did not have to contend with the dark terrors of Calvinism, the sense of sin, fear of the Hereafter, and the truth . . . that only some are foreordained to everlasting life . . . none of that touched Morris in the slightest. 'Whatever is, is,' he was fond of saying and was quite sure in the long run it was all for the best." [11]

[9] Frank Monaghan, *John Jay* (New York, 1935), p. 25; Daniel Walther, *Gouverneur Morris* (New York, 1934), p. 25; George Dangerfield, *Chancellor Robert R. Livingston of New York, 1746–1813* (New York, 1960), p. 91; see also the interesting autobiographical fragment, written by Jay in later life, in William Jay, *Life of John Jay* (New York, 1833), I, 1–9.

[10] J. W. Francis, *Gouverneur Morris: A Fragment* (n.p., n.d.), p. 11; Dangerfield, pp. 91–92.

[11] Howard Swiggett, *The Extraordinary Mr. Morris* (New York, 1952), p. 3.

The draft of the plan of government authored by Jay contained an article stating that "free Toleration be forever allowed in this State to all denominations of Christians without preference or distinction and to all Jews, Turks and Infidels." But this toleration was to be denied "to such Christians or others as shall hold and teach for true Doctrines, principles incompatible with and repugnant to the peace, safety and well being of civil society in general or of this state in particular." [12] Jay's hatred of Catholicism led him thus to propose a virtual *carte blanche* for the state government, granting it a roving commission to inquire into the doctrines of sects to assess their bearing on the public safety. He was willing to accept a power which the English government in a hundred years of rule in New York had never claimed to possess, a power to regulate private religious beliefs as well as public acts.[13]

At some point in the deliberations of the committee on the constitution, the Jay draft article was drastically revised and the proscriptive clauses deleted. Substituted for them was the brief and direct grant appearing in the draft submitted to the full convention: "That the free Toleration of religious profession and worship be forever allowed within this State to all mankind." [14] Jay and his fellow committee members were not at odds on this point, but seem instead to have differed as to the true meaning of the qualifying clauses in Jay's original proposal.

When the religious freedom article came up for debate in the convention on March 20, Jay immediately moved the addition of a proviso clause virtually identical to the passage deleted from his draft by the committee.[15] The convention's journal carries the terse entry, "Many debates arose thereon." It appears that a majority of the delegates were unwilling to

[12] Lincoln, I, 541. [13] *Ibid.* [14] *Ibid.*

[15] The March 20 debates can be followed in *Jour. Prov. Cong.*, I, 844.

turn over such sweeping powers to the new state government as Jay insisted on. Faced with this opposition, Jay withdrew his first amendment, and he was given leave to substitute a second aimed directly and by name at the source of his discontents. He moved the following addition to the grant of toleration:

> Except the professors of the religion of the church of Rome, who ought not to hold lands in, or be admitted to a participation of the civil rights enjoyed by the members of this State, until such time as the said professors shall appear in the supreme court of this State, and there most solemnly swear, that they verily believe in their consciences, that no pope, priest or foreign authority on earth, hath power to absolve the subjects of this State from their allegiance to the same.

The substitute went on to require such persons to "renounce and believe to be false and wicked, the dangerous and damnable doctrine" that they could be absolved of their sins by the pope or of the terms of the oath specified by this amendment.[16]

The Jay amendment, with its stern Reformation logic, was essentially backward-looking but nonetheless evocative. It could well be expected to call up old Protestant suspicions of Catholics among the representatives. It occasioned prolonged debate before it came to a vote and was defeated, 10 votes in the affirmative to 19 opposed. The frontal attack turned aside, further discussion of the article was postponed to the next day, doubtless to allow passions to subside.

On the afternoon of March 21, the convention returned to the religious freedom article.[17] By then the anti-Catholic group had altered its tactics, having decided to achieve the proscription of Catholics by means of a naturalization oath for aliens. In place of the amendment defeated the previous day, Jay moved the adoption of a clause which "provided that the

[16] *Ibid.* [17] *Ibid.*, pp. 845–46.

liberty of conscience hereby granted, shall not be construed to encourage licentiousness, or be used in such manner as to disturb or endanger the safety of the State." This amounted to a reservation of police powers to regulate religious observance where it was deemed injurious to the general welfare, though its vague distinction between advocacy and action apparently troubled several delegates.

Gouverneur Morris saw little difference in fact between this general proviso and the Jay amendment referring to Catholics that had been withdrawn the previous day. The convention, however, rejected his point of order. Robert R. Livingston then moved a more precise substitute in place of Jay's latest proposal. It would apply only to actions specifically violative of state law, rather than to beliefs and actions both. The substitute motion was voted down, and the Jay proviso was then adopted, but Livingston's proposal was later to reappear in a slightly less restrictive form in the final version of the constitution. The implication of these moves is that the convention believed the police power should operate against threatening actions performed in the name of religion, but should move in the realm of sectarian ideas only with great caution and only when specific actions or practices were involved.

On April 1, 1777, the amended article on religious freedom was accepted after some changes in wording had been made, including the alterations in the proviso bringing it more in line with Livingston's earlier motion.[18] Article 38 of the new constitution now read:

WHEREAS we are required by the benevolent principles of rational liberty, not only to expel civil tyranny, but also to guard against the spiritual oppression and intolerance, wherewith the bigotry and ambition of weak and wicked priests and princes,

[18] *Ibid.*, p. 860; the convention journal does not reveal when or for what reasons the last-minute changes in phrasing were made.

have scourged mankind: This Convention doth further, in the name and by the authority of the good people of this State, ORDAIN, DETERMINE and DECLARE, that the free exercise and enjoyment of religious profession and worship, without discrimination or preference, shall forever hereafter be allowed within this State to all mankind. Provided that the liberty of conscience hereby granted, shall not be so construed, as to excuse acts of licentiousness, or justify practices inconsistent with the peace or safety of this State.[19]

The preamble to this article was from Jay's draft.[20] It affirmed the convention's attachment to reason in ordering the affairs of free men and attested its conviction that America, with its enlightened tolerance of religious diversity, was fundamentally different from Europe with its sorry history of bigotry, persecution, and despotism.

A significant change in the final version, unrecorded as was the change in the proviso clause, was the deletion of the word "toleration," and the substitution for it of "exercise and enjoyment." This seemingly minor point was actually quite meaningful. It implied the difference between a concession given and conceivably subject to recall by the state, connoted by the word "toleration," and a right lying beyond the power of earthly authority to rescind. Perhaps the convention wished to avoid comparisons with the English Act of Toleration when it made this change, for that act far from guaranteed the degree of religious liberty that the New York constitution was intended to affirm.

By Article 38 the infant state of New York had wedded its fortunes to the principle of religious freedom for all, whether Protestant, Catholic, Jew, or other. Moreover, the convention had refused to circumscribe this right by any broad reservation of state regulatory power over religious beliefs and prac-

[19] New York [State], *The Constitution of the State of New York* (Fishkill, 1777), art. 38; this is the first official printing of the constitution. [20] Lincoln, I, 541.

tices short of acts harmful to the peace and safety of the community. Despite the presence of anti-Catholic suspicions, it was determined that such feeling should not be permitted to mar the general applicability of this liberal article. Here at last New Yorkers had the explicit guarantee, denied them under English rule, of a right long enjoyed for the most part but never with any certainty that it could withstand the test of political expediency. Now it seemed that they had achieved that certainty.

A subject requiring a good deal less deliberation than the religious freedom article was the formal disestablishment of the Church of England. The Anglican establishments in the four lower counties had already ceased to exist; the local populace had seen to this at the outbreak of hostilities.[21] Only in areas occupied by the British army were Anglican churches reopened, but it is doubtful that any of these were deriving much if any tax support from their communities. The dislocations of war had brought an end to the former arrangements.

Article 35 of the new constitution provided for the continuation of the English common and statute law and the acts of assembly which together comprised the formal law of New York as of April 19, 1775, the date of the opening battle of the War for Independence. Certain classes of laws, however, were excepted from this; one exception being "that all such parts of the said common law, and all such . . . statutes, and acts . . . , or parts thereof, as may be construed to establish or maintain any particular denomination of Christians, or their Ministers , . . . hereby are, abrogated and rejected."[22] This passage occasioned no debate of any importance, and it was accepted without a division.

The draft article, as it had come from committee, had mentioned the Church of England by name, but in its final

[21] New-York Historical Society, *Collections, 1870* (New York, 1871), p. 270. [22] *Const. of N.Y.* (1777), art. 35.

form the reference was deleted in favor of the general phrase "particular denomination of Christians."[23] One explanation for this was the continuing refusal to give substance, even retroactively, to the official English view that the Church of England had legally been established in New York.

But there were other reasons to refrain from heaping special odium on Episcopalianism. The exigencies of war made conciliation of New York Episcopalians seem a reasonable course of action. For years, numbers of the best talents in the province had made their way into the Anglican church. The perilous times dictated a policy of winning over as many as possible of these Anglican lights whose names were stamped with quality and ability. Loyalism was a major threat to the Revolutionary movement in New York partly because of the prominent figures associated with it.[24] In a letter to the Continental Congress of July 11, 1776, the convention had pleaded for action by that body to expunge from the Book of Common Prayer passages objectionable to dissenters and, conversely, to curb the unbridled attacks of dissenters on the Anglican church which were interfering "with the interest of the American cause."[25] A further reason for the conciliatory approach in the convention, that took the form of refusals to single out the Church of England by name for the purpose of imposing special penalties, was the influence of Episcopalians among the representatives. The opinion of men like John Jay carried great weight and enabled Episcopalians to play decisive roles in the deliberations. These were men who were intent upon raising a new, loyal American Episcopal church from the ruins of the old,[26] and they were not inclined to

[23] Lincoln, I, 540.

[24] On Loyalism, see Ellis and others, pp. 114–15; and C. P. Nettels, *The Roots of American Civilization* (New York, 1938), pp. 626, 627, 679.

[25] *Jour. Prov. Cong.*, I, 521.

[26] E. P. Alexander, *A Revolutionary Conservative: James Duane of New York* (New York, 1938), pp. 176–79.

burden themselves in this task by consigning their faith to an inferior position through the terms of the state's constitution. While accepting the necessity, even the wisdom, of disestablishment, they had no desire to fasten the taint of disloyalty on Episcopalianism as a form of worship too. And so, while the connection of the Anglican church with the state was broken, the church itself was left substantially undisturbed.

An aim of the convention related to disestablishment was to prevent clergymen from ever again interfering in politics as they, particularly Anglican clerics, had frequently done during the colonial period. This did not mean that the Revolutionary movement in New York was inimical to religion, far from it. But it did indicate the wide acceptance of a separation policy recognizing that formal, denominational religion had interests and obligations peculiarly its own and that politics and religion ought to overlap as little as possible. This conclusion had slowly developed over the years since Lord Cornbury's administration. Non-Anglican churches had become accustomed to the greater freedom from state interference following that disastrous administration. Moreover, there was the lesson of the great damage that Anglican involvement in politics had created for that church.

Article 39 of the Constitution of 1777 proclaimed that

> ministers of the gospel, are by their profession dedicated to the service of God and the cure of souls, and ought not to be diverted from the great duties of their function; therefore no minister of the gospel, or priest of any denomination whatsoever, shall at any time hereafter, under any pretence or description whatever, be eligible to, or capable of holding any civil or military office or place, within this State.[27]

This article had passed essentially unaltered from the Jay draft into the committee's draft. It was read to the conven-

[27] *Const. of N.Y.* (1777), art. 39.

tion, immediately moved to a second reading, and then adopted without debate or division.[28]

While anti-Catholic pressures to incorporate restrictions on members of that faith in the article on religious freedom had been checked, they reappeared in the discussion of a naturalization procedure for the new state. The committee's draft had stipulated simply that anyone who entered the state, and who remained there purchasing lands or tenements, could become a citizen by taking an oath of allegiance before the Supreme Court of the state.[29] After the religious freedom article had been voted, the convention brought up the section on naturalization for debate. John Jay was first on the floor, moving an amendment to the committee's proposal requiring prospective citizens to "abjure and renounce all allegiance and subjection to all and every foreign king, prince, potentate and state, in all matters ecclesiastical as well as civil." [30] Briefly debated, the motion was then put off because of the lateness of the hour.

When, on March 26, the naturalization article was again taken up, the Jay amendment was accepted by a vote of 26 to 9.[31] Jay now moved that the Dutch churches in New York, which still maintained ties with the governing bodies of the Reformed church in Holland and drew upon seminaries there for ministers, be exempted from the operation of the naturalization oath. But this discrimination in favor of a particular church was unacceptable, probably because it suggested the unpopular idea of special privilege. The convention had already recorded its opposition to any such distinctions in other articles of the constitution.

Undeterred by this setback, Jay moved to drop the reference to the Dutch church, replacing it with a statement that the oath would not be employed to "discontinue the innocent

[28] Lincoln, I, 545–46; *Jour. Prov. Cong.*, I, 846.
[29] Lincoln, I, 547–48. [30] *Jour. Prov. Cong.*, I, 846.
[31] For the March 26 debates, see *ibid.*, pp. 851–53.

connection which non-episcopalian congregations in this State have heretofore maintained with their respective mother churches in Europe, or to interfere in any of the rights of the episcopalian churches now in this State, except such as involve foreign subjection." [32] Jay's purpose was now out in the open. The only "non-episcopalian" or "episcopalian" churches "heretofore" active in New York were Protestant churches. By tailoring the oath requirement to except the former dissenting churches and the Anglican bodies, whose foreign ties were broken by Article 35, the one church with overseas connections left to bear the full onus of the oath was, by process of elimination, the Roman Catholic church. Recognizing this for what it actually was, the representatives rejected the motion decisively, 29 to 6.

During the ensuing debate Jay went so far as to propose giving the legislature the authority—in *ex post facto* fashion—to require already naturalized citizens to subscribe the oath. This was defeated, and the question was turned over to a special committee of three including John Jay, James Duane, and Robert R. Livingston.

Tuesday, April 1, the convention returned to the naturalization article. Morris, seconded by Livingston, presented a motion that the entire provision be "obliterated." Jay, for the special committee of three, moved instead that the naturalization procedure apply only to those aliens "born in parts beyond sea, and out of the United States of America." [33] The significance of this compromise of the prickly issue is apparent from the fact that the thirteen American states, in the absence of any formal national government, were virtually independent entities.[34] The citizens of one state were technically aliens when they moved to another. Thus, in its initial

[32] *Ibid.*, p. 852. [33] *Ibid.*, p. 860.

[34] In the year 1777 the Articles of Confederation government for the new nation still lay ahead; the country was governed by the *de facto* Continental Congress system.

form, the oath requirement would have applied to Americans as well as to foreign nationals. The compromise applied the oath only to the latter. With its incorporation in the oath provision by unanimous vote, and after the Morris motion to obliterate was defeated, the convention went on to adopt the naturalization article. It now read:

> it shall be in the discretion of the legislature to naturalize all such persons, and in such manner as they shall think proper; provided all such of the persons . . . being born in parts beyond sea, and out of the United States of America, shall come to settle in, and become subjects of this State, and [shall] abjure and renounce all allegiance and subjection to all and every foreign King, Prince, Potentate and State, in all matters ecclesiastical as well as civil.[35]

Several motives seem to have figured in this decision to prevent foreign Catholics from settling in New York.[36] One was simply the need for a naturalization procedure to replace that of the English, even if it meant restricting some foreigners. An oath as such was not new; the English had long required one of newcomers to the province. Jay's oath had in fact come directly from the former English Oath of Supremacy. But a majority of the convention also seems to have believed that the oath would be useful against any attempt by popish or other forms of Old World reaction to subvert the new state.[37] Anti-Catholic suspicions, the outgrowth of years of indoctrination, were an emotional and unreasoning but very real thing. Common sense could provide little help here. However, the convention was sufficiently imbued with the

[35] *Const. of N.Y.* (1777), art. 42; *Jour. Prov. Cong.*, I, 861.

[36] Exclusion of Catholics would be the effect of the oath requirement. No faithful Catholic could in conscience forswear his spiritual or ecclesiastical loyalty to the pope and remain a Catholic; this is precisely what the oath demanded.

[37] For the attitudes of Jay, the anti-Catholic leader in the convention, see Monaghan, p. 95; George Pellew, *John Jay* (Boston, 1890), p. 86.

ideal of religious liberty that it made a significant and hopeful break with the "No-Popery" tradition. The representatives, despite the ceaseless prodding of men like John Jay, would not accept any prior restraints upon the worship of Catholics already in the state, though this would have been easy because there were so few of them. But neither would it accept terms that would work the exclusion of Catholics who might come to live in New York from the other American states. These were Americans, the products of a free environment; most of them, like the Carrolls of Maryland, were devoted to the Patriot cause. As for Catholics "in parts beyond sea," raised in conditions of intolerance and despotism among the squalling nations of Europe, these could not be similarly trusted. This was a conviction that would take a long time to modify and that would lie at the root of much of the history of church-state relations in the years ahead.

The constitution adopted by the convention on April 20, 1777, in the name of the people of New York was a conservative document in keeping with the state's colonial past. Property qualifications for voting and officeholding, some of them quite steep, were meant to maintain power in the hands of those who counted for something in this world, the possessors of landed property. This first government of New York State was republican in form; that alone did not make it democratic. But the religious terms of the Constitution of 1777, save for the somewhat limited anti-Catholic naturalization oath, were quite liberal compared with the first constitutions of the other original American states. Moreover, the animus against Catholicism apparent in the constitution seems to have been due less to any fear of Catholic worship than to the fear among eighteenth-century Protestants of papal influence, an influence widely assumed to regulate not only doctrinal faiths but also the political behavior of Roman Catholics. Yet with the exception of this fear, admittedly a very compelling one destined to shape ideas and actions in New York for well over a century to come, the framers of the first state constitution were in the vanguard of the movement to free religious observance from state controls that emerged from the American Revolution. In not attempting to spell out the degrees of approved sectarian belief, as did many of their sister states, the founders expressed their great respect for the religious diversity of their state.[38]

[38] To contrast religion in the New York constitution with the treatment of it in the other Revolutionary state constitutions, see W. C. Webster, "A Comparative Study of the State Constitutions of the American Revolution," *Annals of the American Academy of Political and Social Science*, IX (1897), 404–05; and A. P. Stokes, *Church and State in the United States* (New York, 1950), I, ch. v.

V

The Revolutionary Settlement

WHEN the Constitution of 1777 was adopted by the Convention of Representatives, the state of New York was an active military theater. The populous lower counties were in British hands; the frontier settlements lay in constant fear of surprise attack from marauding bands of Tories and Indians. To the north in Canada, General John Burgoyne was readying his army for an invasion of the state down the Champlain route. Conditions were such that popular ratification of the constitution would have been exceedingly difficult if not impossible, even had it been provided for. The constitution went into operation immediately following its passage by the small group of men who had framed it. The verdict of the people would have to wait for the return of more settled times.

There was little public comment on the details of the new constitution at the time of its adoption. This holds true for the constitution's religious provisions. John Jay, still pursuing his anti-Catholic crusade, complained of one omission disturbing to him. He would have preferred a "direction that all persons holding offices under the government should swear allegiance to it, and renounce all allegiance and subjection to foreign kings, princes, and states in all matters, ecclesiastical as well as civil."[1] Not content with the discriminatory naturalization

[1] H. P. Johnston, ed., *John Jay: Correspondence and Public Papers* (New York, 1890–93), I, 135–36.

article, Jay wanted to exclude Catholics, and any other undesirables, from ever holding public office. But the convention's work was completed; the opportunity for further changes had passed, and any serious thought of such a measure was dropped for the time being.

One of the few recorded instances of church attitudes toward the new constitution appeared in a gratulatory address of the Consistory of the Dutch Reformed church at Kingston to George Clinton, first governor of New York State, in August 1777. The Kingston church had long been "convinced of the unrighteous design of Great Britain, upon their civil and religious privileges." But now, the address continued, "while the Constitution is preserved inviolate, and the rulers steer by that conspicuous beacon, the people have the fairest prospect of happiness, unanimity and success." Clinton's selection as governor was particularly fortunate. The Dutch Consistory "esteem themselves especially happy, in having cause to believe that religious liberty (without which all other privileges are not worth enjoying) will be strenuously supported by your Excellency." [2]

The written constitution of any reasonably free society may appear logical and correct in its formulations but still fail in practice because it does not accurately embody the deeply felt needs of the people from whom it arises. The ultimate test of any constitution lies in the uses to which it is put. If the actions of the New York legislature at the close of the Revolution are any indication, the religious principles contained in the first constitution of the state closely reflected popular expectations.

By 1784, with the war concluded, New Yorkers were turning to the problems created by the successful break with Great Britain and by the years of hostilities. Many of the

[2] Letter, Rev. George J. L. Doll, Kingston, to Governor George Clinton, Aug. 2, 1777, quoted in Marius Schoonmaker, *The History of Kingston, New York* (New York, 1888), p. 269.

provisions of their first constitution would now be tested under peacetime conditions. Among the official acts of the legislature of 1784 was a series of four laws implementing the principles of religious liberty and church-state separation set forth in the Constitution of 1777. The passage of these laws was nearly unanimous; at no time did any of the four bills call forth a major division within the legislature or lead to public controversy outside the halls of government.[3] This composure, not present for example in the discussion of the treatment of Tories, suggests that a broad area of agreement existed over the religious terms of the 1777 constitution.

The first of the four statutes dealt with church corporations. This was one of the long-standing demands of dissenters in New York. Corporate charters would give to the former dissenting churches the legal standing and financial security denied them during British rule. The various sects correctly saw that their fortunes, in this world at least, depended largely upon their ability to receive and convey the property and other donations of their members. By the church incorporation act of 1784, the state also recognized that freedom of religion presupposes the existence of temporalities in the form of church buildings, parsonages, and operating funds by which public worship is made possible.[4] The preamble of this act, pointing to the religious freedom article of the constitution for its authority, described an obvious need:

Many of the churches, congregations and religious societies . . . have been put to great difficulties to support the public worship of God by reason of the illiberal and partial distributions of charters of incorporation to religious societies, whereby many

[3] See the legislative proceedings for the 7th session (1784) in New York [State] Senate, *Journal, 1784*, and Assembly, *Journal, 1784* (New York, 1784), *passim;* and the files of the *Independent Gazette or the New-York Journal Revived* and the *New-York Packet and the American Advertiser* for 1784.

[4] New York [State], *Laws of the State of New York, 1777–1801* (Albany, 1886–87), I, 613–18.

charitable and well disposed persons have been prevented from contributing to the support of religion, for want of proper persons authorized by law to take charge of their pious donations.

Because title to much church property was held by unofficial persons, there was great insecurity among religious groups, the preamble concluded, "to the no less disquiet of many of the good people of this State."[5]

It was accepted as an obligation of free government that religion and virtue be encouraged among the people. Here was a case where the requirements of religious liberty diverged from any conception of a strict and unbending separation between church and state. Only through state action could the physical holdings of religious societies be secured to their rightful ends, for they lay within the temporal domain of the state and were subject to the jurisdiction of civil government. At the same time, care was taken that state regulation did not become a pretext for interference. The law of 1784 established a system of general incorporation to be administered by the local courts. Incorporation need depend only on compliance with certain predetermined general rules, thus freeing the procedure from possible political considerations. The act also denied for the state any intention of working changes in ecclesiastical forms or beliefs:

> Nothing herein contained shall be construed . . . to abridge . . . the rights of conscience, or private judgment, or . . . to alter or change the religious constitutions or governments of . . . the said churches, congregations or societies, so far as respects . . . the doctrine, discipline or worship thereof.[6]

A second act, altering the charter of Trinity Church in New York City, was passed with two purposes in mind.[7] One was to make the charter of this leading congregation of the former Anglican establishment more conformable to the state constitution. The second was to vest control of the church in

[5] *Ibid.*, p. 613. [6] *Ibid.*, p. 618. [7] *Ibid.*, pp. 647–49.

the hands of loyal Episcopalians; the Tory element in possession of Trinity during the long British occupation in the war was to be denied any position of influence. The act pointed out that certain provisions in the 1697 charter of the church were "inconsistent with the spirit and letter of the constitution of this State." These provisions, together with the Ministry Act of 1693, were "contradictory to that equality of religious rights which is designed to be established by the constitution." [8] All such parts of the charter, the Act of 1693, and the other colonial laws relating to the Anglican establishment were "abrogated, abolished annulled repealed and made void." Nothing in the act was to be interpreted as granting "any kind of preeminence or distinction to the Episcopal mode of religious worship within this state but that an universal equality between every religious denomination according to the true spirit of the Constitution . . . shall forever prevail." [9]

As if this last law had not been sufficient, the legislature passed a third repeating the abrogations of the Trinity Church Act, while abolishing several other colonial laws touching on the former establishment and religion in general that had been omitted from the terms of the Trinity Church statute.[10] The opening lines of this act restated the old dissenting arguments against the legality of the Anglican establishment in the four lower counties of the colonial period. Inveighing against the laws that had forced persons in these counties to pay taxes to support the Church of England "contrary to every principle of justice and sound policy . . . ," the preamble states, "by colour of such laws it has been pretended, that the Episcopalian churches were established . . . and claims in consequence thereof have been set up, and prosecutions commenced injurious to the rights and privileges of other religious denominations, to the great vexation and disquiet of the good

[8] *Ibid.*, p. 647. [9] *Ibid.*, p. 649. [10] *Ibid.*, pp. 661–62.

people of this state." While these statutes had been voided by the adoption of the state constitution, the legislature felt obliged, "in order to remove every ground of uneasiness that may arise from such pretended claims in future, that the said laws should be repealed." [11]

The most obvious reason for this law was that the former dissenting sects doubted that the first repealer applying to Trinity Church adequately presented their views of the colonial establishment. The act revising Trinity's charter carried the implicit assumption that the Anglican church actually had been legally established in New York. The other Protestant sects had never accepted this, and their point was emphasized by the reference to "pretended claims" in this general repealer. It was a case of insisting that the new broom sweep absolutely clean, leaving behind not a shadow of a doubt.[12]

Rounding out the legislative program to erase all mention of Anglican privileges from the statutes was an act to alter the charter of King's College in New York City.[13] This brought the charter into line with what the non-Anglicans had always insisted, that the college be monopolized neither by Episcopalians nor by any other sect. The government of the college was entrusted to a board of regents of a newly created University of the State of New York. The board was to represent all shades of opinion, one of its places being permanently set aside to be filled by the majority votes of the clergy of all denominations in the state. Any sect might have a professor-

[11] *Ibid.*, p. 661.

[12] *Ibid.*, p. 662. Of special importance to New York Catholics was the inclusion among the repealed colonial statutes of "an act entitled 'An act against Jesuits and Popish priests' passed the 31st day of July 1700"; *ibid.* This act, together with one passed in the same year disfranchising Catholics, embodied the determination of the provincial regime to prevent Catholic worship or participation in public affairs; see New York [State], *The Colonial Laws of New York* (Albany, 1894–96), I, 453. By the repealer of 1784, the last legal barrier to Catholic worship in New York was now thrown down.

[13] *Laws, 1777–1801*, I, 686–90.

ship in the college for the purpose of instruction in its own doctrines simply by endowing a chair with sufficient funds. Where before the Revolution the college faculty had been restricted to Anglicans, the revised charter stated that "no professor shall be in anywise whatsoever accounted inelligible, for or by reason of any religious tenet or tenets, that he may or shall profess, or be compelled by any bye law or otherwise, to take any religious test-oath whatsoever." [14] With this last act, the revolution in New York's religious condition from a British colony to a free and republican state was completed. By these four laws the elected legislature of the new state had given its approval to the work of the convention of 1777.

The actions of the legislature were not the only indication of support for the Revolutionary religious settlement in New York. There was a similarly favorable acceptance of its terms among sectarian groups ranging from the once-privileged Episcopalians to the formerly proscribed Catholics. The great body of Protestants occupying the middle of the denominational spectrum were publicly silent on this subject, apparently not from any discontents, but simply because the settlement measured up to their expectations so completely. When aroused they were not inclined to be silent, as is known from their reaction to the act of 1784 altering the Trinity charter that brought about an enactment of further legislation more reflective of their interests.

But if the former dissenting sects were content, Episcopalianism was confronted with a humiliating reversal of its lofty position under the English. Episcopalians had to commence anew the difficult task of building up their church without public support and often in the face of hostile opinion. In New York City, the center of Episcopalian strength, there were divided opinions of the job ahead. One group, the patriot or "Whig" Episcopalians, was determined that the church be rebuilt along solidly American lines, with its own

[14] *Ibid.*, p. 688.

ecclesiastical government and no subordination to the mother church in England. Opposing this group was a "Tory" element containing members who had remained within the British lines during the war and who wished to continue its close ties with the English church. The two factions clashed for control of the Trinity Church vestry. It was to resolve this struggle that the state legislature had intervened in 1784 with the act changing Trinity's charter to give the victory to the Whig Episcopalians. While the patriotic sentiments of the legislators were most laudable, if you happened not to have been one of the Tories, this intervention in an internal church dispute seems an ill omen. It suggested that the state could conveniently sidestep the principle of church-state separation if it had a majority sentiment behind it and if the objects of its intervention were sufficiently unpopular and politically powerless. There would be reoccurrences of such behavior in the years ahead.

The Tory faction, defeated in their efforts to retain control of Trinity Church, turned in another direction. They threatened to separate from Trinity and found a new Episcopalian church in New York City with subordinate ties to the Church of England. Their last hope, short of this final step, was a petition to the legislature for redress of grievances. The petition was shunted aside in the state Senate and came to nothing, but the formal break was never consummated. What is of interest in this appeal is that the Tory Anglican group based their case not upon adherence to their former charter privileges, but upon the religious terms of the state constitution. The Tory petition had stated that they "only claim the Privilege of Enjoying their own mode of Religious worship, according to the Dictates of Reason and Scripture, and agreeably to the Spirit and Letter of the Constitution of the State." [15] The petition went on to cite the constitutional article granting the free exercise of religious profession and

[15] Morgan Dix, *A History of the Parish of Trinity Church in the City of New York* (New York, 1898–1906), II, 28.

worship. Here was evidence that even the old Tory Episcopalians had come around to an acceptance of the religious settlement in the Constitution of 1777, not very willingly perhaps, but nonetheless with an awareness of its usefulness for their purposes.[16]

The Catholics of New York posed a different kind of test for the state's religious settlement. They eagerly embraced the constitutional grant of religious liberty, for it permitted their small band in New York City to celebrate the Mass openly for the first time since the seventeenth century. The unknown factor here was the degree of good faith which an overwhelmingly Protestant community would show for this liberal grant when it came to including Catholics within its terms. The anti-Catholic naturalization article of the constitution was not a very promising beginning for the new era. But the Catholics proceeded to form a small congregation. Lacking funds and influential spokesmen, they sought out the assistance of the Spanish and French consuls in the city. These representatives of America's wartime allies allowed the local Catholics the use of their chaplains and chapels.[17]

In March of 1785, Hector St. John de Crèvecoeur, the French consul, presented on behalf of the Catholics a request to the city authorities for assistance in obtaining a church site. The mayor and council were most accommodating, persuading the trustees of Trinity Church to sell certain lots which the church owned on Barclay Street to the Catholics. The congregation incorporated itself under the terms of the church incorporation act of 1784 as St. Peters Church in June 1785 and began to solicit contributions for the erection of a church. At the head of the list of subscribers stood the names of Governor George Clinton and Mayor James Duane, both

[16] The blow-by-blow account of this dispute can be followed in *ibid.*, pp. 1–30.

[17] L. R. Ryan, *Old St. Peters, the Mother Church of Catholic New York,* United States Catholic Historical Society Monograph Series, XV (New York, 1935), 36–39.

staunch Protestants. The generally amicable relations between Catholics and Protestants in this matter says a great deal for the sincerity of Protestant attachments to the constitutional guaranty of worship.[18]

But while reason and justice might oblige the Protestant majority to admit the right of Catholics to free public worship, the old anti-popish prejudices, that had cropped out in the constitutional convention of 1777, remained. In 1788 the state legislature, without any significant opposition, passed a law, long desired by men like John Jay, requiring persons holding offices in the state government to submit to a prescribed oath.[19] Any person elected to the legislature, or as governor or lieutenant governor, or any appointee to state office had to subscribe the following test:

> I ________ do solemnly without any mental reservation or equivocation whatsoever, swear and declare that I renounce and abjure all allegiance and subjection to all and every foreign king, prince and State, in all matters ecclesiastical as well as civil; and that I will bear faith and true allegiance to the State of New York.[20]

Conceivably aimed at former Loyalists, the oath was actually intended to exclude Catholics from state office; as with the naturalization oath, no conscientious Catholic could swear to renounce his ecclesiastical ties to Rome. The act was another manifestation of the same old fears of popish political subversion, for the number of Catholics living in the state at the time was small and politically insignificant. It has been estimated that in 1790 there were only about one thousand Catholics in the state, most of them in the city, out of a total population in excess of 300,000.[21] This small group was more concerned with the enjoyment of its religious rights and the founding of

[18] *Ibid.*, pp. 42–46.

[19] Senate, *Jour., 1788* (Poughkeepsie, 1788), pp. 8, 10, 14–15, 17, 18, 26; *Laws, 1777–1801*, II, 637–39.

[20] *Ibid.*, p. 637.

[21] A. C. Flick, ed., *History of the State of New York* (New York, 1933–37), VII, 10.

a church than with any ambitions to acquire public offices. The oath of 1788 would remain in effect for the next eighteen years until enterprising politicians came to see some merit in the growing political potential of the Catholic population in New York City.[22]

As the eighteenth century, and the first twenty-odd years under the Constitution of 1777 drew to a close, principles of

[22] In 1787 a similar test oath had failed of passage. Alexander Hamilton, a leading member of the Assembly, had said in opposition to the bill: "There are two different bodies in the State to which this has reference; these were the Roman Catholics already citizens and those coming from abroad. Between these two were great distinctions. The foreigner who comes among us and will become a citizen . . . may with propriety be asked these terms. . . . For the natural subject . . . born amongst us, educated with us, possessing our manners, with an equally ardent love of his native country, to be required to take the same oath of abjuration—what has he to abjure? He owes no fealty to any power upon earth; nor is it likely his mind should be led astray by bigotry or the influence of foreign powers. Then, why give him occasion to be dissatisfied with you, by bringing forward a test which will not add to his fidelity? Moreover, the clause in the Constitution confines this test to foreigners, and . . . it was not till after much debate and warm contention that it got admittance, and then only by a small majority in the convention. . . . We should be cautious how we carry the principle of requiring and multiplying tests upon our fellow-citizens, so far as to practise it to the exclusion and disfranchisement of any." The speech, of Jan. 24, 1787, is in R. B. Morris, ed., *Alexander Hamilton and the Founding of the Nation* (New York, 1957), pp. 472–73. While such arguments were successful in preventing adoption of the oath in 1787, they were not the following year.

But if New York succeeded in prohibiting public office to Roman Catholics, the earlier attempt in the convention of 1777 to exclude Catholic aliens by means of a naturalization oath failed. The reason was that the federal government, under the Constitution of 1789, preempted the naturalization process, thus overriding state provisions in this area. And the federal naturalization procedure called simply for a showing of good character and the taking of an oath to uphold the federal Constitution. See 1 *U.S. Statutes at Large* 103 (March 26, 1790); and L. D. White, *The Federalists* (New York, 1948), pp. 394–95.

religious freedom and separation of church and state were firmly joined to the religious and legal framework of New York life. But just what did these ideals mean to people of that time? How were they defined by the jurist, the political leader, or the clergyman? Did they in any way enter into the concerns of ordinary people for the familiar tasks of their daily rounds? If we can judge from the statements of an articulate few, men who held positions of prestige in their communities and who were placed where they could both influence and be influenced by the opinions of their fellow citizens, these ideas had certain rather definite meanings. As for the impressions carried by the rank and file of people, the records are silent. Their opinions of religious conditions have to be judged from the actions of their representatives. The absence of public controversy over the religious clauses of the state constitution, and the tolerant attitudes characterizing simple human relationships in the realms of faith and worship suggest that ordinary people did not materially disagree with those who spoke for them. It is to specific public enactments, then, and to what little exists in the way of expository comment, that we must turn to extract the meaning of the principles invoked.

Article 38 of the state constitution asserted "that the free exercise and enjoyment of religious profession and worship, without discrimination or preference, shall forever hereafter be allowed within this State to all mankind." [23] This expressed the prevailing conviction that each individual should be free to form his own opinions of religion as his reason or conscience permitted. Persons were also free publicly to profess their beliefs, and to join others of like mind for purposes of public worship if they so chose, always provided that any action resulting from their beliefs did not threaten the public safety or infringe upon the similar rights of others. Neither

[23] New York [State], *The Constitution of the State of New York* (Fishkill, 1777), art. 38.

the state nor private citizens could legally force a person to profess a belief or to worship in a manner contrary to his own convictions, although—incongruously—refusal to do so might entail civil restrictions as in the case of Catholic aspirants to public office. John Jay believed that these rights "are, by nature, subject to no control but that of the Deity." They gave to each the liberty "to consider, to adore and to worship his Creator in the manner most agreeable to his conscience. No opinions are dictated; no rules of faith prescribed; no preference given to one sect to the prejudice of others." [24]

This ideal of religious liberty had arisen in part from a very realistic acceptance of New York's religious diversity. There were so many competing sects, none of which could command a majority, that each had sensed the wisdom of living in peace with its competitors for the souls of men. A growing secular spirit, by which people could no longer view religion as the sole object of ultimate human concerns, helped make possible this mutual and largely unuttered agreement to disagree peacefully in matters of faith.

But the commitment to religious freedom was rooted in something more than mere expediency or indifference. The traditional Protestant insistence upon the individual's moral responsibility to mold his life after the example set by Holy Scripture led naturally to the idea that each person was capable of interpreting the teachings of the Gospel for himself, with God his only guide. No external authority of man's devising could generally exert a claim superior to that of private conscience. Bolstering this conviction was the argument based on reason: All men are rational beings able to choose right from wrong if they have free access to the truth, this rational capacity being attributed variously to divine or natural sources. The Rev. John Henry Livingston, a promi-

[24] John Jay, *The Charge of Chief Justice Jay, to the Grand Inquest of the County of Ulster, on the Ninth Day of September, 1777* (Kingston, N.Y., 1777), pp. 9–10.

nent Dutch Reformed pastor who had thought deeply about these matters, explained it this way:

> It is proper that all men within this State should believe for themselves and worship God according to the dictates of their conscience without depending upon fellow subjects, sister churches, or even the civil magistrates in religion. This prerogative all men possess and it is not a new grant, or any gift from the State but the natural right and just demand of every rational creature.[25]

Because freedom of worship was a natural right, not of man's devising but of God's, no human agency could deny it even to those whose beliefs were alien to the community at large. And so one finds Roman Catholics and Jews enjoying its blessings alongside the Protestant majority in late eighteenth-century New York. Yet this same majority could curb Catholic participation in public affairs without seeing any contradiction. This, however, was not an unusual reaction for the large, assured, and unquestioning body of Protestant opinion in the state. The fear of popish political wiles was very real; these were people in some ways much closer in thought to the Reformation and the wars of religion than to our own time. Romish deviousness was to them a condition and not a theory. Because men cannot choose to see what they cannot see, it would only be after developments had altered the surrounding context of ideas and sentiments that New York Protestants would be able to see this particular contradiction between profession and practice.

But if all men were free to believe, were they equally free to disbelieve? The general impression gathered from contemporary actions and statements is that religious freedom was usually thought of as a freedom to worship, not as a freedom

[25] Letter, J. H. Livingston, Albany, to Robert R. Livingston, Feb. 28, 1777, Robert R. Livingston Papers, Bancroft Transcripts, I, 311–27, New York Public Library; the passage quoted is at p. 312.

from worship. To a society steeped in religious piety, the possibility that there could be an equality of rights between the believer and the atheist did not even exist for the great majority. Any consideration of the rights of nonbelievers, like that of the civil rights of Catholics, would have to wait for later generations to whom this was a real question rather than a fanciful one.

It was recognized that religion, to be really free, had to be secured from the intervention of the state. The idea of church-state separation was the offspring of the principle of religious freedom, and not the other way around. This concept of separation was a response to a concrete situation. It was the dissenting answer to the evils of the colonial establishment. No sect would ever again receive the exclusive imprimatur of the state; nor could any sect expect to gain state support for the propagation of its own peculiar doctrines. There was to be a free competition in ideas "without discrimination or preference" on the part of government. On the other hand, there were to be no such sectarian pressures brought to bear on government as the Anglican clergy had exerted in the colonial period. To prevent this, Article 39 of the state constitution expressly prohibited ministers or priests from holding public office in New York.

Separation of church and state, unlike freedom of religion, was at that time regarded not so much a question of immutable principle as it was a matter of simple common sense. Endless difficulties would fall to the government attempting to separate the sheep from the goats, the approved from the disapproved forms of worship, given the number of sects involved. Had not that been the lot of the English colonial regime? Better to let each church stand or fall on its own merits than to hazard the strife and ill will that had accompanied the former Anglican establishment. As John Jay put it, in his charge from the bench to the grand inquest of Ulster County, "the Gospel of Christ, like the Ark of God, would not fall, though unsupported, by the arm of flesh; and happy would it be for mankind, if that opinion prevailed more generally."[26]

The separation of church and state did not imply, however, a separation of religion from public life. The oath taken by the governors and lieutenant governors of the new state was sworn "solemnly, in the presence of that Almighty and eternal God, before whom I shall one day answer for my conduct," and concluded with a prayer to God "to preserve and help me, when in my extremest necessity I shall invoke His holy name, as I do keep this my sacred oath and declaration."[27] These were not the formularies of a secular or anticlerical state. In fact, a great many men, their thoughts shaped by Christian nurture, sincerely believed that religion as a general proposition should be encouraged by the state. For religion contributed to the sense of public morality that any virtuous society requires as a check upon corruption and the countless other evils that human flesh is heir to. This was a very fine distinction, since inevitably there would occur situations where it would be difficult indeed to conceive how religion generally could be encouraged without thereby promoting the interests of specific sects.

But to people of the time, there was no special difficulty in this. Separation was directed primarily against state interference with forms of worship or state support of any one sect. The proposition that the state could promote religion by affording the congenial environment within which all sects might develop their full potential for good in the community, short of interfering directly in the affairs of any of them, would not have occasioned much disagreement. That there were few objections to this is understandable if it is kept in

[26] Jay, p. 10.

[27] New York [State], *Journals of the Provincial Congress, Provincial Convention, Committee of Safety and Council of Safety of New York, 1775–1777* (Albany, 1842), I, 916–17.

mind that the religion of the community was overwhelmingly Protestant. So long as most New Yorkers were in essential agreement on the main outlines of their faith, there would be little opposition to state promotion of the Protestant religion in a broad, nonsectarian fashion. Rev. John Livingston, who so faithfully mirrored the thinking of his time on these questions, summed up this view:

> The State has a right to interfere in the religion of the subjects only in these two respects—first to promote religion in general and secondly defend it from all persecution—in promoting religion the magistrate has no right to judge which is the true and which the false in such a manner as to set up a standard for the people and give exclusive civil privileges to any particular worship; but by promoting I mean that the State judges the fear of God and his service to be of great importance to society and therefore determines to encourage and support their worship in such a legal manner as shall render the poorest subject, or meanest sect perfectly secure in their spiritual privileges.[28]

Only later, when the suspect Catholic church grew strong enough to demand similar encouragement, did people begin to have second thoughts about the wisdom of this attitude.

The pervasive certainty that religion should be encouraged can be seen in several of the early acts of the state government. The church incorporation law of 1784 stated explicitly that

> it is the duty of all wise, free and virtuous governments, to countenance and encourage virtue and religion, and remove every lett or impediment to the growth and prosperity of the people, and to enable every religious denomination to provide for the decent and honorable support of divine worship, agreable [*sic*] to the dictates of conscience and judgment.[29]

In 1781, to cite another instance, the legislature adopted a policy of reserving land for the support of the Gospel and schools in the state tracts then being opened for settlement

[28] J. H. Livingston to R. R. Livingston, Feb. 28, 1777, Bancroft Transcripts, I, 313–14.
[29] *Laws, 1777–1801*, I, 613–14.

upstate.[30] This was meant to encourage the founding of churches in the growing frontier regions, apparently on the assumption that these areas needed the incentive to virtue more than the settled downstate regions. At the same time, education, thought to be intimately related to religion, was to be promoted by this act. In addressing the legislature in 1784, Governor George Clinton remarked:

> Neglect of the Education of Youth, is among the Evils consequent on War—Perhaps there is scarce anyThing more worthy your Attention, than the Revival and Encouragement of Seminaries of Learning; and nothing by which we can more satisfactorily express our Gratitude to the Supreme Being, for his past Favours; since Piety and Virtue are generally the Offspring of an enlightened Understanding.[31]

But despite support for promoting religion, there was no serious consideration of direct state subvention of specific sects, that is to say for establishments literally understood. As one contemporary phrased it, "By providing for religion is not intended the grant of any tythes, . . . but only the putting all sects upon an equal and proper footing." [32] Direct support of any sect smacked too much of state interference. In colonial times such aid had usually been received at the expense of a church's independence.

All this suggests that contemporary notions of church-state separation were much less sweeping than they would become at a later time. So long as the principle of separation was regarded as a defense against state intervention in private church business arising from establishmentarian premises, people were precise about what they meant by separation. Not a great deal of thought, however, was given to the compatibility of public encouragement of religion in general with the

[30] C. Z. Lincoln, *The Constitutional History of New York* (Rochester, N.Y., 1906), III, 499–500.

[31] Assembly, *Jour., 1784*, p. 7.

[32] J. H. Livingston to R. R. Livingston, Feb. 28, 1777, Bancroft Transcripts, I, 315.

separation ideal. But there was simply no reason for defining separation in clearer terms, because few among the Protestant majority, regardless of affiliation, would have been able to see any need for greater preciseness. The possibility that state promotion might lead to difficulties did not arise, and it cannot be expected that they should have proposed answers to nonexistent questions. Of one thing it is certain: at the close of the eighteenth century, most New Yorkers would not have recognized any theory of church-state separation denoting or implying an uncompromising "wall of separation" between the two. This idea was to develop only later under vastly different circumstances.[33]

[33] Thomas Jefferson gave currency to the phrase "wall of separation" in a famous letter of Jan. 1, 1802, to the Baptist Association of Danbury, Conn. (the letter can be read in most editions of Jefferson's writings). The idea implicit in the phrase is that the founding fathers had drawn a rigid line between the affairs of church and of state in the federal and state constitutions with the intention that there was to be absolutely no trespassing across this line from either side. The phrase has since become the rallying cry for those who are opposed to any legislation or other governmental action favorable to sectarian undertakings, especially Catholic parochial schools. The advocates of an absolute, or near absolute, separation of church and state point with pride and authority to these alleged intentions of the framers as their historical justification. Regardless of the later merits of this argument, to insist that it attracted wholesale support in post-Revolutionary New York is to misread the history of the time. While the several churches most certainly opposed any state interference in their affairs, a great many of them and of other public spokesmen of the day, including most government officers, were not similarly opposed to state encouragement of religion. And what was true of New York I suspect was also true in the other original states.

On the other hand, this does not validate the argument from the other side, that the early state governments were fully committed to assist and encourage religion. Those who today hold this idea have read into history a rationalization for their own desires that the modern state be more helpful than it is in promoting religious activities. This view sees too much in state measures, such as church-incorporation and tax-exemption laws, that were meant to help religion generally by affording a congenial legal and social environment for it. There was simply no thoroughgoing concept of state aid for religion, any more than there was one of a "wall of separation."

PART THREE

The Nineteenth Century

IN the nineteenth century New York grew from a rural, thinly populated, provincial-minded society to the urban, thickly settled, cosmopolitan Empire State. Between 1800 and 1825 the port of New York rose to a commanding position in the trade of the new nation. The Erie Canal, completed in 1825, helped transform the state's agricultural economy from essentially one of subsistence to a food supplier for the Western world. By 1820 New York's population surpassed that of any other state, and by mid-century the state was well on its way to industrial leadership. New York City became the country's first great metropolis, vibrant with the labors and headlong drive of a dynamic nation. On the banks of the Hudson and along the route of the Erie Canal from New York to Buffalo—where just a few years earlier could be found only hamlets, isolated crossroads stores, stands of virgin timber, and miasmic swamps—bustling market centers and grimy mill towns sprang up to assault the quiet of the countryside.

Immigrants streamed into New York City from abroad, providing much of the muscle and sweat and blood which made this great transformation in New York's life possible. The first to come were the Irish, proud, brawling, eager to work. Irish pick and shovel men helped dig the "Big Ditch," the Erie Canal, and Irish gandy dancers laid the railroads following hard upon the canal builders. They performed the menial tasks of the great port city and fanned out along river, canal, and rail line to man construction projects or labor in the mills. At first they were a people dwelling apart in a strange land, feared and despised by the native born, forced to seek the solace and identity refused to them in their new environment through their church and in fierce loyalties to homeland. There were also Germans, with their alien language and customs, who came to prosper through hard work and to upset the calm of the Christian Sabbath with their beer-drinking ways. Toward the close of the century even stranger tongues were to be heard in the fitful slums of New York City, where the uprooted poor from southern and eastern Europe were piled tier on tier, alike only in their common struggle to make new lives for their children. Many of these immigrants were Roman Catholics, communicants of the church so long hated and still highly suspect. The newcomers upset not only the repose but also the premises of what had been a predominantly Protestant society, straining to the utmost the liberal tolerance of the eighteenth-century, Protestant-inspired settlement in church and state.

Beset from one side by the assaults of an increasingly militant Catholicism slowly growing in awareness of its power of numbers and demanding equal rights, the older Protestant way of life was also being attacked on other sides. Under the impact of urban and industrial growth, the rise of political democracy, and a galloping secularism, government itself posed disturbing problems for a people whose religious convictions and practices were derived from an earlier and seemingly less complicated time. The state and the local governments were forced to take a greater interest in education and charity work, encroaching on areas long considered to be the special responsibility of religious organizations and the preserves of a strictly Protestant ethic.

Out of the clash of the old and the new, out of the whirlwind of change, forces were generated requiring New Yorkers to rethink the implications of their eighteenth-century concepts of religious freedom and church-state separation. If these ideals were worth saving, they had to be accommodated to the demands of the nineteenth century or else be shouldered aside in the rush. And the conclusion of New York's people was that they were worth-while, thereby justifying the long effort to find a new basis of settlement attuned to present needs while faithful to the best of the past.

VI

On the Frontiers of Religious Freedom

BY the early nineteenth century, the ideal of religious freedom was widely accepted as the right of each individual. It had passed beyond the realm of public speculation and debate, as constitutional principles have a way of doing, and assumed the stature of a self-evident truth. The idea of the state actively interfering in the private beliefs or the worship of persons would have been as alien to the average New Yorker of the nineteenth century as it is to the citizen of our own day. But, to paraphrase George Orwell's famous paradox, while all religious beliefs were equal in the eyes of the law, some were more equal than others. This was not because of any formal policy of favoritism or exclusion toward the various sects, but rather the result of two readily apparent facts. Most New Yorkers believed their nation to be a Christian land, and the great majority of them were Protestants. The moral spirit underlying the laws and customs of early nineteenth-century New York was that of an orthodox and respectable Protestantism. Religious doctrines or practices uncomprehended by this conventional ethic were as likely to be uncomprehended by the law or to be the objects of considerable suspicion in the community. Most people were not consciously intolerant of strange ideas; Catholics, Jews, eccentrics, and atheists went unnoticed and unmolested in most cases. It was just that the majority was so positive of the essential correctness of the familiar concepts of a supreme god, the Trinity, heavenly rewards and hell-fire, the sanctity of the family, and the fact of a high degree of autonomy in their local church governments. Doctrines deviating from these norms could not be taken seriously and were sometimes the object of discriminatory distinctions in secular affairs. It had not yet become accepted that freedom of religion not only requires that the state should not hinder anyone acting in his purely religious capacity, but also that no one should be penalized in his civil capacity merely because of his religious convictions or the lack of them.

As the nineteenth century opened, Roman Catholics were still excluded from holding statewide public office by the oath obliging them to abjure their spiritual allegiance to the pope. Rules governing blasphemy, carried over from English and colonial practice, were still invoked in the courts. On occasion these rules were used to punish those who offended the moral sensibilities of the Protestant majority by calling into question the truth of cherished doctrines. An oath required of witnesses in the law courts assumed a belief in a divine being who would punish the false swearer in the hereafter. It was not unknown for judges to exclude the testimony of persons who could not accept what were unquestioned truths to most Christians. Universalists, who did not believe in eternal punishments, and nonbelievers, who could not admit the existence of a god, might be challenged in a court proceeding and dismissed without being permitted to testify. Unorthodox minority sects, whose practices were deemed offensive to the community, were the objects of popular abuse and, in at least one case, of flagrant legislative interference.

It was not because these penalties worked particular hardships against many people that eventually they were called in question; in fact it was probably because they were employed in so few isolated cases that they were tolerated for so long. In a society whose very ideology causes it to be ceaselessly prodded to correct moral evils operating within it, it is the evil which sears the conscience that is attended to first. But in such a society professing an attachment to a broad, unfettered religious liberty for all without discrimination, these lesser penalties were anachronistic, anomalous. In time they were rooted out as specific instances of their unjust application became known. The most encouraging testimony of the commitment of New Yorkers to the principle of religious freedom, where it is not actually the testimony of a growing indifference to religion altogether, is that these practices were dropped with so very little contention and acrimony.

The first of the civil penalties discarded was the anti-Catholic test oath adopted in 1788 and required of state officers before they could take up their offices. The person taking the oath had to "renounce and abjure all allegiance and subjection to all and every foreign king, prince, potentate and state, in all matters ecclesiastical as well as civil."[1] Because of their ecclesiastical loyalties to the pope, no Catholic could subscribe to this oath without either committing perjury or apostasy. In 1801 the legislature incorporated the act of 1788 in the revised laws of New York without being moved to make any alteration in the original wording.

In 1805 Francis Cooper, a Roman Catholic, was elected to the State Assembly from New York City as a Democratic-Republican. He was the first of his faith to be elected to state office, suggesting the growing political influence of the city's Catholic community. By that time there were a few thousand Catholics living there, most of them of Irish origins.[2]

Cooper, a trustee of St. Peters Church in New York City,

[1] New York [State], *Laws, 1801* (Albany, 1887), ch. 113.

[2] W. H. Bennett, "Francis Cooper: New York's First Catholic Legislator," United States Catholic Historical Society, *Historical Records and Studies*, XII (1918), 29–38; L. R. Ryan, *Old St. Peters, the Mother Church of Catholic New York* (New York, 1935), pp. 83–84, 86.

refused to take the prescribed oath, to test its validity, and was refused his seat when the legislature convened on January 28, 1806. Earlier, on January 6, a general meeting of the St. Peters congregation, held in the church's schoolroom, had prepared a petition for submission to the legislature calling for the repeal of the discriminatory oath. The petition, signed by a sizable number of citizens, proclaimed the loyalty of Catholics to the federal and state constitutions and stated that they were as faithful in observing their civic duties as any other group. The oath was described as preventing the members of the Roman church from fully enjoying "the benefits of the free and equal participation of all the rights and privileges of Citizens." [3]

The memorialists emphasized that, consistent with their religious principles, they were prepared to swear unequivocal allegiance to the state "in all matters not only civil but also ecclesiastical, as far as they may interfere with, or in the smallest degree affect the freedom, independence or safety of the State." But they could not do the same for "matters purely and solely, spiritual" affecting their church ties to the bishop of Rome.[4] They were confident that the legislators would see that justice was done them, but concluded with a thinly disguised appeal to their political interests. Repeal or modify the oath, the petition read:

> so that they and numerous other citizens of the same profession resident in the various districts of the State may have cause to unite with their fellow citizens in general, in self-gratulation for the unshackled enjoyment of the invaluable blessing of living under a liberal government, and the influence of benign laws.[5]

On January 29, State Senator De Witt Clinton, who was also appointive mayor of New York City, introduced the

[3] "Petition of the Catholics of New York in 1806 against a Religious Test for Office," *American Catholic Historical Researches,* XI (1894), 182. [4] *Ibid.,* p. 183. [5] *Ibid.*

Catholic memorial in the Senate. The petition was referred to a select committee, of which Clinton was chairman, for consideration. The next day Clinton reported back a bill for amending the oath requirement in line with the Catholic requests, together with a strong recommendation for its passage. On February 1, it was passed by the Senate with only one dissenting vote. The Assembly debated the bill on February 3 and then the following day adopted it without amendment on a roll-call vote, 63 in favor, 26 opposed. Several Federalists in the lower house had put up a strong fight against the measure, calling upon the old no-popery slanders, but with little success. The bill, hustled through the legislature with a remarkable display of speed, became law on February 7, and Cooper took up his seat the same day.[6] He was subsequently reelected to the Assembly in 1807, 1808, 1809, 1814, and 1826. The matter had been finally settled. The amended oath no longer included the ecclesiastical abjuration clause, simply requiring the swearer to "renounce and abjure all allegiance and fidelity to every foreign prince, potentate, state or sovereignty whatever." [7]

New York Catholics had chosen a favorable time to press their claims. It is an unavoidable conclusion that the speedy passage of the oath amendment was closely related to the factional battle then raging within the state Democratic-Republican party. By 1805 the Federalist party was no longer a serious contender in New York, and the dominant Democratic-Republican party had become the center stage in the struggle for political power in the state. At the turn of the century, the Jeffersonian party in New York had three major

[6] New York [State] Senate, *Journal, 1806*, pp. 9, 10, 12, 20, 30, and Assembly, *Journal, 1806*, pp. 36, 50, 60–61. Also see the letter from Rev. Michael Hurley to Bishop John Carroll, n.d., quoted in Rev. E. I. Devitt, ed., "Letters from the Archiepiscopal Archives at Baltimore, 1790–1814," in American Catholic Historical Society of Philadelphia, *Records*, XX (1909), 275–76.

[7] *Laws, 1806*, ch. 2.

factions: the largest was composed of the followers of old Governor George Clinton and his nephew De Witt; next came the group dominated by the aristocratic, wealthy, and closely knit Livingston clan; and finally there were the Burrites, fiercely loyal to their brilliant if erratic leader Aaron Burr. With the pressure of the Federalists lessened by defeat and defection, the intraparty contest for control began in earnest. The stakes were high: party leadership and control of patronage in the state. The ultimate goals were the power and prestige that went with the top spot in New York politics, a forceful voice in national party affairs, and the chance that the leader of the victorious faction might find himself catapulted into the presidency.[8]

After 1801 the Clintons and Livingstons combined their efforts and concentrated upon reducing the weakest faction, the Burrites. They cut off Burr from the patronage and in time froze him out of inner party councils. Burr's political power in New York was finally finished off by his alleged double dealing in the electoral stalemate of 1801 in which Jefferson seemingly had come close to losing the presidency; by his unwise and unsuccessful race for governor in 1804 against his party's regular candidate, Morgan Lewis, a Livingston man; and by the blast of outraged opinion following his duel with Alexander Hamilton.

With Burr out of the way, the Livingston and Clinton factions turned on one another. De Witt Clinton, mayor of New York City since 1803 and possessing the patronage and emoluments of that office, had considerable strength downstate. The Livingstons reigned upstate. The contest began over control of banking privileges in the city which came under the chartering powers of the state legislature. Banks, from the coffers of which one could gain influence through well-placed loans, were an important political asset. In 1805

[8] For the political infighting see Jabez D. Hammond, *History of Political Parties in the State of New-York,* 4th ed. (Cooperstown, N.Y., 1846), I, 164–235.

Clinton launched an attack on Governor Lewis charging party disloyalty, though actually the reason was that Lewis had backed a charter for a new bank, the Merchant's Bank, that competed with Clinton's own institution, the Manhattan Bank, in New York City. The Livingstons replied in kind.

Clinton now began to gather forces for a showdown. In the autumn of 1805, Clinton's lieutenants entered into negotiations with former friends of Burr. Leaders of the two groups held a dinner celebration in late February 1806, but the alliance was never consummated. A public uproar, fanned by Clinton's enemies, over the corrupt deal suspected between Clinton and the followers of the "treasonous" Burr, brought the negotiations to an abrupt end. It was precisely at the time that Clinton was lining up support in the city against the Livingstons that the Catholics demanded repeal of the test oath. Here was a group worth cultivating. Under the proddings of native prejudice, they seemed to act together; their support might very well become a decisive factor in the struggle between Clinton on one side and the Livingstons and their Tammany allies in the city on the other.

The leaders of the city's Catholics were not blind to this consideration, though they were much less convinced of their abilities to swing a bloc of Catholic votes than were the politicians looking on from the outside. The Rev. Michael Hurley of St. Peters Church wrote to his superior, Bishop John Carroll of Baltimore, who was keeping a close watch over the situation:

> A more propitious time we could not have than the present. At variance with one another, and bent upon determined and open opposition, our Democrats will be more likely to attend to our petition, and grant us the relief we sue for, to ensure for themselves the interest of the Catholic body, at the ensuing election.

Even if the legislators turned down the petition of his group, Hurley doubted that many votes would change. But, he concluded, "it is well for our purpose that the present ruling party entertains the apprehension: all that we have to do is avail ourselves of their fears." [9]

It was Clinton's political journal, the New York *American Citizen,* that gave strong backing to the Catholic petition.[10] Clinton played a leading role in getting the petition before the legislature and managing its successful course through the Senate. During the same session, another bill was passed admitting the charity school of St. Peters to a share of the public funds distributed for the support of free schools.[11] Until then only schools affiliated with Protestant societies had so benefited.

Even the Federalist opposition to the oath amendment in the Assembly, it appears, was motivated more by considerations of political advantage than by principle or religious bias. That party hoped to arouse anti-Catholic prejudice which it would then appropriate to regain its former ascendency in New York City politics. This was one of the first instances, but not the last, when New York politicians would discover that gains might be made from appeals to sectarian emotions.[12]

The episode of the Catholic oath demonstrates another interesting fact. In our society professional politicians are extremely practical men, bent above all on winning elections. When it comes to a question of either courting defeat or else compromising principle or prejudice, they will usually take the second course, unless defeat seems inevitable and it may

[9] Devitt, ed., pp. 278–79.

[10] Dorothie Bobbé, *De Witt Clinton* (New York, 1933), pp. 92–93, 127; "Petition," pp. 182–84.

[11] *Laws, 1806,* ch. 63. Evidence that New York Irish Catholics were grateful for Clinton's help is in D. R. Fox, *Decline of Aristocracy in the Politics of New York, 1801–1840* (New York, 1919), pp. 76–77.

[12] See the interesting letter from Robert Troup, Albany, to Rufus King, April 11, 1807, in C. R. King, ed., *The Life and Correspondence of Rufus King* (New York, 1894–1900), V, 29–31; and Fox, pp. 78–80.

appear useful to go down with a principle. The growing numbers of Catholic voters in the city had become a force to be reckoned with in local politics. To chance alienating them permanently by retaining the discriminatory test act, which even many Protestants were no longer sufficiently exercised about to preserve, was not worth the cost.

While the path of Catholics was smoothed by the influence of their numbers and their almost instinctive feeling for American politics, some other religious minorities in the early nineteenth century often faced greater difficulties. The stranger, the nonconformist, the eccentric invariably have had to struggle for a place in American society. The fact that they have chosen to stand apart and have acted in ways unlike most other people have branded them as queer, unnatural, un-American. While American conformism has seldom had the support of our laws or of a state police apparatus, it has nevertheless exerted strong pressures for uniformity in public behavior and expression through the force of community ostracism and, on occasion, of vigilante justice.

In the nineteenth century, when religion figured much more prominently in the lives of people than today, groups striking out against the current of conventional American Protestantism were apt to be objects of suspicion, ridicule, and even violence. One sect particularly odious to many New Yorkers of that time was the Shakers, a harmless minority dwelling in small, rural communities awaiting a self-imposed extinction because of their doctrine of celibacy. Shakers were detested for their ideas of the proper sexual relationship between man and woman, which was to have no relationship, as they were for their practice of holding property in common out of the certainty that this was what Christ had taught.

In 1818 the New York legislature passed a strange act singling out the Shakers for special treatment. The first section of the law granted a divorce to one Eunice Chapman, whose husband James had joined the Shaker sect. The second section provided that in cases where a husband and wife separated, one of them becoming a Shaker, any children of the marriage could be taken from the Shaker parent and awarded to the non-Shaker parent regardless of the existing law regulating child custody. Shaker communities were subject to search by law officers if the Shaker parent chose to hide the children rather than turn them over to the authorities. Any Shaker who assisted in carrying the children out of the jurisdiction or in secreting them could be fined and jailed.[13]

This was an extraordinary enactment. It penalized persons with families who chose to become Shakers over the objections of their spouses, in what amounted to an interference with the right of individuals to worship freely without discrimination. The history of this law is of some interest. It shows how a community, claiming to guarantee the freedom of religion, can be persuaded to violate that freedom when it involves an unpopular minority sect whose only protection is the forbearance of the majority.[14]

James Chapman, married and the father of three children, had left his wife in 1811 and joined a small Shaker community at Nyskayuna in Albany County the next year. His wife visited him in 1813, but repelled by the stern Shaker regimen, soon departed. Because state law gave the father sole rights to the children of a broken marriage, James took the Chapman offspring away from their home in 1814 while his wife was absent. Shortly afterward, Eunice journeyed once more to Nyskayuna, ostensibly to recover the children. James per-

[13] *Laws, 1818,* ch. 58.

[14] Eunice Chapman, *No. 2d. Being an Additional Account of the Conduct of the Shakers, in the Case of Eunice Chapman and Her Children* (Albany, 1818), is a revealing history of this affair. Despite the author's very obvious interests, she exhibits an innocent candor leading her to relate much that is damaging to her claims. See also N. M. Blake, "Eunice against the Shakers," *New York History,* XLI (1960), 359–78.

suaded her to stay, but in 1815 she was expelled for "trying to seduce her husband back into the wickedness of married life" and warned to stay away from her family. Wife Eunice then began a crusade to obtain her children and discredit Shakers in general. "God has singled me out in this furnace of affliction," said Eunice, "to be an instrument in his hand of exposing the errors and delusions of the Shakers." [15]

If James Chapman believed he was making the best of a bad bargain by fleeing his wife and seeking peace among the Shakers, he was quite mistaken. Eunice Chapman's family, Hawley by name, had rather strict ideas about the responsibilities of a husband to his wife, a wife in this case who was one of their own. More important, the Hawleys had a great deal of political influence. Eunice's father was postmaster of Broome in Schoharie County; one brother held the same office in Ridgeway, Genesee County; another brother was supervisor of the United States customs house at Rochester; and a brother-in-law was a business light and political leader of Harpersfield in Delaware County. The Hawley clan, judging from the patronage it held, was a minor power in upstate politics.[16]

In 1815 the Hawleys obtained a special act through friends in the legislature authorizing the chancellor in equity to return the children to Eunice if he saw fit. James refused to give them up and went into hiding with them. The next year, on the advice of political friends, Eunice petitioned the legislature for a divorce. This was most irregular; but since the New York courts recognized adultery as the only grounds for divorce, and this would be extremely difficult to prove against James, who as a Shaker was living in a celibate state, the only course left was to seek legislative relief. Eunice had an obliging senator present her appeal and arrange a select committee, of which he was chairman, to look into the matter.[17]

[15] Chapman, p. v; Blake, pp. 360–65. [16] *Ibid.*, 365; Chapman, p. 1.
[17] *Ibid.*, pp. 23, 25, 26; *Laws, 1815*, ch. 221; Blake, pp. 366–67.

The Senate committee held hearings, which were not exactly models of impartiality, during the 1816 session.[18] The resulting report, highly favorable to Eunice's petition, admitted that the question was a ticklish one. But Shaker beliefs in the sinfulness of marriage and of sexual union placed normal family relationships "on a footing which absolves them from the legal, moral and religious ties and duties which have always been considered of the utmost importance to the peace and welfare of the community."[19] Having judged Shakers guilty of transgressing the social conventions of the majority, the committee concluded that a law was needed "declaring that all persons having families who attach themselves to this society, shall be considered civilly dead."[20] They were to be deprived of their civil rights relating to the custody of children, the conveyance of real and personal property, and the rules of inheritance.

The committee's report was formally adopted at the next session and a bill prepared to meet its specifications. The bill contained a divorce for Eunice and a general section regulating the civil rights of Shakers. Despite the opposition of a group of senators led by Martin Van Buren, who strongly protested the severe penalties being imposed on the sect, the bill passed the Senate by a two-to-one margin in late March, 1817. In the Assembly the measure was shepherded to a vote by the same legislator who had obtained the child custody law for Eunice in 1815. By a vote of 53 to 43, the closeness reflecting the strength of opposition to the general anti-Shaker provision, the bill received Assembly approval in April. Ahead still lay the hurdle of the Council of Revision, composed of the governor and high judiciary of the state and possessing a veto over laws passed by the two houses. At this particular juncture in New York history, there was growing antipathy between democrats in the legislature and the more

[18] Chapman, pp. 32–36. [19] Senate, *Jour., 1816*, p. 265.
[20] *Ibid.*, p. 266.

conservative state judiciary over charges by the former that the New York courts were undemocratically abusing their powers.[21]

On January 27, 1818, the Council of Revision vetoed the act on the grounds that it deprived Shakers of their marriage rights without due process of law; the Council did not take up the question of religious freedom. The legislature, regarding the veto as another instance of unwarranted judicial intervention, repassed the bill but, significantly, did so in an amended form excluding the most flagrant anti-Shaker terms of the first bill and including only the child custody provision.[22] At the end of February, 1818, the Council again vetoed the measure, stating that divorce and child custody were properly judicial and not legislative matters and terming the bill a violation of the constitutional guarantee of religious freedom "without discrimination or preference."

The Council saw in the bill a form of penalty "whereby the equality of civil rights (as between persons of different religious professions) is essentially impaired." [23] To strip a person

[21] Senate, *Jour., 1816–1817*, pp. 15, 156, 226–27, 235, 245–48, 250; Assembly, *Jour., 1816–1817*, pp. 692–93, 714, 723, 742–44, 745; Chapman, pp. 36–38; Blake, pp. 369 ff.

Newspaper reports of the act aroused the libertarian ire of so staunch a defender of religious liberty as former President Thomas Jefferson. Writing to Albert Gallatin in June 1817, he commented: "Three of our papers have presented us the copy of an act of the legislature of New York, which, if it has really passed, will carry us back to the times of the darkest bigotry and barbarism to find a parallel. Its purport is, that all those who shall *hereafter* [*sic*] join in communion with the religious sect of Shaking Quakers, shall be deemed civilly dead, their marriages dissolved, and all their children and property taken out of their hands. This act, being published nakedly in the papers, without the usual signatures, or any history of the circumstances of its passage, I am not without hope it may have been a mere abortive attempt." See P. L. Ford, ed., *The Writings of Thomas Jefferson* (New York, 1892–99), X, 91–92.

[22] A. B. Street, *The Council of Revision of the State of New York* (Albany, 1859), pp. 381–82; Blake, pp. 370–71.

[23] Street, p. 386.

of some rights by legislative fiat, simply because the person is a Shaker, was a dangerous precedent that someday might be used to deprive men of all their rights even to life itself. The Council went on to examine the police-power reservation in the constitutional article on religion, the amended bill having been based upon it by the legislature:

> There is no evidence that the Society of Shakers are guilty of acts of licentiousness, or any practices inconsistent with the peace and safety of this State; and although we may lament what to us appear absurd errors in their religious creed, yet, so long as they preserve the character which they now possess for sobriety, industry and peaceful habits, the Council cannot regard them as having forfeited the protection secured by . . . the Constitution. To justify such an act of denunciation, the danger to "the peace and safety of this State" must be not merely speculative, remote and possible, but imminent and certain.

The Council concluded that the bill represented a kind of legislative interference with religious beliefs that was "not only unprecedented in the annals of our State, but highly dangerous and alarming in its consequences." [24]

But despite the Council's objections, the bill was passed over the veto by two-thirds majorities in both houses of the legislature and became law.[25] The act seems to have created no great stir of protest in the state. One of the few papers commenting on it, the *New York Evening Post*, treated it as a bore.[26] This astounding display of callousness toward a defenseless religious minority illustrates to what lengths the tyranny of a majority is capable of going. The law's general provision relating to Shakers and child custody, with but minor revisions, still remains on the law books as part of the

[24] *Ibid.*, p. 387.
[25] Senate, *Jour., 1818*, pp. 108–12; Assembly, *Jour., 1818*, pp. 469–70.
[26] *New York Evening Post*, Feb. 21, March 20, 1818.

Domestic Relations Law of the state of New York.[27] In all fairness, however, the law was and is a practical dead letter; no actions were ever brought under it. The bill's primary purpose was to grant special relief to Eunice Chapman in the form of a public bill; it was not a signal for a campaign of persecution against Shakers. But what was the most objectionable in this episode was the cavalier manner with which the elected representatives of a free society could trample on the rights of Shakers in order to dispense a favor to a single individual who happened to have political connections.[28]

The nonbeliever was more incomprehensible to the faithful of that day than were unorthodox believers such as the Shakers. Those who rejected the tenets of Christianity, or of religion in general, often stood outside the pale of civil as well as spiritual respectability. The general conditions of freedom in American society served to restrain organized efforts to curb infidelity; yet unbelievers, at least those unafraid of making their views known, were likely to incur severe penalties for their candor. This was particularly true in places where the

[27] Domestic Relations Law of the State of New York, sec. 71, in *New York Consolidated Law Service*, III (1950), with supplements.

[28] During the 1840's a legislative committee could write a ringing defense of the Shakers' right to freedom from outside interference. Involved were efforts to disallow an earlier statute permitting Shakers to hold lands in perpetuity through incorporated trusts. As to the power of the legislature to intervene, the committee answered: "That the Shakers are a religious society, no one has presumed to doubt. That their principles of religion and mode of worship may be sneered at, scorned, or regretted: that from without the pale of their community, all may unite in the mortification, that such a strange, innocent and deluded people should exist, may be readily conceded, but that they are inhuman, and do not possess moral feelings, all must deny. Hence the panoply of our laws are over them, and they must be allowed, unmolested, to enjoy the free exercise of their religious devotions." See "Report of the Select Committee on the Subject of the Shakers," Assembly, *Documents, 1849*, doc. no. 198, p. 12.

ties binding men to the Christian religion were especially compelling, as in rural communities still untouched by the indifference and anonymity of the materialistic cities, where men were more apt to be judged, if judged at all, by their worldly goods rather than their otherworldly concerns.

In early nineteenth-century New York, the nonbeliever might be subjected to considerably more than social ostracism. The courts were one of the chief formal bulwarks of Protestant orthodoxy against the pernicious inroads of "atheism" and "infidelity." For a careless remark in public, one could be prosecuted for an offense against public morality. Conservative judges, led by Chancellor James Kent, constructed a doctrine of public morality, based upon the English common law, and used it to justify criminal actions against those whose remarks were deemed blasphemous to the Christian religion. One's religious beliefs also affected one's standing as a witness before the law. An act concerning oaths, carried over from colonial times, served to disqualify nonbelievers as competent legal witnesses. This particular act prescribed a mode of oath-taking requiring the laying on of hands and kissing of the Gospel, or raising one hand and swearing by an everlasting god to tell the truth. People with scruples against swearing might affirm their oath so long as they accepted a supreme god and a state of future rewards and punishments. By construction, nonbelievers were excluded from giving testimony under this act.[29]

The leading case for the prosecution of blasphemy was *People* v. *Ruggles*, decided in 1811.[30] Ruggles, a resident of Washington County, was indicted in late 1810 for having said that "Jesus Christ was a bastard, and his mother must be a whore." The indictment specified that the accused "wickedly, maliciously, and blasphemously" uttered these words "in the presence and hearing of divers good and christian people, &c.

[29] *Laws, 1801*, ch. 113, and *Revised Laws, 1813*, ch. 13; secs. xv and xvi in each. [30] 8 Johns. 290 (1811).

of and concerning the christian religion, and of and concerning JESUS CHRIST." Ruggles was adjudged "in contempt of the christian religion, and the laws of this state, to the evil and pernicious example of all others, &c." [31] No statutory authority was cited for the criminal action. Ruggles was held to have transgressed the common law so far as it protected the religion and the public morals of society. At no time was this incident treated as a simple breach of the peace, but rather as a serious moral offense.

In June of 1811, Ruggles was tried in the county court, Justice Ambrose Spencer presiding, was convicted, and then was sentenced to a three-month jail term and fined five hundred dollars. The conviction was appealed to the state Supreme Court, then the highest appeals court in the state, where the verdict of the trial court was upheld in a unanimous decision delivered by Chancellor James Kent.

Counsel for the defendant had argued that there was no New York statute defining blasphemy and making it a punishable offense. He also appealed to the religious-freedom article of the state constitution granting toleration for all beliefs. Moreover, the lawyer contended, the police-power clause of that article, intended to punish licentiousness and practices inimical to the public safety, applied only to actions and not to opinions. Kent ignored these arguments, turning instead to a rather nebulous law of the land concept. After citing English precedents showing that blasphemy was indictable under the common law, he asked why this rule could not be applied to America. There was nothing in our "manners and institutions" which did away with the necessity for incorporating this principle in our common law. The common law, he ruled, "checks upon words and actions, dangerous to the public welfare." Because the public welfare depends upon moral obligation, and our society's morals were derived from Christianity, the common law was applicable to blasphemous words

[31] 8 Johns. at 290.

which "strike at the root of moral obligation, and weaken the security of social ties." [32]

"We are a christian people," Kent asserted.[33] While the state constitution permitted "decent" discussions of religious differences, it was not meant to allow malicious abuse of the religion of the people threatening to the very moral discipline of society. He cited an act against immorality, regulating sabbath observance, and the act concerning oaths, with its religious test, as evidencing the legislature's tacit acceptance of the proposition that Christianity occupied a unique position in the law of the land.

In 1823 a similar indictment was lodged against one William Porter, who allegedly had made blasphemous statements very similar to those for which Ruggles had been penalized.[34] Again the incident occurred in Washington County, whose people seem to have been very zealous or else very wicked. Porter, charged with having committed the offense at a whortleberrying party, based his defense on having been "so beastly drunk that he did not know what he did." [35] Denying that this was sufficient excuse, the judge directed the jury to return a verdict of not guilty on procedural grounds, while cautioning that this was in no way to be regarded as affecting the holding in the Ruggles case. Nonetheless, indictments for blasphemy disappear from the court dockets after the Porter case, apparently as public indifference gradually gave way to growing doubts about the wisdom of the Ruggles ruling.

The issue of the competency of witnesses was a somewhat more serious one, involving not the scrutiny of random remarks but judicial excursions into the private religious convictions of persons. Unlike blasphemy, which was punishable by fine and imprisonment, the disqualification of a witness carried no further legal penalties. It was probably because dis-

[32] 8 Johns. 290, at 296. [33] 8 Johns. 290, at 295.

[34] *People* v. *William Porter*, 2 Parker's Criminal Reports 14 (1823).

[35] 2 Parker's Criminal Reports 14, at 15.

qualification did not seem a very serious matter, together with the pertinacity with which Protestants clung to the idea of the intimate connection between religious belief and the trustworthiness of a citizen, that this disability was countenanced for so long.

The case of *Jackson ex dem. Tuttle* v. *Gridley*, decided in 1820 by the New York Supreme Court, was the first important attempt to define the law concerning oaths as it applied to the question of competency.[36] Amos Gridley had been a defense witness in a proceeding where the verdict was found for the defendant. When Gridley had been called to testify, the plaintiff objected that he was incompetent. The witness was alleged to have recently declared his disbelief both in a god and a future state of rewards and punishments and to have said "man was like a beast, and when he died there was an end of him." [37] The trial judge overruled the objection and permitted Gridley to be sworn in. On appeal, the plaintiff asked for a new trial, contending that Gridley had been incompetent to testify and that his testimony had materially affected the verdict.

Chief Justice Ambrose Spencer, for the appellate court, ordered a new trial and commanded that Gridley be excluded as a witness. Spencer cited the English legal doctrine, incorporated in the law of New York, that anyone who did not believe in a god and future rewards and punishments could not be a witness in a court of law. It had only to be proved that a witness was an infidel and it followed that the witness could neither be sworn to refute the assertion nor be allowed to testify without taking the oath. Proof of infidelity consisted of "avowals and opinions expressed by the witness within such time, as to induce the presumption that his infidelity still exists." [38] Conversely, evidence of an intervening "change of mind," which might consist of proof of faithful attendance at

[36] 18 Johns. 98 (1820). [37] 18 Johns. 98, at 102–03.
[38] 18 Johns. 98, at 105.

church or public expressions of a belief in God, would justify the swearing in of the witness. Spencer concluded:

> Religion is a subject on which every man has a right to think according to the dictates of his understanding. It is a solemn concern between his conscience and his God, with which no human tribunal has a right to meddle. But in the development of facts, and the ascertainment of truth, human tribunals have a right to interfere. They are bound to see that no man's rights are impaired or taken away, but through the medium of testimony entitled to belief; and no testimony is entitled to credit, unless delivered under the solemnity of an oath, which comes home to the conscience of a witness, and will create a tie arising from his belief that false swearing would expose him to punishment in the life to come.[39]

In other words, the law's pursuit of truth is superior to any religious conviction. Those who cannot conform to orthodox Christian doctrine cannot be depended upon to tell the truth in a court proceeding and therefore must be treated as second-class citizens in so far as their privileges as witnesses are concerned.

One of the first indications that there was some popular disapproval of judicial interference with religious beliefs occurred at the New York Constitutional Convention of 1821. The convention was responsible for the first thorough revision of the state's constitution since its adoption in 1777. Its work marked a minor triumph in New York for the advancing spirit of political democracy that had been steadily gathering force since the election of Thomas Jefferson in 1800.

Church-state issues were not among its primary concerns, but the question of religious freedom did receive attention from the convention. Although agitation for an end to all remaining religious distinctions and tests was unsuccessful in 1821, it did inspire opponents of judicially imposed orthodoxy

[39] 18 Johns. 98, at 106.

to press on their attack against all forms of privilege arising from religious considerations.[40]

Scrutiny of the constitutional article on public worship in the convention provided the occasion for a debate on religious tests. Erastus Root, a leader of the most advanced democrats, moved an amendment that "the judiciary shall not declare any particular religion to be the law of the land; nor exclude any witness on account of his religious faith." [41] Root strongly protested indictments for blasphemy, the contention of certain judges—some of them present in the convention hall—that Christianity was the law of the land, and judicial snooping into the religious beliefs of witnesses. Root wished for "freedom of conscience. Where that existed, true religion would flourish. But where such punishments were inflicted, commiseration would be excited for the accused, and execration for the ministers of the law. If judges undertake to support religion by the arm of the law, it will be brought into abhorrence and contempt." [42]

Chancellor James Kent then rose to say that Root was mistaken. The courts had not declared Christianity to be established under the law, but only that blasphemous remarks directed at the Christian religion were indictable offenses against public morality. He reviewed his decision in the Ruggles case, remarking that the Supreme Court of New York had adjudged blasphemy to be as much a breach of public morals as indecent exposure. The fathers of the constitution never meant to destroy Christianity, nor would the courts permit this. Judges sought "to preserve, so far as it came within their cognizance, the morals of the country,

[40] For the 1821 convention generally, see Hammond, II, 1–85; C. Z. Lincoln, *Constitutional History of New York* (Rochester, N.Y., 1906), I, 613–756.

[41] N. H. Carter and others, eds., *Reports of the Proceedings and Debates of the Convention of 1821* . . . (Albany, 1821), p. 462.

[42] *Ibid.*, p. 463.

which rested on christianity as a foundation." "Are we not a christian people?" he asked. The use of the common law to punish blasphemy is merely "the application of common reason and natural justice to the security of the peace and good order of society." [43]

On the competency issue, Kent seemed to be astounded that anyone could sincerely believe that the required oath was an invasion of the rights of conscience. This was the only means available to the courts "to check atheists and blasphemers." Did Root want even this protection against infidels removed? To do so would "endanger the security of life, liberty, and property, and the comfort and happiness of our families." [44]

The following day, Root divided his original amendment into two separate motions. The first, altered slightly to read, "It shall not be declared or adjudged that any particular religion is the law of the land," was brought to a vote without further debate and adopted, 62 ayes to 26 nayes. It soon became apparent that some who supported this motion did not fully understand its implications or agree with them, but the vote also revealed the existence of a body of opinion opposed to any further blasphemy prosecutions. Kent himself said that he had voted for this clause because it was quite harmless and might even be useful someday. But in the future he would not hesitate to render the same decision he had in the Ruggles case if the need arose.[45]

Root then presented his second motion, reading that "no witness shall be questioned as to his religious faith." One delegate believed that "the testimony of the atheist and infidel, ought not to be placed upon an equality with others, as he could feel no responsibility." Chancellor Kent expressed his

[43] *Ibid.;* it was probably due to statements like this last from Kent that the more nebulous concepts from the natural law began to lose favor with lawyers and the public in the nineteenth century.

[44] *Ibid.*, p. 464. [45] *Ibid.*, pp. 464–65.

agreement with this. Olney Briggs, another of the root and branch democrats with probably the most liberal views on religion of any in the convention, replied that it was impossible to say definitely who was or was not an atheist. "In this age of light and knowledge, he regretted to see such narrow views entertained; we should be above such prejudices, and act on the broad principles of liberty." In defense of his amendment, Root said that he wanted to "purify the morals of the people and the incorrect practice of our courts." The existing oath requirement put a premium on hypocrisy and lying. He "wished all men might be religious, but not hypocrites and liars, for there was enough of them in all conscience." After a rather scornful rejoinder from Kent, the proposed clause was defeated by the overwhelming vote of 94 opposed to only 8 in favor.[46] In 1821, the notion that the rights of persons who questioned the very bases of religious faith should be protected along with those who accepted these bases was, it seems, still a very unsettling one.

During subsequent debate on the final wording of the religious freedom article, Chief Justice Ambrose Spencer moved that the Root amendment stating that no religion was the law of the land, adopted earlier, now be dropped. He believed that this addition "would go to prevent punishment for blasphemy, and thereby endanger the morals of the community." Sufficient leeway for differences of opinion was already afforded by existing law. Spencer warned that the courts must be allowed to continue to regulate blasphemy in order "to prevent men from reviling the Savior of mankind, and from reviling the religion which the great mass of the community have adopted." Briggs retorted that "he had yet to learn, that a person had not the right to discuss the question of the truth of the Christian religion." [47]

Rufus King, the old Federalist who represented the most conservative religious views in the convention, delivered a

[46] *Ibid.*, pp. 465–66. [47] *Ibid.*, p. 574.

lengthy speech for striking out the Root amendment. King argued that while the first state constitution had ended the Anglican establishment, it did not similarly disavow those English laws recognizing and protecting Christianity. Hence, Christianity was carried over into the laws of New York State. Therefore, "while all mankind are by our constitution tolerated, and free to enjoy religious profession and worship within this state, yet the religious professions of the Pagan, the Mahomedan, and the Christian, are not, in the eyes of the law, of equal truth and excellence." King advocated the rejection of the clause under discussion, for "while the constitution tolerates the religious professions and worship of all men, it does more in behalf of the religion of the gospel." [48]

Out of these debates emerged a consensus that it would be best to retain the existing Article 38 of the 1777 constitution, rather than make any doubtful or troublesome innovations. Conservatives sided with Kent, who observed that "the present constitution had gone quite far enough with the freedom of toleration of religious opinion. We had better leave it as it is, without any new provision on the subject, and especially any that might be construed to allow of still increasing latitude of discourse and action." [49] Moderate democrats, led by astute politicians like Martin Van Buren, also favored making no changes. They seem to have been motivated not by any agreement with the views of Spencer, King, or Kent, but by a desire to avoid disrupting the convention through religious contention.[50] In the constitution finally voted by the convention, Article 38 of the constitution of 1777 was carried over

[48] *Ibid.*, p. 575. [49] *Ibid.*, p. 576.

[50] Van Buren was a leader of the dominant group in the convention which, on most questions, consistently followed a middle of the road course between the extreme democrats, who wanted the politically impossible, and the extreme conservatives, who thought that no improvements over the existing constitution were possible at all. For Van Buren's position on the religious freedom article, see *ibid.*, p. 574.

intact as section 3 of article 7, with only the preamble deleted as superfluous.

The religious freedom debates in the convention of 1821 reproduced the spectrum of contemporary opinion on the subject. For the time being, expediency and the influence of Protestant conventionalism were capable of keeping men firm in opposing the growing pressures for an equal freedom of thought and action for minorities who differed from the dominant Christian outlook.

In the quarter century following the constitutional convention of 1821, New York, in step with the rest of the nation, underwent a time of peaceful if not exactly quiet revolution. This was the age of what we now call, though not always with great accuracy, Jacksonian democracy, a time of restless and exciting change, of the growing popularity of democratic ideas, and of seemingly unlimited opportunities for getting ahead. The Jacksonian era was in part a revolution in attitudes, a reaction against the dead hand of the past. In politics, the control of the electoral process by a small group of congressional and state officers was weakened by the onrush of the common man demanding a larger say in his government. National political parties as we know them appeared, directing their appeals to a broadly based, mass electorate created by the extension of the suffrage and the proliferation of grass roots organization in most of the states. This was the age when national party conventions were born, and the older spoils system took on new life; it was a time of almost frenzied adulation of democracy. In economic life, men turned against state-chartered "monopolies," with their special privileges, and against government interference. Old barriers were battered down, and a mad scramble for the wealth of a rich continent ensued. It was a time for making the most of one's opportunities, the devil take the hindmost, and for laissez-faire. It was also an age of social reform, as the effervescent enthusiasm for political democracy spilled over to encompass all human rights and inspired assault after assault upon social evils impeding the march of human progress. Out of this quarter century came a new militant abolitionism, the temperance movement, the crusade for women's rights, demands for improved public education, and a humanitarian concern for society's unfortunates: the pauper, the insane, the diseased, and the criminal.[51]

In religion, the stern Calvinistic spirit of colonial American Protestantism was challenged by a newer emphasis in belief. The earlier Old Testament conception of a vengeful and exclusive god was confronted with the nineteenth-century's New Testament vision of a god of love who sacrificed his only son, Christ, that all men might be saved. Organized religion also had to contend with the augmented forces of secularism and materialism in this worldly, speculative, grasping age. For many reformers, preoccupation with the needs of this world inevitably meant that religion, with its concern for the hereafter, was relegated to a role of only secondary importance in their thoughts. Religious orthodoxy was subjected to pressures for change from many directions; demands for the removal of the last impediments to a universal enjoyment of religious freedom made headway. Social and political distinctions arising from religious differences came under increasing attack from democrats, secularists, and religious liberals. The separation of church and state, as it was understood to mean a complete separation of government and religion, gained new adherents. Tolerance for the religious eccentric and the nonbeliever became more widespread as the practices of orthodox Christianity were made to seem unenlightened and undemocratic.

The campaign against religious distinctions and tests took many forms in New York. Among the more extreme reform-

[51] For the social history of this reform era, see Alice Felt Tyler's engaging *Freedom's Ferment* (Minneapolis, 1944).

ers, a pronounced anticlericalism was popular. There were crusades to end the tax exemption of church property and to prohibit the appointment of chaplains to state institutions. Charges were made that the conservative Protestant clergy and aristocratic politicians were attempting to unite church and state. Reformers contested the justice of sabbath laws and fought against the movement conducted by sectarian organizations to end Sunday mail deliveries. In 1833 the Democratic state legislature was prevailed upon to pass a law stopping the payment of the chaplains in the two houses who led daily prayers during sessions, although within a few years this departure from long-standing custom was rescinded. In 1835 Thomas Herttell, a radical returned to the Assembly by New York City Democrats, obtained the passage of a bill in the lower house declaring that religion should not be a determining factor in judging the competency of witnesses in the courts. Scores of petitions in support of this bill were received in Albany, but it failed to get by the Senate.[52]

Herttell typified the radical reforming spirit of the day. From the 1820's to the 1840's he devoted much time and energy to exposing religious inequities embedded in the laws of New York. In speeches before the Assembly and through a series of pamphlets, he attacked the wisdom of Sunday-observance laws, the system of state-appointed chaplains, the opening of legislative meetings with formal prayer, and the exclusion of nonbelievers as legal witnesses.[53] Herttell firmly believed that "any law enacted to enforce conformity to sec-

[52] Fox, pp. 388–90; *Laws, 1833*, ch. 87; *Laws, 1839*, ch. 390.

[53] Among Herttell's pamphlets are *The People's Rights Reclaimed* (New York, 1826), charging that sabbath laws were unconstitutional; *The Demurrer* (New York, 1828) and the *Rights of Conscience Defended* (New York, 1835), both upholding the equal rights position on the competency issue; and *Remarks on Prayers in the Assembly of the State of New York* (New York, 1854), a speech delivered against such prayers in 1840. All are rich sources for the ideas and the exaggerated rhetoric of the religious reformers.

tarian religious tenets, carries with it intrinsic evidence of its unrighteous principle; because if people conscientiously believed in the tenet intended to be favored by the law, no law would be necessary to enforce it." [54] Such laws, he wrote, "are hostile to the spirit and genius of our free political institutions, adverse to the benevolent principles of rational liberty, the equal rights of man, and the express provisions of our constitution." [55]

The radical reformers such as Herttell obtained little in the way of concrete reforms. Their proposals, looking toward a total separation of church and state, were too alien to the great mass of citizens. These might be more tolerant of religious dissent and nonconformity than formerly, but they still considered themselves to be Christians and America a Christian state. Nevertheless, the radicals did serve a useful function; their gadfly tactics aroused many to the injustice of prosecutions for blasphemy and of the test oath required of witnesses, thereby advancing the cause of equal religious rights. On the competency of witnesses issue radicals and moderates found common ground and were able to combine their efforts to overthrow this distinction. Side by side with the Herttells were to be found the cautious young Buffalo lawyer, Millard Fillmore, and others who joined their voices with the radical reformers in the attack upon religious tests.[56]

Some sects heartily supported the movement for equal rights in religion. Baptists, for example, reaffirmed their traditional opposition to any connection between church and state and directed verbal fire at conservative fellow Protestants who were adverse to any changes that might weaken the

[54] Herttell, *People's Rights*, pp. 32–33. [55] *Ibid.*, p. iv.

[56] Fillmore, pseud. "Juridicus," *An Examination of the Question, "Is It Right to Require Any Religious Test as a Qualification To Be a Witness in a Court of Justice?"* (Buffalo, 1832); R. J. Rayback, *Millard Fillmore, Biography of a President* (Buffalo, 1959), pp. 65–67, and 67 n.

influence of conventional Christianity.[57] But other Protestant groups were moved to strong attacks upon what they saw as the gathering forces of infidelity. Herttell was castigated as a spokesman for Locofocoism, the epithet applied to the more extreme political, economic, and social reform movements of that day in an effort to saddle them with the image of mad revolutionaries run riot.[58] The growing influence of secularism was attributed by the *Christian Advocate* to "the anti-Christian tenets disseminated by the notorious Fanny Wright" and her following among the radical reformers.[59] The *Methodist Quarterly Review* was opposed to any change in the law governing oaths and the competency of witnesses. Its editors maintained that radicals such as Herttell incorrectly assumed "that the constitution of the state of New York is based upon atheism, and that it guaranties to atheists all the rights, privileges, and immunities of other men." [60] The very shrillness of such statements, however, was an indication that the more extreme supporters of religious tests realized that they were now on the defensive; they moved increasingly in futile opposition to the reforming spirit of the times.

In the late 1820's a movement to safeguard the Christian sabbath from the inroads of infidelity led to the formation in New York of The General Union for Promoting the Observance of the Christian Sabbath. But it was unable to elicit any lasting enthusiasm for organized political action in behalf of the cause.[61] Agitation to prohibit Sunday travel on the Erie Canal flared in the 1830's. But in 1842 the president of the state canal commission could write in answer to a petition

[57] *Signs of the Times* (Old School Baptist periodical published at New Vernon, Orange County), VIII (1840), 146–50, 151–52.

[58] *Albany Evening Journal* editorial, Jan. 8, 1840.

[59] [New York] *Christian Advocate*, Jan. 17, 1840.

[60] *Methodist Quarterly Review*, XXV (1843), 12.

[61] T. F. Savage, *The Presbyterian Church in New York City* (New York, 1949), pp. 83–84.

from a sabbath convention in Rochester that "the statute of this State, prohibiting travelling and servile labor on the Sabbath, is nearly a dead letter; and, like similar regulations, its rigid enforcement would create more immorality than it would suppress. The secular arm has always been a poor coadjutor of both morality and religion." [62]

One result of the growing secular and tolerant outlook in New York was that the courts and legislature began to retreat from the sweeping interpretation of competency requirements laid down by the state Supreme Court in 1820. The New York Supreme Court, as early as the 1823 case of *Butts* v. *Swartwood*, in effect decided that a Universalist might be sworn as a competent witness even though he did not believe in eternal punishments for perjury.[63] In 1824, a lower court decision established the rule that a witness did not have to accept the idea of everlasting damnation for lying. He was free to believe that punishment could come either in this world or the next; it was immaterial so long as he acknowledged some form of penalty for perjury.[64] In the Revised Laws of 1828, the state legislature modified the oath requirement in line with the ruling of 1824. At the same time it specified that a witness must not be interrogated directly concerning his religious beliefs; the determination of competency on religious grounds would have to depend on other testimony.[65] The state Supreme Court, in 1837, judged that no objection to a witness' competence on grounds of religion could be entertained after the witness had been sworn, al-

[62] *Proceedings of the Sabbath Convention Held at the City of Rochester, July 20th and 21st, 1842* (Rochester, 1842), p. 68.

[63] 2 Cow. 431 (1823).

[64] *People* v. *Zerubbabel Matteson* (1824), 2 Cow. note at 432–36.

[65] New York [State], *Revised Statutes, 1828* (Albany, 1829), II, secs. 87, 88.

though evidence as to the sworn witness' credibility would be admissible.[66]

As another convention to revise the state constitution prepared to convene in 1846, there was considerable evidence that opinion had come around to accept the removal of discriminatory religious tests and to recognize the wisdom of admitting nonconformists and unbelievers to the full and equal right to religious freedom long enjoyed by other New Yorkers.

The constitutional convention of 1846 met as the age of Jacksonian democracy was drawing to a close in New York. The great work of reformers in democratizing New York's political life had been all but completed. It fell to the 1846 convention to round out the triumph of popular government begun in 1821 and carried forward by the legislature over the intervening years. In the area of religious rights, the convention's commitment to an enlarged democracy resulted in the erection of additional constitutional safeguards around the freedom of conscience and belief.

During the closing debates on the religious freedom section in the convention, Moses Taggart of Genesee County moved an amendment specifying that "no man shall be deprived of any rights or rendered incompetent to be a witness on account of his opinions or religious beliefs."[67] A similar amendment had been accepted with relatively little opposition in the committee of the whole, but had been deleted from the final draft prepared by a committee of revision in favor of the religious section adopted in 1821.

One horrified delegate expressed alarm at Taggart's motion. He warned that "a more dangerous idea could not be spread

[66] *People* v. *Edward M'Garren*, 17 Wend. 460 (1837).

[67] S. Croswell and R. Sutton, *Debates and Proceedings in the New-York State Convention for the Revision of the Constitution* (Albany, 1846), pp. 807–08.

through the state, than that a witness was to be tolerated who was a disbeliever in the existence of a Supreme Being, and in his moral government to punish false swearing." [68] It would imperil the rights of the people to liberty and property. Another delegate replied that the religious test for competency was "hostile to that entire liberty of conscience and freedom to worship in that manner which every man's conscience might dictate." This test not only affected witnesses, but also parties to legal actions. He mentioned several instances where sound causes had been irreparably harmed because respectable witnesses had been disqualified for incompetency on religious grounds. In conclusion, "he asked not for favor for any peculiar opinions; but . . . for those equal rights which we all profess to be willing to have every man enjoy, leaving his religion as a matter to be settled with his conscience and his God." [69]

One member believed it risky to leave the determination of a person's religious qualifications to any earthly tribunal. Some witnesses might deserve to be excluded, but as a general rule the courts should not be the ones to decide. He thought that "the general moral deportment of a man may be better evidence of his belief in a Deity than any expression of his religious opinions." [70] Taggart added that the oath test led to hypocrisy. Such a test was not required by the federal Constitution. "He believed that neither religion nor the religious community longer desire this test." [71]

Taggart suggested that if religious belief could actually affect the testimony of a witness, let the matter be decided by the jury as a question of credibility and not one of competency. A motion to this effect was presented, but was decisively rejected by a vote of 92 to 12. Then the original Taggart amendment, with some minor changes in wording, was adopted by the comfortable margin of 63 to 46.[72] A clear

[68] *Ibid.*, p. 808. [69] *Ibid.* [70] *Ibid.* [71] *Ibid.*, pp. 808–09.
[72] *Ibid.*, p. 809.

majority had decided that the last remaining religious test in the laws of New York was to be discarded in the interests of a more perfect freedom of religion. It was not, however, that the arguments against the test oath had changed materially since 1821, but rather that they now commanded the attention of a majority where they had not at the preceding constitutional revision convention. An even greater number of the delegates in 1846 had voted against permitting evidence of a person's private religious opinions being used to impeach his credibility as a witness before a jury; this rejection of the credibility test went directly contrary to a practice then allowed in the state courts as a result of the ruling in the M'Garren case of 1837.[73]

Section 3 of article 1, of the Constitution of 1846, as finally adopted, read:

> The free exercise and enjoyment of religious profession and worship, without discrimination or preference, shall forever be allowed in this State to all mankind; and no person shall be rendered incompetent to be a witness on account of his opinions on matters of religious belief; but the liberty of conscience hereby secured shall not be so construed as to excuse acts of licentiousness, or to justify practices inconsistent with the peace or safety of this State.[74]

This version has remained basically unchanged as the fundamental constitutional guarantee of religious freedom in New York down to the present. Its durability has testified to the broad agreement among New York's diverse millions, with

[73] Admittedly, part of the vote against the Taggart amendment relating to credibility reflected opposition to any restrictions on the imposition of tests by judges or juries. But the vote favoring the Taggart amendment on competency, when compared with the vote on credibility, suggests that there was a respectable majority in the convention opposed to any religious test for determining either the credibility or the competency of witnesses.

[74] Croswell and Sutton, p. 841.

their many creeds and interests, that religious freedom is the right of all peaceable men and of no concern to secular authority short of specific acts working harm to the welfare of the community or to the rights of other individuals.[75]

Outside the convention, opinion was favorable to the decisions affecting the rights of religion. There was no public controversy generated by the competency question, a good indication that people accepted the convention's disposition of it quite matter-of-factly and with few regrets. Several of the leading secular and religious newspapers in New York did not even bother to comment editorially on the matter, confining their coverage of the convention's work to straight factual reports of its proceedings. Horace Greeley's *New York Tribune*, in a fairly representative editorial assessment, was highly laudatory of the treatment of the competency problem, commenting:

The New Constitution provides more effective safeguards for absolute Liberty of Conscience. . . . The time has been, and that not long ago, when erroneous belief, or want of belief, was held to disqualify men altogether for giving testimony. . . . Public Opinion has in good part corrected this monstrous judicial ab-

[75] Another interesting action of the 1846 convention (*ibid.*, pp. 430–32, 809) was the deletion of the constitutional prohibition on clergymen holding public office. This disability, inserted in 1777 to promote the separation of church and state, was retained for so long apparently because of the bitter memories of clerical intervention in politics in the time of Jefferson's presidency. On this, see Martin Van Buren, *Inquiry into the Origin and Course of Political Parties in the United States* (New York, 1867), pp. 278–79, 365–66. But by 1846 the old objections had lost their former appeal. Increasingly it was felt that this penalty was an infringement of the equal rights of ministers. It was undemocratic to single out this class because its members happened to be clergymen. Thus it was from a sense of the injustice of this provision, and not from any desire to encourage ministers to take up political careers, that the prohibition was deleted in 1846.

surdity; the New Constitution utterly annihilates it and provides against its recurrence.[76]

It remained, however, to test the tolerant spirit of the convention of 1846 in the courts, and here—despite Horace Greeley's optimism—it was not very evident that religious tests had been "utterly annihilated." In the 1858 case of *Stanbro* v. *Hopkins*,[77] the Supreme Court of New York ruled on an appeal from a trial judge's instruction to the jury that the religious opinions of a witness could be used in weighing the credibility of the witness' testimony. The plaintiff below, over the objections of the defendant, had been allowed to compel a defense witness to admit that he did not accept the existence of a supreme being capable of punishing false swearing. The Supreme Court's opinion acknowledged that a witness could no longer be dismissed as incompetent for religious reasons following article 1, section 3 of the 1846 constitution. But a person's religious views may render him less credible as a witness:

> Inasmuch as the barrier against admitting unbelievers in anything heavenly or divine to testify has been thrown down in this state, witnesses may be compelled to disclose, on cross-examination, their opinions on matters of religious belief. . . . This rule only carries out that doctrine of the common law which permits the laying open, as far as possible, the minds of witnesses to those who are compelled to pass upon their evidence.[78]

[76] *New York Tribune*, Oct. 14, 1846. In the same editorial, the *Tribune* commented on the dropping of the anticlerical officeholding restriction: "This most unique restriction (originally a crotchet of the great and good John Jay) is abolished by the New Constitution, and the People are left free to require or reject the services of Clergymen in a Political capacity, the same as other citizens. We deem this a great improvement. . . . The State has no right to make or meddle with ecclesiastical matters."

[77] 28 Barb. 265 (1858).

[78] 28 Barb. 265, at 271.

This decision, disregarding the obvious intent of a majority of the convention of 1846 on the matter of credibility, allowed the courts to continue to permit counsel to question a man's private religious convictions and to permit juries to weigh those convictions in assessing the integrity of testimony given. The Stanbro rule announced in 1858 remained until 1903. This was chiefly because it was not put to a test sooner, suggesting that in fact trial courts were much more flexible in applying this rule than the rule itself seemed to require.

In 1903 a majority of the New York Court of Appeals, now the highest appellate court in the state, overturned the Stanbro rule, declaring that witnesses could not be questioned concerning religious belief or disbelief in order to test their credibility.[79] The opinion of Judge Edgar M. Cullen, concurred in by four of his six colleagues, was also the first clear recognition by the higher courts of New York that nonbelievers possessed the same legal rights as believers in actions at law.

Judge Cullen stated that the ruling of the trial judge in the case under appeal, which had followed the Stanbro decision of 1858, had been erroneously arrived at. Cullen went to great lengths to trace the history of this question from its common law origins in England to the Constitutional Convention of 1846, where, he said, the competency issue had been settled once and for all. The action of that convention made "the divorce between the state and religious creeds complete." [80] What was more, "when the Constitution abrogated all disqualifications from office or civil rights, the consideration of a witness's religious belief on the question of his credibility necessarily fell at the same time." [81]

Cullen cited with approval an opinion of 1868 where it

[79] *Brink* v. *Stratton*, 175 N.Y. 150 (1903). Cullen's opinion, beginning at 156, was a concurring opinion signed by a clear majority, giving it the force of law.

[80] 175 N.Y. 150, at 158. [81] 175 N.Y. 150, at 160–61.

had been said that religious belief was no sure test of a person's character. Both the believer and the unbeliever are subject to the same human weaknesses and failings. As the court had observed in that earlier case, "Conduct and life, as distinguished from belief, give the standard of character." [82] Judge Cullen warned of the great danger to individual rights in resting the determination of credibility upon religious opinions. "Doubtless, no wise advocate will interrogate a witness as to his religious faith," he said, "unless it be obnoxious and unpopular in the community. But that is the very case in which the exposure of a witness's religious belief would probably lead to injustice." [83] Some might contend that the fate of the atheist was not important enough to concern society, but "the principle involved here is in itself important." [84]

With this ruling, the last major hurdle to a realization of the full guarantees of the rights of conscience for all of New York's citizens was crossed. Official practice, encompassing now even those who denied religion altogether, was at last brought into alignment with profession, and in the main it has remained so ever since. The differences that have occurred on this score in the years since 1903 have not been over the broad categories of ideas and actions protected by the religious freedom article, but over the inclusion within them of borderline cases.

[82] *Gibson* v. *American Mutual Life Insurance Co.*, 37 N.Y. 580 (1868), at 584.

[83] 175 N.Y. 150, at 161.

[84] 175 N.Y. 150, at 162.

VII

Church, State, and Education

ONE of the most challenging, persistent, and embittered church-state problems confronting New York in the nineteenth century resulted from the development of a system of publicly supported schools. First, there was the friction generated by the rise of the public elementary school to fulfill a function which, to a great extent, had been met by religious and private groups in the colonial period. Then came the impact of a rapidly growing Catholic population upon a predominantly Protestant society whose institutions reflected this predominance. Catholic educational views inevitably clashed with the doctrines of Protestant Christianity which permeated the educational philosophies of the young state. The major sources of contention between Protestant and Catholic were the issues of religious instruction in the schools and of public support for private sectarian schools.

In colonial New York, under both the Dutch and the English, it had been a natural assumption that the education of the young should be closely related to the religion of the community. Elementary schooling in the traditional reading, writing, and arithmetic was informed and guided by principles of religion and morality. Schools were viewed as adjuncts of the churches in what was regarded as the noble task of instilling Christian piety in the minds of the younger generation. Colonial theory and practice were themselves a reflection of New York's European heritage. In the post-Reformation Netherlands, education had been reserved to the established Reformed church by the civil authorities. In sixteenth- and seventeenth-century England, elementary education, whether in private or ecclesiastical, Anglican or Calvinist schools, was an accepted means for the inculcation of Protestant tenets. English schooling reflected the fierce absorption with religion which left its indelible mark upon the life of that age.[1]

As in the mother country, so in New Netherland, the Dutch church was the primary source for what education there was. The civil government of the colony felt little responsibility for education beyond examining prospective teachers to see that they conformed to the doctrines of the Reformed religion. To the Amsterdam Classis of the Dutch church, which exercised ecclesiastical jurisdiction over New Netherland, was reserved the nomination of schoolteachers, who were considered to be as much officials of the church as were clergymen. While the representatives of the governing Dutch West India Company and the people of the colony might disagree over the responsibilities of each for the support of schools, both were agreed that religious instruction was a basic aim of formal schooling. Thus such schooling should be left in the first instance to the institution which by authority and competence was best suited to conduct it, the Dutch church.[2]

Following the English conquest in 1664, responsibility for educating children was placed solely with the parents after the prevailing practice in England. The state required only that schooling consist of instruction in religion and the laws of England; town officials were instructed to see that all parents complied with this. What resulted was a patchwork system of

[1] C. J. Mahoney, *The Relation of the State to Religious Education in Early New York, 1633–1825* (Washington, D.C., 1941), ch. i.

[2] *Ibid.*, pp. 24–50.

education in which heads of families made use of the most accessible means, which were bound to differ from household to household and community to community.[3]

The English inclination to view education as the obligation of parents and not of the state, so long as it was of a religious and civic nature, meant that schooling was left to the home, to privately hired teachers, to local town governments, and to religious societies. Those who could afford it employed tutors or sent their children to private tuition schools. Where a town had a majority of one sect, it might decide to support a teacher, usually the town's minister, at public expense, as was the case in Hempstead and other of the English dissenting towns on Long Island settled by New Englanders. Otherwise children obtained their education through the churches of their parents or, as was true of many, received no formal schooling at all. The Dutch church, while now deprived of public support for its schools, continued to maintain them wherever possible as annexes of local Dutch churches. In New York City parochial elementary schooling for the poor of each sect became the general practice in the eighteenth century and continued to be so after the Revolution. These church schools were essentially institutions for the propagation of the doctrines of the various sponsoring sects. But regardless of the type of education provided, most people agreed that all schooling should be intimately related to religion.

The multiplicity of competing sects in colonial New York and the opposition of each sect to any kind of education which did not include instruction in its own peculiar doctrines were largely responsible for the absence of any comprehensive system of publicly financed schools in the province. There was no majority sentiment for such a system, and the provincial government preferred to leave things as they were

[3] The summary of educational developments in the period of English colonial rule given here is based upon *ibid.*, pp. 50–85.

rather than provide another source of sectarian unrest that might upset the always tenuous religious settlement in the colony. In this atmosphere of official indifference, the responsibility of private, including religious, institutions for education became fixed in the popular mind, as did the conviction that instruction in religion should form an essential part of any educational curriculum.

After the Revolution the leaders of the new state's government developed an interest in the encouragement of education. Now there was a sound reason for desiring an educated citizenry. It was clearly seen that under a republican form of government, where the people were the ultimate sovereign power, the success of that government depended upon the enlightened and informed interest of the people. The grand vision of New York's founding fathers of a republic marching onward and upward, proudly demonstrating the superior qualities of the American experiment for all the world to behold and marvel at, required a people with sufficient education to rule themselves wisely and virtuously. From the earliest days of this nation, Americans have had this noble, sometimes naïve, faith in the powers of education to solve their own as well as the world's ills. Governor Morgan Lewis, in his annual message to the New York legislature in 1804, voiced these sentiments when he remarked: "In a government resting on public opinion, and deriving its chief support from the affections of the people, religion and morality cannot be too sedulously inculcated. To them science is an handmaid—ignorance, the worst of enemies. Literary information should, then, be placed within the reach of every description of citizens."[4] The rising demands for public support of schools rested upon the growing conviction that not only parents, but the state itself, had a responsibility for the education of the young. No longer could the public's interest in the civic

[4] S. S. Randall, *History of the Common School System of the State of New York* (New York, 1871), p. 13.

training of future generations be satisfied by the haphazard school arrangements which were the legacy of the colonial period.

Despite a sputtering and half-hearted initial effort, an early demonstration of the paradoxical niggardliness Americans have often displayed when it came to paying for the schools most of them professedly desired, a start on a state-supported school system was made in 1795. The legislature voted a five-year program of grants to elementary schools already in being or which were to be set up in the localities. Initiative was left entirely to the local communities, and the sums appropriated were much too small. The arrangement proved unsatisfactory for encouraging the establishment of new elementary, or as they were then called, common schools. Rather than correct these defects, the legislature allowed the program to lapse at the close of the five-year period.

Through the unceasing efforts of the friends of state-supported education, however, the legislature was persuaded in 1801 to establish a state common school fund with the proceeds of four public lotteries. In 1805 it was enacted that the interest accruing on the invested moneys derived from the sale of certain state-owned lands was to be added to the school fund.[5] By 1810 the common school fund had grown to sufficient size to warrant new attention to the problem of creating a system of state aid to schools. There was also the insistent pressure of demands for state assistance from the recently settled upstate areas to which New England Yankees were flocking. These people were usually too money poor and too thinly settled to establish town schools, like those of their native New England, through their own unaided efforts, while the local churches were too poor and too unstable to

[5] J. D. Hammond, *The History of Political Parties in the State of New-York*, 4th ed. (Cooperstown, N.Y., 1846), I, 87–88, 158–59, 216–17; Mahoney, pp. 93–94.

provide schools of their own. The state's answer was to appoint a commission in 1811 to devise a plan for the utilization of the common school fund. The next year the commission recommended the establishment of district common schools throughout the state with the exception of the city of New York. The districts were to be formed within the existing townships. Each year the state would allot the interest from the common school fund to the several districts on a per capita basis, for the payment of teachers' salaries. The elected trustees in each school district were to raise an equal sum for salaries and maintain a schoolhouse by means of local taxes and rate bills or tuition payments. In 1812 the commission's report was embodied in a law governing the upstate regions. With the passage of a school law applying to New York City in 1813, the state was now committed to the idea of the public's obligation to assist the education of the state's youths.[6]

But while New York's leaders accepted responsibilities for financing education, they saw little reason for interfering in the traditional common school curriculum with its pronounced religious flavor. New Yorkers were as certain as their colonial predecessors that elementary schooling should not only impart practical knowledge, but also stress Christian virtue and morality. Religious instruction continued to be the means utilized to accomplish this end. To Governor Daniel D. Tompkins, recommending the support of education to the legislature in 1810, common schooling for the young should not only "enable them to perceive and duly . . . estimate their rights" and "render them useful citizens," but also "inculcate correct principles and habits of morality and religion."[7] In the opinion of the school commission of 1811–1812, common schools were the "best plan that can be devised

[6] The two education statutes are in New York [State], *Laws, 1812*, ch. 242, and *Laws, 1813*, ch. 52; see also Mahoney, pp. 94–98, and S. S. Randall, pp. 17–23. [7] *Ibid.*, p. 15.

to disseminate religion, morality, and learning throughout a whole country." Of these goals, "morality and religion," the commissioners reported, "are the foundation of all that is truly great and good; and are, consequently, of primary importance." [8]

Little wonder, then, that New York's first publicly supported schools were as devoted to religious as to secular instruction. Bible reading, prayers, hymn singing, and the use of instructional materials derived from religious sources were root and branch a part of the common school curriculum.[9] There were few objections to this religious emphasis in the early common schools, despite the state's commitment to a separation of church and state, because of the religious homogeneity of New York's people in the early nineteenth century. The state was predominantly Protestant, and most people saw little reason to complain of using the schools to complement the work of their churches. Besides, there were no compulsory school laws which required parents with conscientious objections to send their children to the common schools. If they were unsatisfied, let them find other means to educate their young. Another factor which contributed indirectly to the widespread acceptance of religious exercises in the schools was the great diversity of sectarian belief represented among the school children. The common school authorities in the districts created by the act of 1812 usually were quite careful to avoid any sign of favoritism toward one Protestant sect as against another. The retention of public favor for the common school system dictated that the religious instruction of the upstate schools should consist of a

[8] *Ibid.*, pp. 18–19.

[9] There is a vivid account of a Protestant revival conducted by the enthusiastic teacher of an upstate common school in Ontario County in 1817 in the *Methodist Magazine*, I (1818), 70–73, 117–19. While this was a more extreme example of such exercises in the schools, it does not seem to have been regarded as unusual.

nondenominational Protestantism with emphasis on those Christian doctrines which united, rather than divided, the several Protestant sects.[10]

The state's initial provision for the educational needs of New York City was radically different from that applied to the upstate areas in 1812. It was thought that the city already had suitable facilities. These consisted of charity schools, dating back in many cases to the colonial period, which were attached to several of the churches for the instruction of the children of each sect; the schools of the Free School Society, a nonsectarian Protestant philanthropic group founded in 1805 for the education of poor children who had no church affiliations; a few free schools conducted by private charitable institutions; and many private tuition schools serving the children of the well-to-do. By the New York City common school act of 1813, the state legislature continued the policy first adopted in 1795 of dividing the city's share of the school fund among the already existing private schools offering free schooling to the poor. These schools were classed as public schools for this purpose. The private tuition schools were deemed capable of caring for themselves without state assistance.[11]

Thus, under the act of 1813, public funds were allotted to sectarian schools in which the tenets of particular sects provided the content of their religious exercises. The explanation for this arrangement, seemingly contradicted by the policy of

[10] Mahoney, pp. 111–13.

[11] *Ibid.*, pp. 114–18; E. G. Hobson, *Educational Legislation and Administration in the State of New York from 1777 to 1850* (Chicago, 1918), pp. 86–88. Additional details on the grant of funds to sectarian schools in New York City, including the free school of St. Peters Roman Catholic Church, are in J. W. Pratt, "Boss Tweed's Public Welfare Program," *New-York Historical Society Quarterly*, XLV (1961), 402 n.

publicly managed schools enacted for upstate in 1812, was that the idea of public education did not yet include a clear-cut distinction between "public" and "private" means of instruction. The state saw as its objective the encouragement of teaching in good citizenship. Schools as physical entities were but means to this end, requiring the public's serious attention only where such buildings were nonexistent, as was the case upstate but not in New York City. To a government of limited means, there were also obvious economies in such a policy. For twelve years the various church schools, the Free School Society schools, and the few other charity schools constituted the publicly supported school system of New York City. During this period the Free School Society, aided by influential politicians and the state legislature, extended its system with the help of special public appropriations until it was the largest single educational force in the city. Its trustees, however, motivated by an ideal of nonsectarian education as the wisest course for a pluralistic society, increasingly doubted the wisdom of state aid to the city's sectarian schools.[12]

The first major clash between these competing philosophies occurred in 1822. The Bethel Baptist Church was given authority by the legislature to use its surplus state funds for the construction of additional parish schools. The Free School Society, which had benefited from a similar privilege since 1817, saw in this grant a precedent for the future aggrandizement of the sectarian school ideal at the expense of its own nonsectarian principle. There was also an economic motive. If children were won away from its schools by the church schools, which is what the Bethel Church was trying to accomplish, the society's share of the school fund, determined by the numbers of children educated gratuitously each year,

[12] E. M. Connors, *Church-State Relationships in Education in the State of New York* (Washington, D.C., 1951), pp. 1–3; Mahoney, pp. 119–28.

would be diminished and it would have to cut its services.[13]

The society appealed to the legislature to rescind the Bethel grant. While awaiting action on its petition, the Free School Society began a public campaign aimed at curbing not only Bethel's schools, but all church schools. For the first time the issue of church-state separation in education was raised when the society contended that state aid to sectarian schools represented a misapplication of public funds. Spokesmen for the society argued that clergymen and priests should not control public moneys, that the state must "save untouched the sacred principle of our constitution, that church and state shall not be united." [14] The representatives of the city's church schools replied that they were using their shares of the school fund not to further any sectarian interests, but to educate children, which was in the best interests of the state. Moreover, they maintained, religious training was essential to the growth of public morality, and such training could best be given through instruction in the creeds of the various sects.

Faced with the gathering storm clouds of religious controversy, the legislature took what seemed the wiser course in 1824 by turning its authority to designate the city's recipients of school funds over to the New York City Common Council. The next year, on the advice of its legal committee, the Council voted to end the allotment of public funds to ecclesiastical schools. Thereafter, only the Free School Society's system and a few other nonsectarian charity schools were to receive a share of the school moneys. The report of the Council's law committee asserted, as grounds for this ruling, that "true religion requires and admits of no aid from the secular power; that her only resources are from heaven, and the contributions of willing hearts; that she seeks only for protection, and not for support; and that the arm of the State . . . has no potency or legitimate control beyond such

[13] The Bethel dispute is treated at length in *ibid.*, pp. 134–201.

[14] Quoted in the *Albany Argus*, Nov. 9, 1824.

protection."[15] By this decision, New York's only major experiment with the financial support of private religious schools was brought to an end. The venture had been struck down from a growing realization of the incongruity of such aid in the light of the ideal of church-state separation.

But if the Common Council's action ended the practice of assisting sectarian schools, it did not overthrow the belief in the need for some kind of religious instruction in the state-supported schools. Teaching the children of many sects, the quasi-public Free School Society, like the upstate common schools, offered a general nonsectarian type of religious teaching in its institutions to meet this recognized need. The society had long made use of the King James version of the Bible and of widely accepted devotions like the Lord's Prayer in its curriculum. As a result of the Council decision of 1825, nonsectarianism may have triumphed over sectarianism in the public schools, but religious instruction was still very much to the fore, and it was invariably an exclusively Protestant instruction. While nonsectarian perhaps to a Protestant, it was very much sectarian to a non-Protestant. Only as long as New York remained a Protestant community would this practice be tolerable to the vast majority of its people.

In the 1820's the population of New York was already undergoing far-reaching changes which were to have profound effects upon older ways of life. From some one million inhabitants at the close of the War of 1812, New York grew to almost two and one half million people in 1840. The great port city of New York increased its population more than threefold from 1814 to 1840; where there had been 95,000 in the former year, there were in the latter year over 300,000 human beings crowding the lower half of Manhattan Island.

[15] Quoting the report given in full in W. O. Bourne, *History of the Public School Society of the City of New York* (New York, 1869), p. 719.

By 1855 the 1840 figure had doubled itself. Between 1814 and 1855 New York's neighbor, Brooklyn, had exploded from a rural village of less than 4,000 to a bustling city of 200,000 population. These population trends were repeated in the upstate cities of Albany, Rochester, and Buffalo as well as in many of the rural counties.[16]

Much of this growth came from natural increase and from the movement of New Englanders out of their stony hill farms and into the fertile regions of upstate New York, but immigration from Europe began to play an important part. After the close of the Napoleonic Wars, at first in fits and starts, and then in a gathering stream, Europeans made their way to America in search of a better life. A great proportion of those who emigrated entered the United States through New York City, the first port on the Atlantic Coast of America. Many moved on, but thousands of others, because of a lack of funds and the necessity of finding immediate work, remained in New York. There they found jobs in the burgeoning commercial city or moved upstate to labor on the Erie Canal and later on the railroads.[17]

Of the early immigrant groups, the Irish and Germans were the most numerous, and of the two Irish immigration was the larger until surpassed by the Germans in the 1850's.[18] Almost two-thirds of the Irish newcomers were Roman Catholics. A good index of their growth in New York is to be found in the estimates of the Catholic diocese of New York. In 1815 it was calculated, on the basis of parish reports, that there were thirteen thousand Catholics in the diocese, which included the entire state plus part of New Jersey. The bulk of these were

[16] F. B. Hough, ed., *Census of the State of New-York for 1855* (Albany, 1857), pp. xii, xvi, xx, xxii–xxiv, xxxiii.

[17] The standard work on immigration in this period is M. L. Hansen, *The Atlantic Migration, 1607–1860* (Cambridge, Mass., 1940), especially chs. iv–xiii.

[18] A. B. Faust, *The German Element in the United States* (New York, 1909), I, 582.

Irish and were congregated in New York City and Albany. Eleven years later the diocese had an estimated 150,000 communicants, 25,000 of them in New York City. By the end of the 1820's there were four Catholic churches in that city, with a fifth about to be built, where only two had existed in 1820. In the decade of the 1820's, Roman churches were built or being constructed in Brooklyn, Albany, Troy, Utica, Carthage, Salina (soon to become Syracuse), Auburn, Rochester, and Buffalo, where none had been before. By 1830, the gregarious Irish of New York City comprised a virtually self-sufficient community with their own newspapers, social clubs, professional men, merchants, churches, and schools.[19]

The coming of the Irish Catholics seriously threatened the predominance of Protestantism in New York City. Catholics, through their clergy and lay leaders, brought new points of view to leading questions of the day, such as education, sometimes in opposition to old habits of thought. The Catholic church has insisted as a matter of doctrine upon the control of education for its own children wherever possible. It has sought to protect the faith of these children by uniting their secular schooling with instruction in the beliefs of the Catholic church through the medium of the parochial school. As the Catholic church in America grew in numbers during the first half of the nineteenth century, the hierarchy turned its attention increasingly to the educational needs of its children.[20]

Clerical demands for the establishment of parochial schools reflected a growing alienation from the education offered in the schools of America. In New York, the nonsectarianism practiced in the schools, which had seemed to native Protestants a reasonable compromise between the commonly ac-

[19] J. G. Shea, *History of the Catholic Church in the United States* (New York, 1886–92), III, 176–77, 196, 199, 204–05; A. C. Flick, ed., *History of the State of New York* (New York, 1933–37), VII, 47.

[20] Peter Guilday, *The National Pastorals of the American Hierarchy (1792–1919)*, (Washington, D.C., 1923), pp. 3–135 *passim.*

cepted need for religious instruction and the diversity of sectarian beliefs, was repellent to Catholics. To them, the religious teaching of the schools was little more than rank Protestant sectarianism. While the reading of the King James Bible, without note or comment, was a fair alternative in a Protestant society to the divisive teaching of creeds peculiar to each Protestant sect, that particular version was the very symbol of anti-Catholicism to the Catholics.

Until the 1840's, however, the poverty of the church in New York prevented it from organizing sufficient parochial schools to care for the increasing Catholic school-age population. Catholic youths had either to attend the state-supported schools at the risk of violating their consciences or else go without formal schooling, as many did in New York City. As early as 1834 the Catholic bishop of New York placed the Public School Society of the city, formerly the Free School Society, on notice that he was dissatisfied with the Protestant teaching presented in its schools under the guise of nonsectarian instruction. Nothing came of this early protest, but it was a harbinger of contention to come over the school question.[21]

To some Americans the Irish Catholic immigrants were welcomed as needed additions to a young nation's labor force, but to others they were cause for alarm. Those who feared them were aroused by the clannishness of the Irish and by their intense national and religious loyalties, which they exhibited in their veneration of Ireland's native heroes and in their devotions to the Catholic church. At a time when American nationalism was on the rise, the seeming indifference of Irish newcomers to becoming full-fledged Americans with strictly American habits and expectations was ample grounds for dislike and suspicion. The Irish taste for whisky, their seeming penchant for brawling, and their poverty appeared as congenital defects of character to the apprehensive. Above all

[21] Connors, pp. 12–15. The society changed its name in 1826; see *ibid.*, p. 2.

there was their attachment to the Catholic faith, which American Protestantism had always feared as the very antithesis of freedom. In New York City in the 1820's, Protestant clergymen and periodicals began to herald the dangers arising from increased Catholic immigration and from the rapid growth of the church in city and state.[22]

In the mid-1830's the anti-Catholic agitation led to direct political action. A Protestant Association was organized in the city in 1834 to rally the defenders of gospel truth against the inroads of the popish invaders. By the spring of 1835 native-born citizens were forming groups in several wards to contest city elections with the Democrats who had attracted the bulk of the Irish vote. The local Whig organization, a beleaguered minority because of its not entirely deserved reputation for "conservatism" and "aristocracy" that placed it in opposition to the mainstream of Jacksonian democracy then at full tide in the city, grasped at this incipient nativist movement. By associating with anti-Catholicism, the Whig leaders hoped to identify their party with a popular new cause, far removed from past issues in the public mind, thereby regaining political initiative in the city. At municipal elections in 1836 and 1837, Whig-nativist fusion tickets were able to win control first of the Common Council and then of the mayorship. The Whigs soon absorbed the antiforeigner movement, and nativism as a distinct political force went into a period of decline until events in the 1840's called it forth once more. But the feelings against Irish Catholics did not disappear; they had become politically useful and would be employed again and again for partisan advantage.[23]

Where some politicians found political capital in attacking the immigrant Irish, others were attracted to them by their

[22] Carl Wittke, *The Irish in America* (Baton Rouge, 1956), pp. 40–50; Ray Billington, *The Protestant Crusade, 1800–1860* (New York, 1938), ch. ii; L. D. Scisco, *Political Nativism in New York State* (New York, 1901), pp. 20–21. [23] *Ibid.*, pp. 21–32.

growing strength at the polls. In that democratic age when party success was increasingly dependent upon the ability to sway large blocs of voters, the Irish Catholics were a prize worth winning. From the 1820's onward, New York City Democrats eagerly courted the Catholic Irish, who initially were predisposed to support the Democratic party because of the libertarian appeal of its name and who later had this choice confirmed by the anti-Irish attacks of Protestant Whigs. The Irish responded to Democratic attentions with their fervent loyalties and contributed their skills at practical politics to the Democratic cause. This identity of the great majority of the foreign-born Irish with the local Democratic party was a major reason for the Whig courtship of the anti-Irish nativist movement in the 1830's. Unable to compete with the Democrats for Irish votes, the city Whigs sought to win elections by attacking the Irish.[24]

But while the New York City Whigs were lining up against the foreign born, a group of young upstate Whigs in the late 1830's were trying to cultivate the immigrant vote. They were convinced that the future of their party lay not in trying to stem the rise of the common man, but rather in accepting the popularization of American politics as an inescapable fact and moving on from there. There were lessons to be learned in the remarkable success of the Jacksonian Democrats, whose nimbleness in attaching their fortunes to popular currents in American political life had been most profitable for them. To Whig leaders such as William Henry Seward and Thurlow Weed, the only way to overcome the taint of privilege and reaction, which the Jacksonians had riveted so

[24] G. G. Van Deusen, *Thurlow Weed: Wizard of the Lobby* (Boston, 1947), p. 91. For a recent assessment of foreign-born Irish Catholic identification with the Democratic party in New York during this period, see Lee Benson, *The Concept of Jacksonian Democracy: New York as a Test Case* (Princeton, 1961), 187–91, 321–24. Benson states, "Probably about 95 per cent of the 'Catholic voters' supported the Democrats in New York State" (p. 187).

successfully upon their party in the public mind, was to broaden the appeal of their organization.[25] Following the Panic of 1837, which voters blamed on the incumbent Democrats, and a division in the Democratic ranks, Seward was elected to the governorship in 1838. The Seward Whigs, encouraged by the victory, went in search of the electoral support that would convert their fortuitous majority into a more durable combination. As part of this campaign, Thurlow Weed, master strategist and tactician of the Seward faction, was determined to detach the pivotal Irish vote in New York City from Tammany Hall.[26] Governor Seward co-operated fully with his cohort in this plan. In his first annual message to the legislature in January 1839, Seward launched a broad appeal for the favor of the immigrant population. He stressed the importance of making the newly arrived foreigner feel at home in America by extending to him the full rights of citizenship and the "immunities of religious worship." The immigrants should also be provided with schools "in which their children shall enjoy advantages of education equal to our own, with free toleration of their peculiar creeds and instructions."[27] Behind the scenes Weed was hard at work with his pen and his control of patronage cultivating the favorable sentiments of New York City Irish leaders both among politicians and the priesthood.[28]

On one question, the education of immigrant children,

[25] The ultimate expression of this new, popular approach was the Whig ballyhoo presidential campaign of 1840, but the techniques employed to elect Harrison had already been tried out in party battles at the state level, as in New York.

[26] Van Deusen, p. 91; Benson (p. 188) supports this view, writing: "Seward, Weed, and Greeley clung to the hope that naturalized Catholic voters eventually would cease to go *en masse* for the Democrats."

[27] G. E. Baker, ed., *Works of William H. Seward* (New York, 1853–54), II, 199.

[28] Letters from James Bowen, New York City, to Weed, Aug. 5, 1839, and B. Birdsall, New York City, to Weed, Jan. 18, 1840, Thurlow Weed Papers, University of Rochester.

Seward's interest in winning votes was reinforced by his long-standing desire to promote better schooling in New York. He had become convinced that the schools of New York City were not reaching thousands of children of foreign parentage. Many of this number were Catholic; they could not attend the schools of the Public School Society without endangering their morals nor were there adequate parochial facilities to care for them. After consulting with political colleagues, Seward devised a plan to aid these neglected youths.

The governor presented his proposal in his message to the legislature of January 7, 1840. Each word, each phrase, was carefully measured for its maximum political effect; here was a plan which, if successful, would help ensure the continued supremacy of the Whigs in New York by breaking the hold of the Democrats upon Catholic voters. The proposal was couched in terms appealing to the widely shared interest in improving public education, while clearly guarding against unnecessarily arousing the ire of Protestant Americans:

> The children of foreigners, found in great numbers in our populous cities and towns, and in the vicinity of our public works, are too often deprived of the advantages of our system of public education, in consequence of prejudices arising from difference of language or religion. It ought never to be forgotten that the public welfare is as deeply concerned in their education as in that of our own children. I do not hesitate, therefore, to recommend the establishment of schools in which they may be instructed by teachers speaking the same language with themselves and professing the same faith. . . . The responsibilities of education are in most instances confided by us to native citizens, and occasions seldom offer for a trial of our magnanimity by committing that trust to persons differing from ourselves in language or religion. Since we have opened our country and all its fullness to the oppressed of every nation, we should evince wisdom equal to such generosity by qualifying their children for the high responsibilities of citizenship.[29]

[29] Baker, II, 215–16. Also see Weed's *Autobiography*, ed. by H. A. Weed (Boston, 1883), p. 483, and F. W. Seward, ed., *Autobiography*

Seward was suggesting that the state support sectarian schools, more specifically Catholic schools. There could be little doubt that the governor was aiming his general remarks at the particular situation in New York City. It was the only "populous" city in the state where there were Catholics in sufficient numbers to constitute an educational problem by their refusal on religious grounds to patronize the existing common schools. Governor Seward was being less than candid when he referred to this problem as one of language, as well as religious, differences. By far the greater number of foreign children in the city were Irish, and they had no particular language difficulties. This attempt to divert attention from the religious aspect fooled no one. It gave to his remarks a deviousness which tended to confirm the suspicions of many that this was all a political deal hatched between Seward and the Catholic hierarchy of New York.

Catholics in New York City interpreted Seward's educational recommendation as an invitation to submit a request for public aid to their parochial schools. Any lingering doubts were removed by consultations between Rev. John Power, vicar general of the New York diocese, and friends of the governor at Albany. The Albany politicians even went so far as to suggest a plan of attack to the Catholics, opening with an appeal to the Common Council of the city for a share of the school moneys. In February 1840, the trustees of seven Catholic schools in New York City submitted a formal request to the Common Council for public assistance.[30]

The petition elicited a storm of outraged opinion from the metropolis. It reopened the question of the Public School Society's privileges, as well as the nativist issue which had muddied the political waters of the 1830's. The defenders of

---

of William H. Seward from 1801 to 1834, with a Memoir of His Life . . . 1831 to 1846 (New York, 1877), pp. 460–61.

[30] Connors, pp. 16–17; J. R. G. Hassard, *Life of the Most Reverend John Hughes* (New York, 1865), pp. 227–28.

the School Society argued that any grant of funds to Catholic schools would be unconstitutional, "because it is utterly at variance with the letter and spirit of our chartered rights, and with the genius of our political institutions, that the community should be taxed to support an establishment in which sectarian dogmas are inculcated."[31] If the city's school funds were subdivided among a greater number of schools, the society's share would be decreased, to the detriment of its thriving and beneficial school system. Nativist elements in the city supported the society's position as a means to strike again the hated Catholic monster.

The Democratically controlled Common Council was placed in an unenviable position by the Catholic petition. It had either to deny the request of the party's Irish Catholic supporters or else—by granting it—appear to be reacting to Seward's initiative while at the same time risking the alienation of Protestant Democrats. The Council's solution was to reject the Catholic petition, but on the high ground of church-state principle rather than on the facts of this particular case. A committee of the Council reported, "An appropriation . . . to the support of schools, in which the religious tenets of any sect are taught . . . would be a legal establishment of one denomination over another, would conflict with all the principles and purposes of our free institutions, and would violate the very letter of . . . our Constitution."[32] In this manner, the Council was able to say no to the Catholics without singling them out by name as deserving of special censure.

Undaunted by this initial rebuff, the Catholics in New York City organized a formal association to press on with their demands. In mid-July of 1840, leadership of the movement was assumed by Bishop John Hughes, coadjutor of the diocese, who had been abroad when the school controversy first broke out. Hughes, a powerful figure in the American

[31] Bourne, p. 180. [32] Quoted in Connors, p. 18.

hierarchy, was convinced that Catholics would have to fight for every concession they hoped to wring from an alien and inimical American society. He combined in his person a priestly sense of mission, the commanding authority of a general, the manipulative skills of a professional politician, and the crowd-pleasing and occasionally elevating oratory of an accomplished public speaker. With Hughes at the helm, the school question soon developed a militancy and emotionalism which spread far beyond the original issues, helped ignite a new burst of nativist bigotry in the Northeast, and doomed whatever political prospects Seward and Weed ever had of winning the allegiance of Irish-Americans.[33]

Through the summer and early autumn of 1840, Hughes conducted frequent protest meetings of Catholics to strengthen the resolve of his flock. Always the refrain of these meetings was the same: the schools of the Public School Society, while claimed to be nonsectarian, were actually sectarian in the extreme and patently anti-Catholic. The only version of the Bible used in these schools was the King James or Protestant edition. Reading selections, employed in both historical and religious instruction, were taken from Protestant sources which were biased toward the Catholic church and unsuitable for use in the instruction of Catholic children. It was only right and just, in view of the constitutional guarantee of religious freedom, that if Catholic youths could not conscientiously attend the School Society's schools, they be taught in parochial schools which would receive a portion of the common school funds for performing this public service.[34]

The School Society and Protestant clergymen replied that the charges of sectarianism were absurd. The attack was carried to the enemy by frenetic assaults upon the church as a despotic monster and an un-American institution. The secular press, particularly James Gordon Bennett's *New York Her-*

[33] *Ibid.*, pp. 19–20. [34] *Ibid.*, pp. 23–24; Bourne, pp. 189–95.

ald, the *Commercial Advertiser*, and the *Journal of Commerce*, joined in the anti-Catholic crusade.[35] The latter two papers were spokesmen for the Whig leadership of New York City. Their editorial position on the school question reflected the growing disillusionment of the city Whigs with Seward and Weed's efforts to popularize their party by appealing to the masses, particularly foreign-born Catholics. Long identified with the nativist cause, these Whigs were dismayed by Seward's pandering after the votes of their sworn enemies, the Irish Catholics. Democrats, in turn, used the nativist reputation of the city Whigs to convince Irish voters that Seward was deceiving them, that he could not deliver on his school proposals because his party was not behind him.

In the fall elections of 1840, Seward's gubernatorial majority was cut in half from that of 1838 by Whig defections and the refusal of the Irish to desert the Democratic column. Although the Whigs carried the state that year, Seward ran well behind the rest of his ticket. The governor and his friends had done their utmost to refute the Democratic and anti-Seward Whig attacks, but the election revealed the weaknesses of Seward's school campaign.[36] He had underrated the power of nativism within his own party, as well as the durability of the Irish-Democratic alliance. The New York City Whig merchant, Philip Hone, attributed Seward's poor showing to "the ill-judged favour which he has shown the Catholics, by which he has lost many of his friends, and not gained the votes of those whom he sought to propitiate."[37] Seward, himself, attributed his shrunken majority to the anti-foreignism of his party. Irish voters were turned against him

[35] L. Kehoe, ed., *Complete Works of the Most Rev. John Hughes* (New York, 1864), I, 126 ff.; Connors, pp. 28–29.

[36] Letter from Patrick Carberry, Auburn, N.Y., to Weed, Oct. 18, 1840, Weed Papers; also see Philip Hone's *Diary . . . 1828–1851*, ed. by B. Tuckerman (New York, 1889), II, 52.

[37] *Ibid.*

because he was the representative of the Whig party and all it stood for, and, as he described himself, the victim of foul slanders from "Americans in both parties, representing me as insincere and deceitful." But Seward meant to carry on his fight to secure to the immigrant his full rights, as "it will relieve me," he wrote, "from the self-reproach of seeing the fairest political prospects of our party destroyed without my protest." [38]

True to his expressed intentions, Governor Seward again attacked the school problem in his third annual message of January 5, 1841.[39] He mentioned that New York City's problem still existed and that something had to be done soon for the many children there who were not attending the schools. At the same time he retreated from his proposal of 1840, a recognition that his former position had repelled rather than attracted public support. "I have no pride of opinion," he observed, "concerning the manner in which the education of those whom I have brought to your notice shall be secured . . . ," although he noted that no alternative plan had been suggested.[40] Seward, somewhat disingenuously it would seem, denied he had ever suggested that the public should support religious schools. He also praised the common schools as republican institutions and hinted that the children of immigrants might well be accommodated under the existing public school system. Seward was in fact searching for some acceptable arrangement that would permit the schooling of Catholic children, under morally unexceptionable conditions, short of his previous suggestion of public aid to parochial schools.

A few days after Seward's message to the legislature, the Board of Aldermen of the New York City Common Council again refused a Catholic petition for a share of the city's school funds. The Catholic Association had claimed in its memorial:

[38] Baker, III, 387–88. [39] *Ibid.*, II, 279–81. [40] *Ibid.*, p. 279.

The rights of conscience, in this country, are held by both the Constitution and universal consent, to be sacred and inviolable. . . . Your petitioners only claim the benefit of this principle in regard to the public education of their children. They regard the public education which the State has provided as a common benefit, in which they are most desirous, and feel they are entitled, to participate; and therefore they pray your Honorable Body that they may be permitted to do so, without violating their conscience.[41]

While the Catholics appealed to the ideal of religious freedom, asserting that they were denied this freedom in the School Society's schools, the aldermen based their rejection once more upon a general view of the principle of church-state separation. Despite this resort to principle, however, it was evident that the Democratic Common Council was still adhering to its previously expressed determination not to become a party to a religious dispute. With its feet in both the Protestant and Catholic camps, the Democratic party preferred to leave things as they were. There was the lesson of Seward's unfortunate excursion into the stormy sea of religious differences to keep it from committing any similar mistakes. Though the aldermen were deeply sympathetic to the plight of the Catholics, to grant their request would only lead to "the awakening of the spirit of intolerance, which, in our country, is of all calamities, the one most to be dreaded." When government "begins to legislate with particular reference to any particular denomination . . . it oversteps a boundary which public opinion has established; violates a principle which breathes in all our Constitutions; and opens a door to that unholy connection of politics with religion, which has so often cursed and desolated Europe." [42]

[41] "Report of the Special Committee to Whom Was Referred the Petition of the Catholics . . . ," *Documents of the Board of Aldermen of the City of New York*, VII (1840–41), 569–70.

[42] *Ibid.*, p. 563. Benson, ch. ix, points out with considerable emphasis what I suggest in this paragraph: sectarian differences presented a

After this second defeat, the Catholics concluded that they had exhausted the possibilities for obtaining favorable action from the city. The issue was now transferred to the state capitol in Albany. The Public School Society had already presented its case to the legislature. The Catholics sent off a petition, containing some seven thousand signatures, to Albany in March of 1841. An indication of how politically explosive this question was can be seen in the legislature's decision to pass the buck. The Catholic petition and the several counterpetitions were turned over to the Whig secretary of state, John C. Spencer, ex officio state superintendent of common schools, for his recommendations.[43]

Spencer, a close friend as well as party colleague of Seward, presented his findings to the Senate on April 26, 1841. Spencer's report embodied a new approach by the Seward group to the New York City school question. The secretary found that religion was so intimately bound up with the education provided in the Public School Society's institutions that it could not easily be separated from the curriculum, nor would public opinion favor any such attempt. The religion offered in the society's schools was Protestant. Since the state ought to be concerned only with the secular education of all children, and since Catholics could not attend the society's schools for religious reasons, there should be no objection to assisting their education in secular subjects in schools of their choice. The question of religious instruction in these schools could safely be left to a majority of the citizens concerned, as was the case in the upstate school districts.[44]

Spencer advised extending the district system in operation

---

complex and delicate situation requiring both Democratic and Whig politicians to exercise considerable caution and even timidity when obliged to deal with them.

[43] Bourne, pp. 350–51; Connors, pp. 29–31.

[44] Spencer's report is in New York [State] Senate, *Documents, 1841*, doc. no. 86.

upstate to the metropolis. The schools of the School Society would become district schools, under the supervision of district commissioners, while retaining their existing management. In districts where a majority did not wish to support the School Society, it could establish new schools which would also be supported as public district schools. The effect of this plan, unstated in Spencer's report but implicit in the situation, would be to continue the present School Society system for Protestant children, while in areas where Catholics were in the majority they would have their own schools. Both types would receive public funds for the secular instruction of their pupils, but the choice of religious instruction would be left solely to the locally elected trustees.

Bishop Hughes was satisfied with Spencer's proposals, but the Public School Society and nativists in New York City were outspokenly opposed. The society's trustees sent off a lengthy protest to Albany against any alteration of their present responsibilities for public education in the city. Several New York newspapers, long characterized by antiforeign sentiments, took up the hue and cry. Anti-Catholic literature was placed in the hands of each state senator. Confronted with this outburst of religious emotionalism, the Whig Senate decided to postpone further consideration of the matter until the opening of the next session due to convene in January 1842.[45]

The next act in the drama unfolded around the fall elections in New York City, where the makeup of the city's delegation to the 1842 session of the legislature would be decided. A nativist group, the American Protestant Union, was formed to oppose any Catholic school bill. The School Society appealed to both major parties to nominate candidates who would be unfavorable to any change in the existing city school system. The Whigs named a ticket committed to vote

[45] Connors, pp. 32–34; New York [State] Senate, *Journal, 1841*, p. 498.

against the Catholic position, while the Democrats seemed to be wavering under the shower of threats and inducements.[46]

Four days before the election, Bishop Hughes and several lay Catholic leaders determined upon a fateful course. At a mass meeting in Carroll Hall on October 29, 1841, Hughes presented an independent party list to the cheering Catholic assemblage as the candidates of the Catholics for the state legislature. Included on the ticket were ten of the thirteen regular Democratic nominees for Assembly, whose sympathetic assurances won them the endorsement of the Carroll Hall meeting, plus three independent Catholics nominated for the remaining three Assembly places on the Catholic ticket. The Catholic party endorsed no Whigs for Assembly, nor did it accept either major party's choices for two State Senate seats, preferring two of its own people for these places. Hughes made it clear to the gathering that Catholics had been forced into this action by the indifference of both parties to their legitimate requests. This ticket did not offer much hope of success, he told his listeners, but at least it had been ascertained that it was not unfavorable to the Catholic claims. "There is but one course for you to take," he said, "stand up for yourselves, and, I will be bound for it, public men will soon come to your aid!"[47]

The purpose of what became known as the "Carroll Hall ticket" was to frighten Democratic and Whig politicians into a better frame of mind for entertaining Catholic requests. The means employed were those most politicians understand best—the threat of defeat at the polls. If appeals to reason and justice had brought nothing but rejection and vacillation from a Democratic city government and a Whig legislature, then the Catholics would resort to the inducements of the ballot.

On election day in the city, the ten Democratic Assembly

[46] Scisco, pp. 34–35.

[47] Kehoe, I, 280. Accurate accounts of the "Carroll Hall ticket" are in *ibid.*, pp. 275–84; Hone's *Diary*, II, 96–97; Bourne, pp. 478–82.

candidates, who had received the Catholic endorsement, were elected. The failure of enough Catholic voters to support the three unendorsed Democrats resulted in the election of Whigs to the remaining three Assembly seats. A comparison of votes made it evident that the last-minute Catholic effort had attracted enough Catholics away from their traditional Democratic allegiance to form a balance of power in city elections capable of overcoming the normal Democratic majority.[48] This Catholic venture into politics sent a shiver of horror through nativist ranks in America and figured in the rise of the Native American party later in the decade, but it had more immediate effects in New York.

The Democrats swept the fall elections throughout the state and won majorities in both houses of the legislature. No doubt with the lesson of the recent city elections well in mind, the party's leaders executed an abrupt about-face on the school question. Where for two years they had opposed any changes in the present system in New York City and had excoriated the Seward Whigs at every opportunity for trying to inject sectarianism into politics, they now became the exponents of the democratization of education in the city. Yet any attempt to settle the vexatious school controversy, it was realized, would have to thread a cautious course between a Catholic Scylla and a Protestant Charybdis. But it was imperative that this disruptive issue be removed from the political arena. The ideal solution would be a compromise capable of meeting enough of the Catholic objections to quiet their protests while not completely alienating Protestant opinion.[49]

Governor Seward did not allow the Democratic legislators to ignore their responsibility. In his last annual message, in

[48] Compare the Carroll Hall list with the votes received by the elected assemblymen and by the three defeated Catholic candidates, *ibid.*, pp. 479, 481.

[49] *Ibid.*, pp. 496–97; for general background see again Benson, ch. ix.

January 1842, he called for a school settlement following the recommendations in Secretary Spencer's report of the preceding session. Another reminder came in the form of a monster petition, organized under Catholic lay auspices and signed by 14,000 citizens of New York City, asking for the extension of the upstate district school system to the city.[50]

William Maclay, one of the Carroll Hall endorsees, was named chairman of the Assembly's committee on schools by the Democratic leadership of the house, an indication there was to be action on the school question.[51] After consultations with leaders of his party and communications with Hughes, Seward, and Weed, Maclay brought in a school bill which followed the main lines of the Spencer report.[52] The unanimous report of the Assembly's school committee, which accompanied the bill to the floor, concluded that the Public School Society had "failed to accomplish the great object of its establishment—the universal education of the children of the city of New-York." [53] In true Jacksonian fashion, the private School Society system was attacked as a privileged and dangerous monopoly over which the public at large had no control of policy and in which the people could have no confidence.

While the Democratic *Albany Argus* sang the praises of Maclay's bill, and sectarian journals such as the Methodist

[50] Baker, II, 306–09; and Seward, pp. 585–86. [51] Bourne, p. 497.

[52] Hassard, p. 249. Seward and Weed were also in direct touch with Hughes on the school question through Greeley and other intermediaries. They were trying to recover what they could of Seward's political fortunes, first, by influencing the final version of the bill along desired lines and, second, by shaping plans to attack the bill if it did real violence to Seward's and Hughes' specifications. See the letters from Horace Greeley, New York City, to Weed, Feb. 9, 1842, Weed Papers; and Jacob Harvey, New York City, to Seward, March 2, 9, 1842, William Henry Seward Papers, University of Rochester.

[53] New York [State] Assembly, *Documents, 1842*, doc. no. 60, p. 7.

Christian Advocate damned it as a cowardly surrender to Catholic intimidation, the Assembly proceeded to pass the measure by a vote of 64 to 16. Over forty members of the lower house found the task of reconciling clashing points of view so difficult that they preferred to abstain from voting. Linking the recent city elections to the outcome of the vote in the Democratic Assembly on the Maclay bill, Thurlow Weed's *Albany Evening Journal* concluded, "It waked up old Tammany and opened at least *one* of the hundred eyes of the Argus." [54]

In the Senate, the New York City school bill ran into the opposition of the city's entire delegation, two Democrats and two Whigs, all favoring no change in the existing school arrangements. Their opposition ordinarily would have meant the defeat of the bill, but two significant events cleared the way for its final passage. The chairman of the Senate's school committee, Senator Henry A. Foster, Democrat of Oneida County, secured an amendment which attracted several undecided members to the measure. The Foster compromise amendment prohibited the granting of public funds to any district school in the city in which "any religious sectarian doctrine or tenet shall be taught, inculcated, or practiced." Where the Maclay version would have permitted the public schools in Catholic wards to be conducted as virtual parochial schools, the amendment advanced the principle of no sectarian instruction in any public school in New York City, presumably including those of the School Society. Meanwhile, with the Senate seeming to drag its feet on the school bill, the Catholic Association in the city reorganized and nominated another independent ticket to contest the upcoming municipal elections. After the Senate stirred itself and passed the Maclay

[54] *Albany Evening Journal*, March 19, 1842. *Albany Argus*, Feb. 15, 1842; [N.Y.] *Christian Advocate*, Feb. 16, March 9, 1842; New York [State] Assembly, *Journal, 1842*, pp. 562–65.

bill on April 9, 1842, the Catholics withdrew their slate of candidates on April 11. Passed in the Senate by the slim margin of one vote, the bill with its Senate amendments was then accepted by the Assembly, 80 to 21.[55]

The new school law was greeted with anguished outcries in New York City among the supporters of the School Society and nativists. On the day that Governor Seward signed the measure, the general committee of his own Whig party in the city condemned it. That night an angry mob stoned the residence of Bishop Hughes. Political papers, such as Horace Greeley's *New York Tribune*, and religious publications, such as the *Christian Advocate* and the nativist *American Protestant Vindicator*, condemned the law as a cheap political deal, in the words of the *Tribune*, "to bring back the stray sheep to the fold of Tammany." [56]

Like most compromises, the law did not suit anyone completely. While it allowed the School Society to continue to operate its schools as district public schools, they were placed under the supervision of an elective Board of Education. This body, with the assistance of the state legislature, placed restrictions on the further growth of the society's system while energetically fostering the rapid development of the popularly controlled ward schools created by the Maclay law. In another ten years the society would give up the uneven battle and deed its property to the city. On the other hand, Catholics failed to achieve their original demand for the incorporation of parochial schools into the public system.[57]

But out of this involved political and religious controversy emerged one lasting result. This was a conviction that in a

[55] Bourne, pp. 520–21; *Albany Argus*, and *New York Tribune*, April 11, 1842; Hassard, p. 250; Senate, *Journal, 1842*, pp. 456–67; Assembly, *Journal, 1842*, pp. 887–88; New York [State], *Laws, 1842*, ch. 150.

[56] *New York Tribune*, April 11, 1842. See also *Tribune*, April 12; *Christian Advocate*, June 8; *American Protestant Vindicator*, April 20, 1842; and Connors, pp. 42–43.

[57] *Ibid.*, pp. 44–45.

religiously diverse society, such as New York City contained with its large and estranged Protestant and Catholic groups, the best interests of a democratic polity were served by restricting the teaching of sectarian religion in the public schools where children of all sects were intermingled. For New York City at least, the outcome of the school controversy represented an advance for the principle of church-state separation. The conclusion that in a society based upon the ideal of equal civil rights for all, the state was properly responsible only for secular instruction, leaving religious instruction to the home and the church, was slowly gaining popular approval in the metropolis.

Despite the prohibition on sectarian instruction in the New York City schools, there were still difficulties; several schools, particularly those of the Public School Society, persisted in using Protestant teaching materials after 1842. It was maintained that the antisectarian clause of the 1842 school law did not exclude the teaching of the general truths of the Christian religion. After protests to the legislature, the prohibitory section in the 1842 law was amended in 1843 by a clause denying public funds to any school "in which any book or books containing any sectarian compositions shall be used in the course of instruction." [58] This was interpreted, however, as not applying to Bible reading. In 1844 the legislature determined that Bible reading might be required of students, but it was to be performed "without note or comment," and the particular version to be used was left to the discretion of the trustees in each school district of the city. By this compromise, schools with Protestant majorities continued to use the King James version, and schools in Catholic districts were free to adopt the church-approved Douay edition. But these Bible exercises were a far cry from the religious instruction re-

[58] *Laws, 1843,* ch. 216. Also see *Laws, 1844,* ch. 320, and Connors, pp. 59–61.

quired in days past. For fifty years the school law of 1842 with its subsequent amendments continued in force in New York City.

Though the city's schools were subject to prohibitions on sectarian instruction from the 1840's onward, there were no similar regulations for the upstate common schools for many years. Catholics, who were settling there in growing numbers, encountered the Protestant bias of the religious instruction in the public schools. But they lacked the numbers and the influence of their city brethren which might have enabled them to pose an effective political challenge to this condition. At the same time most of the Catholic parishes outside New York City were too poor to provide parochial schools. The Irish and German laborers who made up a majority in most parishes had all they could do to finance the building of their churches, let alone consider the establishment of parish schools. Consequently, large numbers of Catholic children had to attend the local common schools.[59]

In no position to demand or expect public funds for their own schools, upstate Catholics, before the Civil War, sought to secure relief from the Protestant religious exercises of the public schools. At first Catholics made little headway against the ingrained Protestant exclusiveness of the great majority of the upstate population. In the year 1838 a group of upstate Catholic parents memorialized the state Assembly for a law "to prohibit the practice of praying, singing, reading the Bible, and other religious exercises, in such schools . . . as receive aid from the public treasury." [60] The petitioners were of the opinion that the Protestant orientation of the public schools was a violation of the equal rights of conscience.

Assemblyman Daniel D. Barnard, for the committee on

[59] Wittke, pp. 25–26, 35; Shea, IV, 126, 132.

[60] Assembly, *Documents, 1838*, doc. no. 55, p. 1.

colleges, academies, and common schools, replied that when parents join together to establish a common school, the majority decides and the minority abides. Applying this reasoning to religious exercises in the upstate public schools, a question over which the state exercised no authority, the conclusion was obvious that "a majority of the parents sending children to a public school . . . may rightfully agree and direct that the proper business of the school shall be opened or closed, or both, daily with religious exercises."[61] The minority has no choice but to submit to this decision so long as it is not a violation of public morality. Obviously, there could be nothing objectionable in religious instruction intended to convey sound principles of morality. In other words, the Catholic minority had no grounds whatsoever for complaining of the long-settled practice in upstate Protestant communities of teaching Protestant morality and doctrines in the public schools. The Assembly voted 120 to one to accept Barnard's report.

However, Roman Catholics were soon to find some relief from an unexpected quarter—the state officer appointed to oversee the administration of the public schools. Since 1822 this official has had authority to hear appeals on all local disputes arising under the state school laws, with the quasijudicial power to render decisions binding on all parties. From the late 1830's it has been the usual position of this officer that to maintain the well-being of the public school system the schools must avoid all religious practices which lead to formal complaints of sectarian bias.[62] As early as 1838 Superintendent of Common Schools John A. Dix ruled that a teacher could not require formal prayers during regular school hours or

[61] *Ibid.*, p. 4.

[62] T. E. Finegan, ed., *Judicial Decisions of the State Superintendent of Common Schools . . . from 1822 to 1913* (Albany, 1914), pp. 524 ff.

exact the attendance of any student at such exercises whose parents objected to them.[63]

In 1853 a dispute arose in Rensselaer County requiring the state superintendent, Henry S. Randall, to rule on the practice of requiring school children of all faiths to read from the Protestant version of the Bible. Randall was aware that the "great increase and diffusion throughout the State of a Roman Catholic population" had created this problem. Personally favorable to religious instruction as part of the school curriculum, Randall also recognized that the common schools were public institutions where children of all sects went to be educated. "To introduce into them . . . a course of religious instruction conformable to the views of any religious denomination, would be tantamount to the adoption of a government religion—a step contrary to the Constitution." [64]

The broad principle governing religious teaching in the public schools was concisely articulated by Superintendent Victor Rice in 1866:

> Common schools are supported and established for the purposes of imparting instruction in the common English branches; religious instruction forms no part of the course. The proper places in which to receive such instruction are churches and Sunday schools. . . . The money to support schools comes from the people at large, irrespective of sect or denomination. Consequently, instruction of a sectarian or religious denominational character must be avoided, and teachers must confine themselves, during school hours, to their legitimate and proper duties.[65]

This principle, which continued to guide the administration of the New York school laws throughout the remainder of the nineteenth century, was as crucial to the development of

[63] *Ibid.*, p. 532.

[64] H. S. Randall, *Decision . . . on the Right to Compel Catholic Children to Attend Prayers, and to Read or Commit Portions of the Bible, as School Exercises . . . 1853* (n.p., n.d.), pp. 4–5, 6.

[65] Finegan, p. 527.

the upstate schools as were the school regulations of the 1840's for the New York City schools. It was another recognition of the practical wisdom to be found in the separation ideal when applied to the emerging public institutions of a diverse society.

The decisions of the several state superintendents of common schools were shaped by a secular view of education that was becoming increasingly evident in New York. Many Protestant clergymen and lay leaders objected strongly to these rulings. But to others the secularization of public education represented the most expedient, though regrettable, alternative to destructive religious strife over the schools. The benefits of public education were deemed too vital to society and to the individual to hazard their loss by an obstinate insistence upon a religious regimen in the schools that, in many places, did not fit the facts of a community in which Protestantism no longer reigned supreme.

From the 1850's onward the secular view of public instruction, first opposing compulsory religion in the schools and then the very concept of religious exercises, was embraced by many influential leaders of opinion. Among these were Henry Ward Beecher, popular pastor of Brooklyn's Plymouth Church; the Rev. Joseph P. Thompson of the Broadway Tabernacle Church in New York City; and E. P. Hurlbut, a former judge of the New York Supreme Court. Horace Greeley's *New York Tribune* and E. L. Godkin's weekly magazine *Nation* also favored the secularization of the public schools.[66]

Public officials, in the courts and in the legislative forum, were increasingly receptive to this idea. In 1851 a three-judge panel of the state Supreme Court could rule, "Our common schools are not confined to any *class*, but are open to *all*. . . . They are bound to instruct all the children who present

[66] Connors, pp. 71–76.

themselves, without regard to their social relations, their station in life or their religious faith." [67] When in 1853 Catholic residents of several cities in the state appealed to the legislature for state-supported parochial schools, the committee on schools of the Assembly reported that

> the government has never listened for a moment to the suggestion of fractionizing this system in favor of or against any political party, or any religious sect, or denomination. . . . The fathers, of our system of common schools . . . seem sedulously to have avoided all affinity with systems of faith or sects, whether religious or political. In their wisdom, they seem to have left the religious education, the sectarian discipline, the instruction in religious creeds and practices, where they rightfully belong—to the genial influence of the domestic fireside; to the family altar; to the church; to pastoral instruction, the Sabbath school and the Bible class.[68]

While inaccurate as history, this report was a most accurate reflection of the growing contemporary conviction that secular education was preferable to religious contention in view of the many creeds represented in the school population. Only by stripping public schooling of any feature which might be construed as favoring one denomination over another could Protestants be justified in refusing public aid to sectarian schools. "Give us the Free Schools without Religion, rather than no Free Schools at all," concluded Charles Loring Brace, minister and social worker, in the 1870's.[69]

To Brace the practice of conducting Protestant religious exercises in the public schools afforded useful arguments to the Catholic clergy in its campaign to obtain public support

[67] *People ex rel. Roman Catholic Orphan Asylum Society* v. *Board of Education of Brooklyn*, 13 Barb. 400 (1851).

[68] Assembly, *Documents, 1853*, doc. no. 97, p. 5.

[69] C. L. Brace, *The Dangerous Classes of New York*, 3d ed. (New York, 1880), p. 428.

for separate schools. Many were agreed with Brace's statement:

> The Free School under our system does not need any influence from the Church. The American trusts to the separate sects to take care of the religious interests of the children. We separate utterly Church and State. There may be evils from this; but they are less than the danger of destroying our system of popular education by the contests of rival sects.[70]

While upstate Catholics were struggling against Protestant religious exercises in the public schools, their church was generally silent on the question of state aid to parochial schools. Catholics had not given up their claims, but other pressing concerns temporarily absorbed their attentions. After 1842 Bishop Hughes was engaged in expanding the parochial school system of New York City. In the 1850's the Know-Nothing mania placed the Catholics of the state on the defensive. Then came the Civil War and the suspension of interest in education.

With the war ended, Catholic pressures for public assistance to their schools once more began to mount. These appeared at a time when many Protestants believed the school problem had been settled. For several years they had accepted the necessity of removing objectionable Protestant religious exercises from the public schools. They had acquiesced in the secularization of public education in order that no sect, especially the Catholic, might have cause to repudiate the system and endanger its continued development. Having given in completely, or so they thought, to Catholic demands that the schools be made truly nonsectarian, Protestants were hurt and angered by this new Catholic attack upon the very foundations of public, secular schooling for the state's children.

The first major evidence that Roman Catholics had re-

[70] *Ibid.*, p. 427.

newed their campaign to obtain public school money appeared in 1869. Boss William Marcy Tweed, the crafty rogue from Tammany Hall who was then sitting in the state Senate, introduced a bill "relative to schools." The key provision permitted any city or county board of supervisors to support "any free school or schools, in which not less than two hundred children have been or are taught and educated gratuitously." [71] The law was to apply to any city in the state, but it seems to have been understood that it applied only to the parochial schools of New York City. These were about the only schools with the prescribed enrollment which were not already the recipients of some form of public aid. Boss Tweed, never forgetful of his dependence upon the votes of the city's Catholic population, was seldom guilty of neglecting the church's interests.

It soon appeared to the Republican Senate majority that the Tweed measure was a bill in aid of Catholics; few Protestant or Jewish church schools could meet the enrollment requirement set in the bill. According to the *Albany Argus*, which was partial to Tweed, the Republican Senators "smelt a savor of Popery in the provisions, and called a caucus and agreed to kill it." [72] The Presbyterian *New York Observer* breathed a sigh of relief at the bill's defeat by the Senate, but its editors cautioned that "soon some other measure will be proposed with a similar purpose, and unless the Legislature is watched vigilantly, the Romanists will yet get their hands on the money." [73]

The *Observer's* warning proved an accurate prophecy. The Tweed forces, repulsed on the ill-disguised parochial school bill, resorted to more devious means. To the annual tax levy bill for New York City, a routine measure authorizing the raising and apportioning of operating funds for the city's

[71] *New York Times*, March 26, 1869; Senate, *Journal, 1869*, p. 277.
[72] *Albany Argus*, March 27, 1869.
[73] *New York Observer*, April 1, 1869.

government, a school provision was inserted. Section 10 of the bill reserved 20 per cent of the excise funds received by the city in 1868 "for the support of schools, educating children gratuitously in said city who are not provided for in the common schools thereof."[74] The measure was finally forced through in the hectic rush of legislation at the close of the session by a combination of secrecy and bribery. At no time was there any significant outcry raised against section 10.

Not until two days after the bill's passage did the *New York Times* discover that section 10 of the 1869 tax levy law threatened the city's public school system. In September the Republican state convention at Syracuse took a platform stand against "every attempt on the part of our State Legislature to appropriate any money of the people to the support of sectarian schools." The Methodist *Christian Advocate* saw in section 10 proof that a "general Papal conspiracy against the 'free school system' of the country, exists."[75] Aroused by these warnings, irate citizens throughout the state deluged the 1870 session of the legislature with petitions for the repeal of the now notorious section 10. Only later did it become apparent that much of this protest was artificially stimulated by the Republicans. The archconservative Republican Union League Club of New York City was charged with having sent hundreds of petition forms to upstate communities to be signed and forwarded to Albany.[76]

Contemptuous of these initial protests, the Tweed-controlled legislature refused to accept any repealer of section 10. But the uproar continued to mount. A repeal meeting convened at Cooper Union in the city on the evening of March 30, 1870. Such respectables as Peter Cooper, Henry Ward

[74] *Laws, 1869*, ch. 876, sec. 10.

[75] *New York Times*, May 11, Sept. 30, 1869; [N.Y.] *Christian Advocate*, Oct. 15, 1869.

[76] Senate and Assembly *Journals* for 1870, *passim;* Assembly, *Documents, 1870*, doc. no. 169; *New York Times*, Feb. 16, 1870.

Beecher, and the prominent lawyer William Dodge urged those in attendance to fight for the recall of section 10. Beecher proclaimed: "In America, American ideas shall prevail. And these ideas are the broadest religious toleration and the fullest and freest secular and unsectarian education. . . . The appropriation sought to be repealed violates this principle." [77] A state Council of Political Reform was organized at Albany on April 11, largely through the efforts of Protestant ministers and laymen opposed to the Tweed measure. It charged that the obnoxious section 10 contravened the "American doctrine of equal toleration and protection to all religious sects, but public support to none" and that the refusal to repeal it was certain to "introduce sectarian rancor into American politics, and array at the ballot box the Protestants against the Roman Catholics." [78]

Boss Tweed may have been a corrupt and dictatorial ruler of his own domain, but as a politician he was not insensible to opposition from those he could not control. In the face of the growing uproar from every corner of the state against his pet school scheme and conscious of its possible impact on the fall gubernatorial election, the outcome of which could directly affect the newly won hegemony of Tammany over Albany, the Tweed legions beat a strategic retreat. With the Boss himself remaining silently in the background, a repeal of section 10 was voted, but not before it was amended to protect Tweed from the ill-feeling of Catholics. It was provided that the repeal would take effect only after the annual grant to parochial schools in New York City had been distributed for the 1870–1871 school year. The reason given for this was that the affected schools had already made out their budgets for the coming year with the grants in mind. In 1871, again under

[77] *Albany Evening Journal*, April 1, 1870; *New York Times*, March 31, 1870.

[78] New York City Council of Political Reform, *Political Reform* (New York, 1870), p. 4; also *Albany Argus*, April 6, 1870.

outside pressure, the Tweed machine accepted reluctantly a blanket legislative prohibition on any future appropriations by the city or county of New York to private or sectarian schools. After this the controversy gradually subsided for the time being.[79]

Away from Albany and the legislative halls, Catholic efforts to achieve public assistance for their schools continued. To already aroused Protestants, these, like the Tweed machinations, had the appearance of a well-planned Catholic plot to subvert the public school system. In several communities scattered throughout the state, local Catholic parishes were quietly making arrangements for public aid to their church schools. The priest of St. Peters Church in Poughkeepsie entered into a formal agreement with the city board of education in 1873 to place two parochial schools at the disposal of the public school authorities. Under this arrangement, the city leased the two schools for a nominal annual rent of one dollar each. No religious instruction was to be permitted during regular school hours; students of all faiths could attend the two schools; and the board was to have powers to examine the schools and appoint teachers. In return, the city was to pay the teachers and maintain the buildings. The priest would retain control of the school premises outside the school hours. In practice, this plan permitted poor Catholic parishes to avoid the added burdens of maintaining parochial schools, while allowing them to retain many of the advantages of church education. At Poughkeepsie the teachers hired by the city for the two schools were invariably nuns of the order which had staffed the schools when under Catholic direction. Religious instruction was given to Catholic pupils before school opened officially in the morning, during the noon hour, and at the close of the school day.[80]

What became known as the "Poughkeepsie Plan" was later

[79] *New York Times*, April 23, 24, 26, 1870 and April 7, 1871; *Laws, 1871*, ch. 583, sec. 6. [80] Finegan, pp. 560–68; Connors, pp. 110–16.

adopted at Suspension Bridge in Niagara County; at West Troy, which later became part of Watervliet; at Lima in Livingston County; at Corning in Steuben County; and at Roundout in Ulster County. Attracting little attention at first because of the usually amicable interfaith relations enjoyed in the localities which embraced the plan, the "Poughkeepsie Plan" became a leading issue in the 1890's, when the school question again erupted with even greater intensity.[81]

At the same time that politicians and Catholic priests and laymen were spontaneously, as it were, seeking to bring about local arrangements with school officials, leaders of the national and state hierarchies were speaking out on the school question. One of the most prominent and vocal spokesmen for state assistance to Catholic schools was Bernard McQuaid, bishop of Rochester. Beginning in the early 1870's, Bishop McQuaid unceasingly expounded his views. McQuaid contended that the state, by its secularization of education, had flagrantly interfered with "the primary and natural right of parents to procure for their children the best education they can (and no education is worth having that leaves out religious culture)." The bishop characterized this as "the blot and disgrace that is upon the country by the wrong and unjust system of public schools that is now upheld in the land simply and solely by the power of the majority." [82]

McQuaid proposed that the state define the amount it wished to spend on education and then pay it on a per capita basis "for that education wherever it finds it under the conditions imposed, whether it be in a large school or a small one, private or public, religious or purely secular." This would ease the double and unjust tax burden suffered by Catholic

[81] Finegan, pp. 533–60, 568–74; "The Education of the People . . . ," *Independent*, XLII (1890), 1–13; Connors, pp. 117–18, 123–25.

[82] F. J. Zwierlein, *The Life and Letters of Bishop McQuaid* (Rochester, 1925–27), II, 122.

parents who had to support both public and parochial schools. Ideally McQuaid would have preferred to abolish the public schools and to replace them by publicly financed schools attached to the churches of each sect.[83]

The bishop counseled Catholics to employ their united strength at the polls to secure their rights. He told a lay German Catholic convention in Rochester that "Catholics number one-third the population of the State of New York. . . . Our numbers are daily and rapidly increasing. . . . Remember that it is the duty of laymen, of citizens, of voters, to speak for the right and maintain it whenever and wherever they can."[84] Naturally, McQuaid's opposition to the public schools and his calls for Catholic political action angered New York Protestants and anti-Catholics. His preachments on the school question provided additional reasons for suspecting the Catholic church of evil designs. Further proof was at hand in the statements of the Vatican and the American hierarchy on the evils of the public schools and in their exhortations to the faithful to forward the work of building parochial facilities for every Catholic child in the land.[85]

The Roman Catholic educational campaign occurred at a time when anti-Catholicism was on the upswing in New York as well as in the nation at large. Both Protestant and secular fears contributed to this renewal of ancient animosities. On one hand, Protestant groups were alarmed by the growth of the Catholic church in America. To secularists and nationalists, the influence of growing Catholic numbers was suspected in the corruption of the cities with their large Catholic populations and in the gathering social unrest, as well as in the school controversy. American institutions and ideals seemed in imminent danger from an alien and un-American religion.

[83] *Ibid.*, pp. 122, 131. [84] *Ibid.*, p. 141.

[85] D. F. Reilly, *The School Controversy (1891–1893)*, (Washington, D.C., 1944), p. 22; Guilday, pp. 243–46.

A specter of Catholic domination was haunting the minds of ever larger numbers of Americans in the late nineteenth century.[86]

Protestant militants and alarmed secularists turned to organized action to counter the Catholic threat to American institutions. As one Methodist pastor warned, if Protestants did not take preventive steps, they would one day soon "find Papists in all the high places of the nation, with the control of cities and states, our Sabbath abolished, our educational system in ruins, Romanism established and sustained by law . . . our religious freedom gone." [87] With mounting frequency after the Civil War, annual conventions and assemblies of the various Protestant denominations passed anti-Catholic resolutions in defense of the ideal of religious freedom for all and against public favors to any.

Prominently featured were ringing appeals to support public education against the inroads of the Catholic enemy. One leading New York anti-Catholic saw behind Catholic attempts to gain public school funds the guiding hand of the pope himself. His aim was "the destruction of our free non-sectarian system of popular education." In its place the pope planned to substitute "his own system of church or parochial schools, that is schools whose text-books and teachers are selected, appointed and controlled by the Church, though the State may be permitted to pay all the bills." [88] During the 1880's action groups sprang into being throughout New York. Typical of them was the Central Committee for Protecting and Perpetuating the Separation of Church and State. Prominent figures, among them John Jacob Astor, John D.

[86] D. L. Kinzer, "The American Protective Association: A Study of Anti-Catholicism" (unpub. dissertation, University of Washington, 1954), pp. 6–69.

[87] H. Mattison, "Romanism in the United States," *Methodist Quarterly Review*, L (1868), 531.

[88] D. A. Hawkins, *Report on Compulsory Education* (New York, 1874), p. 9.

Rockefeller, and Cornelius Vanderbilt, were persuaded to act as sponsors for this committee. Pamphlets were sent into every corner of the state, aimed to arouse "every voter in the State to support, as candidates for the Senate and Assembly, only those . . . who will steadfastly sustain the American principle of The Separation of the functions of Church and State." [89]

As the 1890's drew near, the lines of battle between New York Catholics and non-Catholics were once more being formed for a contest over the proper role of the Catholic church and of religion in general in the public life of the state. In the forefront was the issue of public secular education as opposed to the claims of the Catholic church to state-supported, private sectarian schools.

[89] The Central Committee for Protecting and Perpetuating the Separation of Church and State, *The Separation of Church and State Endorsed by Pres. Grant* . . . (New York, 1885), p. 4; this pamphlet is bound with others appearing under the general title *Appeals to the People of the State of New York* (n.p., n.d.), New York Public Library.

VIII

Sectarian Charities and the Public Welfare

AFTER the Civil War, the issue of public assistance to sectarian charitable institutions further complicated the church-state question in New York. As with the debate over public education, this issue had its origins in the growing Protestant fears of the Catholic church and secular opposition to public favoritism for any sect. The controversy revolved about the question of whether a people committed to the ideal of church-state separation could aid religious societies caring for the poor without violating this ideal. There was an important consideration which made the application of the separation principle much more difficult and uncertain than in the school question: the recognition that private charitable institutions were performing a vital service for society. If the state had a responsibility to care for its destitute and neglected, and there was a growing number convinced than it did, then by assisting private charities the state was helping to meet its obligation. At the same time, it was saving itself the expense of creating new public facilities for purposes which private groups were already meeting.

The policy of public support for private charitable institutions was developed almost by accident in the first half of the nineteenth century.[1] It was intimately connected with the rise

[1] D. M. Schneider and Albert Deutsch, *The History of Public*

of the humanitarian movement in America after the Revolution and the consequent awareness that poverty and dependency were much more complex problems than had once been thought. From earliest colonial times, government had accepted some responsibility for the care of the poor. But because poverty was attributed to such sins as immorality, intemperance, and shiftlessness, this care was usually perfunctory and inadequate. Public charity was intended to be so Spartan that it would discourage all but the most dissolute from applying for it. Those fortunate enough to be granted assistance in their own homes were the lucky ones. In the late eighteenth century, however, this arrangement was being replaced by the hideous public almshouses and the so-called New England system, whereby the poor in the various towns were auctioned off to a low bidder who would provide minimal food and shelter in return for the labor of his charges or a small fee paid by the local overseers of the poor.[2]

In the early decades of the nineteenth century, the poorhouse system became increasingly popular throughout the state as the most economical method of caring for the poor. Town and county poorhouses were built to centralize the administration of public poor relief. In a typical poorhouse one could find all types of dependents congregated together under the most miserable and inhumane conditions. The unemployed, widows, orphans, neglected and delinquent children, the aged poor, the diseased, and the insane all were housed in these institutions.[3]

Concurrent with the expansion of the poorhouse system, humanitarian reformers and philanthropists were beginning to object to the treatment of all groups of dependents in the same manner and in a single institution. Private societies were organized to relieve special classes of unfortunates. Humani-

---

Welfare in New York State, 2 vols. (Chicago, 1938–41), is the standard work on welfare policies in New York.

[2] *Ibid.*, I, chs. i, ii, and pp. 60–75, 87.

[3] *Ibid.*, chs. xii, xiii.

tarians were attracted early to the problems created by the practice of mingling children with the other classes of poor under the unwholesome conditions of the public poorhouses. Overcrowding, inadequate educational opportunities, and harsh treatment of children in the mixed poorhouse moved these private organizations to establish orphan asylums and homes for neglected children where the inmates would have care better suited to their special needs. This was an increasingly typical response to adversity in nineteenth-century America: finding government too antiquated in its thinking about problems of poor relief and too slow in meeting new needs, citizens resorted to voluntary associations to overcome these deficiencies.[4]

In 1806 the New York Orphan Asylum was founded in New York City by public-spirited women. Incorporated by the state in 1807, the group commenced the building of an orphanage. The society's privately solicited funds were rapidly depleted by this project, and in 1808 it felt compelled to appeal to the legislature for assistance. Lottery proceeds were granted to the orphanage, and in 1811 the legislature ordered an annual grant of five hundred dollars paid to the society by the state. This experience was repeated in many other places throughout New York. During the 1830's several special homes for dependent children were established in Albany, Brooklyn, Troy, Utica, Buffalo, and Rochester. Originally supported by voluntary contributions, but soon discovering that private donations were insufficient to sustain them, these homes invariably turned to the state and to local governments for aid. Most of them were successful in their entreaties for public subsidies.[5]

While many of these early institutions were nonsectarian in character, they nevertheless emphasized Protestant religious instruction for the children under their care. As in the case of

[4] *Ibid.*, pp. 141, 167–76, 185–87. [5] *Ibid.*, 187–90, 191.

the common schools, it was naturally accepted that a basic purpose of these societies was to teach Christian morality and virtue. Like the early schools, this teaching reflected the Protestant backgrounds of the societies' founders. Catholic objections to the Protestant indoctrination of Catholic orphans led the clergy and the laity to establish asylums specifically for youths of their own faith. A Roman Catholic Benevolent Society was organized in New York City in 1817; it later became the Roman Catholic Orphan Asylum. Soon after its foundation, it too began to receive regular public grants from the state and subsequently from the municipal government. In the 1820's similar Catholic ventures were undertaken in Brooklyn and Albany.[6]

There were parallel developments in the care of delinquent and neglected children. The growing belief that delinquent children should not be confined in jails with adult criminals led directly to the formation of the Society for the Reformation of Juvenile Delinquents in New York City in the early 1820's. A House of Refuge was opened in 1824 through private efforts. The following year the state began to appropriate annual sums to the House of Refuge, and in 1831 the legislature empowered the city of New York to grant funds to it. In time public assistance outweighed private contributions in the support of the House of Refuge. The private New York Juvenile Asylum was opened in New York City in the early 1850's to care for neglected and abandoned children, the flotsam tossed upon the streets of the city by the heavy waves of immigration in the 1840's. The state legislature authorized the city and county of New York to appropriate yearly per capita grants to the asylum in return for having powers of commitment to the institution. In 1853 a group of Protestant philanthropists initiated the Children's Aid Society of New York City for vagrant children. Protestant religious

[6] *Ibid.*, pp. 190–91.

instruction and the placement of its charges in Protestant rural homes were primary objects of the society. New York County was ordered by the legislature to make an annual grant for the support of this program in 1865. Children's aid societies and juvenile asylums organized in Brooklyn and Buffalo also had the backing of public aid.[7]

The proselyting activities of such Protestant groups as the Children's Aid Society, particularly the policy of sending children to Protestant foster homes in the West, resulted in Catholic complaints. Many of these children of immigrants had been born to the Catholic religion. To counter this, Catholics in New York City organized a Society for the Protection of Destitute Roman Catholic Children in 1863. The society received vagrant Catholic children from parents, the courts, and the local commissioners of charity and correction and undertook to bring them up in the Catholic faith. Commencing in 1864, the society was granted lump sum aids from the state as well as public funds from New York County.[8]

Through these various steps a system of private charitable institutions had grown up in New York State by the middle years of the nineteenth century. Many of them were operated by Catholic or Protestant organizations. Several benefited from the support of local governments, while others were recipients of both local and state aid. Called into being by social welfare problems arising from immigration, urban growth, economic depressions, epidemics, and the effects of civil war, these institutions soon became integral parts of the poor relief system in the state. Charitable legislators and local officials found it quite easy to vote subsidies to these charities, especially since it relieved government of the necessity for shouldering the burdens of direct care for their inmates in publicly operated asylums. Until the 1860's there was little

[7] *Ibid.*, pp. 317–25, 328–34.   [8] *Ibid.*, pp. 334–36.

open dissent from this system of grants to private secular and sectarian institutions.[9]

In the late 1840's and during the 1850's the state legislature began to rationalize the hitherto piecemeal support arrangements for private charities. By a law of 1849, a lump sum was appropriated for distribution among incorporated orphan asylums outside of New York City in proportion to the numbers of children cared for in each institution during the year. In 1855 a similar grant was made for orphanages throughout the state to be divided on a per capita basis. This policy was continued through the medium of annual charities bills in the years that followed. As of 1857 twenty-six orphanages were sharing in the division of a sum of $35,000. By 1866 the amount had grown to $80,000 divided among sixty-three participating institutions. This increase was largely due to growing population and a rise in the numbers of orphans and half-orphans created by the Civil War.[10]

Not only did the state provide for the maintenance of orphaned and destitute children, it also made funds available for their education. In 1850 a law permitted private incorporated orphan asylums outside of New York City to participate in the distribution of school moneys on the same terms as the common schools of the district in which each asylum was situated. The next year, the legislature extended this privilege to the major child-care institutions of New York City. While these institutional schools received public school funds and were subject to inspection by local school authorities, they remained under the management of the asylums. No restrictions were placed on any sectarian religious instruction which might be required by the parent institutions.[11]

During the 1860's state aid to private charities increased

[9] *Ibid.*, chs. xiv, xv, and pp. 338–39.

[10] New York [State], *Laws, 1849*, ch. 368, and *Laws, 1855*, ch. 538; Schneider and Deutsch, I, 338–39.

[11] *Laws, 1850*, ch. 261; *Laws, 1851*, ch. 386.

measurably over what it had been in the preceding decades. To the growing numbers of orphanages and similar child-care institutions sharing in the distribution of funds from the public treasury were added other classes of charitable institutions. Hospitals and dispensaries, given occasional assistance in the past for treating indigent patients, were now regular recipients of public moneys. In return for such grants, they provided care for wounded and sick New York volunteers sent back home for treatment during the Civil War. Charity weekday schools for the children of the poor and a few private institutions for the insane and the deaf and dumb also benefited from the annual charity appropriations of the legislature.[12]

In addition to general appropriations, divided among the several institutions on a per capita basis, special grants to individual institutions were made by the legislature with increasing regularity. During the 1850's all state grants to private charitable institutions averaged about $90,000 a year. Over the decade of the 1860's the average annual appropriation to the same source stood at close to $150,000. In the three years from 1870 to 1872, when a stop was put to these large-scale subsidies, no less than a total of $2,250,000 was expended by the state on aid to private charitable organizations.[13]

A great many of the private institutions receiving state funds were sectarian. Of the sixty-five orphan asylums granted assistance at one time or another in the twenty years from 1847 to 1866, twenty-nine were sectarian in nature. The great majority of these were maintained by the Roman Catholic church. Others, while clearly Protestant in motivation,

[12] This paragraph is based on a study of charity appropriations acts in the annual session laws of New York for the period; see *Laws, 1860–1869, passim.*

[13] New York [State], *Journal of the Constitutional Commission of the State of New York, 1872–1873* (Albany, 1873), p. 313.

were usually operated by laymen acting in their individual capacities, rather than by official Protestant bodies, enabling them to claim to be nonsectarian in the literal sense because they had no affiliation with any church. Several of the hospitals and charity schools which obtained state grants in this period were also attached to one denomination or another, the Catholic again claiming the majority of these.[14]

The rapid increase in state aid and the tendency of sectarian institutions to monopolize the funds appropriated were viewed with growing alarm by many New Yorkers in the 1860's. Most vocal in their opposition were taxpayer groups and Protestant organizations. The former objected to the idea of any public assistance to private charities; the latter were chiefly aroused by the amount of money granted to Catholic institutions. With a constitutional convention due to convene in 1867, the opponents of state aid found common ground in a campaign to place constitutional restrictions upon the power of the legislature to make such appropriations. Both the economy-minded and anti-Catholics frequently founded their arguments on the principle of church-state separation.

The Citizens' Association of New York City, a typical group of leading business and professional men devoted to retrenchment in state finances, campaigned vigorously for an end to all public assistance to private charitable institutions. The association was unfriendly not only to state appropriations but also to those made by the municipalities. It canvassed the state to arouse public support for its views, and it flooded the constitutional convention, which opened at Albany in June of 1867, with appeals for economy and honesty in government. "The applications of private charities to the Legislature for pecuniary aid," warned the association, "are becoming yearly more numerous and successful, and the burdens thus imposed upon the tax-paying community more diffi-

[14] New York [State], *Documents of the Constitutional Convention of the State of New York, 1867–1868* (Albany, 1868), III, doc. no. 55.

cult to be borne." The tax rates for the support of public charities were already high enough without also forcing the taxpayer to assist private institutions. Voluntary giving was more than adequate to take care of all legitimate private charities. The Citizens' Association took a stand on high principle when it asserted "that it is against the theory of our Government to compel the people to support these private charities, which are, in fact, but the appendages of our various sects of religion." [15]

While angered taxpayers harped on economy, spokesmen for Protestant opinion concentrated their attacks upon the Catholic church. The church, it was argued, was reaping most of the benefits accruing to private charities from state aid. After a detailed study of the money appropriated by the legislature to sectarian charitable institutions in 1866, calculated to amount to $129,029.49, the *New York Tribune* commented: "The remarkable fact appears that only $3,855.35 of this sum was for the benefit of Protestant and Hebrew Associations, the balance being for Roman Catholic institutions." [16] The Presbyterian *New York Observer*, in an editorial titled "Our State Religion: Is It Roman Catholic?" appearing in 1867, claimed: "The Roman Catholics comprise a comparatively small portion of the entire population of the State, but our Legislature, in its munificent concern for the sustentation and propagation of Popery, has actually given to the Roman Catholics more than nineteen twentieths of the charitable funds of the State." The *Observer* was especially alarmed by the fact that Catholics never had a majority in the state legislature; it was a case of Protestant politicians seeking Catholic votes by squandering "the people's money in this unscrupulous and inordinate manner." [17]

[15] The Citizens' Association of New York, *The Constitutional Convention: Alterations in the Fundamental Law of the State, Proposed by . . .* (New York, 1867), p. 17.

[16] *New York Tribune*, June 1, 1867.

[17] *New York Observer*, June 6, 1867.

The convention, which gathered at the state capital in mid-1867 to revise the state constitution, soon felt the full force of the campaign against sectarian appropriations. Petitions by the score poured in from all corners of the state. They invariably called for an end to public aid for sectarian institutions. The memorials came from Protestant clergymen and their congregations, from the annual meetings of Baptist associations and Presbyterian synods, from local political clubs, and from irate citizens' groups.[18] "The manner in which the petitions were got up and signed and forwarded," reported the *Albany Argus*, "indicated concert of purpose and an organization." [19]

In late August, the convention's Committee on Charities and Charitable Institutions, to which many of the petitions had been sent, submitted a report dealing with the issue of sectarian appropriations. The report, signed by six of the seven committee members, recommended that any private institution receiving state funds would have to demonstrate that it was "not religious or sectarian in character, and that a majority of its managers are not members of one religious denomination." [20] The committee evidently intended to separate the functions of church and state in the field of charitable relief, but there was another construction which could be given to the proposal that made it especially appealing to anti-Catholic opinion. Most Protestant charities could claim to be nonsectarian in that their directors did not officially represent any Protestant sect, but rather organizations of private citizens banded together for a charitable purpose. Nevertheless, these institutions were Protestant in so far as the religious services they offered to their charges were generally Protestant oriented as distinct from Catholic or Jewish. On the other hand, most of the avowedly sectarian institutions were oper-

[18] New York [State], *Proceedings and Debates of the Constitutional Convention of the State of New York, 1867–1868* (Albany, 1868), I, II, III, *passim.*

[19] *Albany Argus,* Sept. 3, 1867.

[20] *Documents . . . Convention, 1867–1868,* IV, doc. no. 106, p. 3.

ated by the Catholic church and managed by one of its religious orders. In effect, the committee's proposal would exclude Catholic charities from further state aid while permitting many Protestant institutions to continue receiving such assistance.

The lone dissenting committee member objected strongly to what he termed an "unjust distribution" in the report of the majority. The report was unfair to religious benevolence and discriminated against denominationally managed institutions. He believed that the just course for the public would be "to cut off entirely all State aid from institutions not owned exclusively by the State, or to throw the door wide open *on equal terms* to all." [21]

What had begun as a reasonable debate over state policy toward private charities quickly developed into a bitter clash between Protestant and Catholic. When the report of the charities committee came before the committee of the whole for discussion, the chairman of the former group, Erastus Brooks, accused politicians in New York City—and he could only have meant Republicans—of playing politics with the charities question. The minority party in the city had long tried to saddle the ruling Tammany Hall Democrats with the charge of favoritism toward the Catholic church. Brooks stated that the many petitions which had come before the convention had originated in party councils in New York City. Brooks was aware that sectarian charities performed a praiseworthy service, but to forestall political strife over religious differences the committee had thought it best to apply the principle of church-state separation to the administration of public charity.[22]

George W. Curtis, Republican delegate from New York City, then rose to say that New York was a Protestant state and that "Romanists" were receiving an undue proportion of

[21] *Ibid.*, doc. no. 105, p. 2.

[22] *Proceedings . . . Convention, 1867–1868*, IV, 2710–20.

the state's money. A delegate from Columbia County characterized the Catholic clergy as "vampires and ghouls who stood at the bedsides of the dying to rob them of their property." [23] Catholics and their supporters in the convention replied in kind. It was charged that the proposed test to determine whether an institution was sectarian in character amounted to a grant of inquisitorial powers over religious belief. Anti-Catholic opinion in the convention arrayed itself behind the Brooks committee's proposal. Opposed to them were the few Irish Catholic members. A third group of delegates objected to the draft amendment as having no proper claim to inclusion in the state constitution. They contended that sectarian charities fulfilled a need which the state would otherwise have to meet by establishing many new and expensive public charitable institutions.

With the convention threatening to break up into warring sectarian factions, cooler heads took charge. Leaders of the Republican majority, such as Brooks and Thomas Alvord of Onondaga County, reminded the convention that state aid to dependents was not extended to welfare institutions as such but rather to needy individuals on a per capita basis. So long as this class of persons was cared for, no matter by what kind of institution, the state had no reason for delving into the religious convictions of the organizations affording the care. Francis Kernan, a Democratic leader and Irish Catholic of Utica, warned that the state needed the services provided by sectarian charities much more than Catholic charities needed state aid. The church would prefer to give up both the aid and the public obligations which went with it rather than suffer an unpopular church-state connection. A majority of the delegates followed their leaders and voted to table the charities report. It remained in this parliamentary limbo for the rest of the convention. The advantages redounding to the state from

[23] *Albany Argus*, Jan. 17, 1868.

the existing system of public aid, and the desire to avoid a religious dispute mutually destructive to the fortunes of both major parties, had won out over the demand for an end to sectarian appropriations.[24]

During the years following the convention of 1867–1868, the open-door policy of assistance to private charities was continued and even expanded. These were the years of Boss Tweed's suzerainty at Albany. Tweed always prided himself in being the friend of the poor in New York City; the poor, true to Tweed's expectations, showed their gratitude by supporting Tammany at the polls. Tweed made sizable personal contributions to charity, his party machine dispensed food and coal with a liberal hand to the unfortunate during hard times, and the city treasury was always open for a worthy cause. Between 1869 and 1871, the Tammany-controlled city government granted over $1,250,000 to the Catholic church, the spiritual home of the greater number of Tweed's supporters. Some $300,000 was given to Protestant, Hebrew, and other private charitable groups in the same period.[25]

Tweed's entrance into state politics in 1867 presented him with a broader field in which to demonstrate the Democratic party's munificent regard for the poor. Under his driving hand, the legislature became strangely bipartisan in its support of the annual appropriation for private charities. Tweed's philosophy was simple and direct. "I believe," the Boss told his Republican Senate colleagues, "in supporting all deserving charities, without asking what denominations control them. . . . We, on this side, are in favor of aiding all the charities. So now, gentlemen on the other side, offer your amendments,

[24] *Proceedings . . . Convention, 1867–1868*, IV, 2720–54; *Albany Argus*, Jan. 17, 1868. See also New York [State], *Journal of the Constitutional Convention . . . 1867–1868* (Albany, 1868), pp. 829–30.

[25] Gustavus Myers, *The History of Tammany Hall* (New York, 1901), p. 230; M. R. Werner, *Tammany Hall* (New York, 1928), p. 194.

inserting deserving charities, and we will accept them."[26] Of course, Tweed's beneficence was repaid many times over. Control of state funds added immensely to the resources already available in New York City for cementing the allegiance of the city's poor to the Democratic party. By assisting upstate Republican legislators to obtain grants for their home districts, he gained support for his own less elevated schemes for plunder. It was even rumored that Tweed raked off a share of the charity appropriations into his own pocket, though this—like so many other charges against Tweed—has never been conclusively proven correct.[27]

From 1869 to 1871, the high noon of Tweed's career and of his power in state politics, the annual charity appropriations grew by leaps and bounds. State grants, which never before had reached $200,000 a year, surpassed $400,000 in 1869, and thereafter were never less than a half million dollars annually. The money voted in 1871 was in excess of $900,000. Inevitably abuses began to creep into the charity bills, which had become a logroller's delight. Besides orphanages, hospitals, and charity schools, the politicians were sneaking in institutions whose charitable motives were at least questionable. Since 1866 parochial schools in New York City had been appearing among the recipients of charity grants; equally doubtful items of expenditure for upstate institutions were also voted. In 1870, $2,000 was given to a Baptist church in Tonawanda to assist in its renovation. The appropriations for the same year included an item of $5,000 for a college at Le Roy, Genesee County, "for the construction of an Art Gallery, and the purchase of a Cabinet of Natural History."[28]

The abuses associated with charity appropriations encouraged the opponents of sectarian grants to renew their cam-

[26] *New York Times*, April 7, 1871. [27] Myers, p. 229.

[28] *Laws, 1870*, ch. 704; also *Journal . . . Commission, 1872–1873*, p. 313, and E. M. Connors, *Church-State Relationships in Education in the State of New York* (Washington, D.C., 1951), p. 93.

paign against them. Since these excesses were linked with the Democrats in the public mind, the Republican party was receptive to pleas that the annual practice of granting funds to sectarian and other private charities be brought to an end. In the fall elections of 1871, popular revulsion at the corruption of the Tweed regime in city and state resulted in a sweeping victory for the Republicans. The 1872 session of the legislature contained large Republican majorities committed to reform and retrenchment.

One of the more important acts of the 1872 legislature was its refusal to pass the annual charity bill. An Assembly resolution calling for discussion of the usual appropriation measure for private charitable institutions, moved by a Kings County Democrat, was tabled indefinitely by a large majority. Both houses of the legislature also passed a resolution calling for a constitutional amendment forbidding state or local grants to sectarian organizations.[29] The Republican *Albany Evening Journal*, pleased with the defeat of the charity bill, concluded that "nearly a million dollars has been saved, which heretofore has been annually given mainly to the institutions of one religious sect. This alone is a strong point for the Legislature." [30] The *Albany Argus*, frequent defender of the Democratic-sponsored charity grants of the Tweed years, bemoaned the fact that "there was time and money for everything but Charity, and the promotion of good will." "The plea of sectarianism," complained the *Argus*, "sealed up all the generous fountains of the heart, and while money could be voted freely to other purposes, not a dollar could be given to the orphan, the sick, or the unfortunate." [31] The Democratic party deeply regretted the loss of this particular source of good will.

[29] New York [State] Assembly, *Journal, 1872*, II, 1193, 1230, 1282, and Senate, *Journal, 1872*, p. 1129; *New York Tribune*, April 18, 1872.

[30] May 15, 1872. [31] May 15, 1872.

The crusade against sectarian appropriations, so successful in the 1872 legislative session, was carried forward into the deliberations of the Constitutional Commission of 1872–73. Since there was no existing law to prevent future legislatures from passing charity bills, the ultimate goal was to secure a constitutional amendment outlawing sectarian grants. The constitutional commission was appointed to suggest revisions in the state constitution, the work of the 1867–68 convention having been rejected by the voters.[32] One of the proposals introduced before the commission was a constitutional prohibition on public aid to sectarian institutions. From its deliberations came two amendments pertaining to this general issue. One forbade the state to assist any private association, corporation, or undertaking by loans of money or grants of public credit. The second extended this prohibition to the county, city, town, and village governments of the state. The commission had purposely failed to single out sectarian institutions in these proposed amendments, preferring a blanket restriction on certain public aids to all private groups.[33]

However, the two amendments contained very significant qualifying clauses reflecting the commissioners' belief that there was merit in certain forms of public aid to private charities. The restriction on state appropriations was not to extend to funds granted for the education and support of the blind, deaf and dumb, and juvenile delinquents in private institutions. Neither was it to include the public school funds which long had been distributed among private orphan asylums for the education of their charges. At the same time, local governments were permitted to aid and support the various classes of their poor in private institutions if they so desired. The two amendments simply provided for a transfer of responsibility for aiding most types of private charities

[32] *New York Times*, March 19, 1873.

[33] *Journal . . . Commission, 1872–1873*, pp. 191, 223–24, 255, 284, 350, 471; *New York Times*, March 18, 1873.

from the state to the localities. No distinction was made between sectarian and nonsectarian institutional recipients of public assistance in either amendment.[34]

Both amendments were incorporated in the state constitution as sections 10 and 11 of article 8 by popular referendum in 1874.[35] The former policy of indiscriminate aid to private orphan asylums, hospitals, dispensaries, and charity schools was now forbidden by the state's basic law. Nevertheless, state support was continued in certain special cases. In addition, many local governments willingly assumed the support of private charities which was no longer permitted to the state, for they saw that the drive for economy and the demand for a separation of church and state should not destroy the important contributions of private, including sectarian, charitable institutions to the public welfare.

Humanitarian concern for the welfare of dependent children soon led to another breach in the new policy of curbing public aid to private charities. The continuing plight of children confined in the public poorhouses throughout the state resulted in a significant reform in 1875. The legislature enacted a law preventing the further commitment of orphaned and vagrant children to the county and municipal poorhouses and requiring that all children presently confined there be transferred to other institutions. Henceforth, these youths were to be placed in orphan asylums or other similar places, whether of a public or private nature. The key clause provided that each child be sent to "an orphan asylum, charitable or other reformatory institution that is governed or controlled by officers or persons of the same religious faith as the parents of such child, as far as practicable." [36] In other words, private

[34] *Journal . . . Commission, 1872–1873*, p. 471.

[35] F. J. Zwierlein, *The Life and Letters of Bishop McQuaid* (Rochester, 1925–27), III, 314.

[36] *Laws, 1875*, ch. 173; Schneider and Deutsch, II, 63.

sectarian asylums would be the primary reception centers for children coming under this law.

The "Children's Law" of 1875 in time reopened the whole question of public support for sectarian charities. It encouraged the expansion and revitalization of sectarian orphan asylums, many of which had been experiencing financial difficulties since the shutting off of state aid in 1872. At the close of the year 1874 there were 132 private orphanages and homes for the friendless caring for almost 12,000 dependent children under sixteen years of age. By 1885 there were 204 such establishments with over 23,000 youths under their charge. Public aid to these institutions also increased substantially. Both the state and local governments contributed to the care of this class of public wards placed in the keeping of private institutions. The localities were especially active in this respect. New York City, for example, had supported 9,000 dependent youths in both public and private institutions in 1875 at a cost to the city of about $750,000. In 1888 the city was maintaining almost 15,000 children in private institutions alone at a cost of $1,500,000. The great majority of the twenty-eight private child care establishments assisted by the city in 1888 were sectarian.[37]

The importance of the "Children's Law" of 1875 for the church-state question lay in its recognition of the advantages of private sectarian institutional care for dependent children over the type of care available in the public poorhouse. Moreover, the state was now obliged to delve into the sometimes explosive question of religious affiliation when placing its wards in private institutions. The law of 1875 also assumed a high degree of co-operation between the officers of sectarian asylums and the public authorities.[38] Out of this emerged a

[37] *Ibid.*, pp. 64–65.

[38] L. A. Stidley, *Sectarian Welfare Federation* . . . (New York, 1944), pp. 148–49.

closer working relationship between church and state in one important area of public policy at a time when there was growing sentiment in some quarters for an even broader application of the principle of church-state separation in all areas of public life.

Opposition to public aid for sectarian charities in the 1880's, like the campaign against public grants to sectarian schools, was closely connected with the rise of anti-Catholic feeling in America over the last three decades of the nineteenth century. Protestants and secularists both believed that there was a gigantic, centrally directed Catholic movement under way to break down the separation of church and state in the United States. It manifested itself in Catholic efforts to secure public support for their parochial schools and state aid for their charitable institutions. One militant anti-Catholic New Yorker defined the issue this way:

> The constant attempts of the Romish Church . . . to obtain grants of the public real estate and donations of public moneys sufficient to support its numerous so-called eleemosynary institutions and its army of non-producing priests, monks, and nuns, and its Brothers and Sisters of various orders—in a country like ours, where not only is a State religion and a State Church prohibited by both the State and National Constitutions, but where even the State Constitution goes so far as to prohibit any "*discrimination or preference*" in favor of any one form of religious profession or worship over another—should arouse a tolerant public to protective and preventive measures before the evil becomes too deeply rooted for safety.[39]

The frequently expressed solution of the anti-Catholics was to erect tighter constitutional barriers in New York against all forms of public aid to sectarian institutions. Only then could non-Catholics feel confident that American principles of

[39] Dexter Hawkins, *Archbishop Purcell Outdone! The Roman Catholic Church in New York City and Public Land and Public Money* (New York, 1880), p. 1.

church-state separation would not succumb to the assaults of an insidious enemy.

But while there was wide agreement among non-Catholics on the need for stronger legal safeguards for the public school system, many of these same people were less certain that there was a similar need for action in the area of welfare policies. Here was a case where two values were in conflict. One was the belief in the public's responsibility for the care of destitute and neglected human beings. The other was the ideal of church-state separation. The former took precedence in the thinking of many. Charles Loring Brace, a Protestant long engaged in charitable work, represented an influential segment of public opinion when he wrote:

> The object of a State Legislature in all these matters is *bonum publicum*—the public weal. If they think that a private charity is accomplishing a public work of great value, which is not and perhaps cannot be accomplished by purely public institutions, they apparently have the same right to tax the whole community, or a local community, for its benefit, that they have now to tax it for the support of schools, or Almshouses, or Prisons, or Houses of Refuge. In such a case it need not be a matter of question with the Legislature whether the charity is "sectarian" or not; whether it teaches Roman Catholicism, or Protestantism, or the Jewish Faith, or no faith. The only question with the governing power is, "Does it do a work of public value not done by public institutions?" If it does . . . the Legislature . . . is perfectly right in granting aid to such institutions without reference to their "sectarian" character.[40]

The views of Brace were very close to those of Catholics on the question of public aid to the poor. Catholics believed that every sect and charitable organization should maintain asylums for the poor of their own faith. When private means were inadequate for this purpose, it was proper for "the State

[40] C. L. Brace, *The Dangerous Classes of New York*, 3d ed. (New York, 1880), p. 378.

to lend its assistance to all impartially in proportion to the numbers they relieve, asking of none, 'Are you Methodists? Are you Catholics?' . . . but only requiring proof that the recipients of public money are honestly engaged in work for the public good." [41]

Again, as with the school question, the areas of difference over the issue of state aid to sectarian charities had been well delineated by the late 1880's. It was obvious that two systems of competing values were in conflict on this question. But already events were moving toward a dramatic confrontation of these opposing beliefs in the political arenas of the 1890's.

[41] The Catholic Publication Society, *Private Charities, Public Lands, and Public Money* . . . (New York, 1879), p. 23.

IX

The Constitutional Convention of 1894

AS the decade of the 1890's opened, tensions between Catholics and their opponents in New York were rapidly mounting. Anti-Catholics saw in these frictions the portents of an approaching showdown over the school question and the issue of sectarian appropriations. A public school official in New York City was convinced that "a conflict between the advocates of denominational schools and the friends of the purely secular public schools is forever impending, and . . . glaze over it as we will, this conflict must someday be fought without gloves and fought to a finish." [1] The editors of a New York Baptist journal characterized the intensifying church-state controversy as an irrepressible conflict between Catholicism and the American system. The villains in this drama, according to John Jay, a leading New York anti-Catholic, were "the Roman hierarchy, with whose widely organized and relentless hostility to American schools and American principles our people, whatever their past credulity or indifference, are fast becoming familiar." [2]

[1] *New York Herald*, Oct. 12, 1890, in E. C. Putnam Collection, consisting of newspaper and periodical clippings on the subject of education, Harvard Divinity School Library.

[2] John Jay, "Moral Education in the Public Schools," *Magazine of Christian Literature*, IV (1891), 66; also "A New Phase of the School Question," *Baptist Quarterly Review*, XIV (1892), 104.

The heaviest verbal skirmishing took place around the question of the public schools. Catholics and their adversaries discharged volley after volley of abuse and recrimination against each other's positions. This was partly due to the prominence the Catholic hierarchy gave to this issue. As one cleric after another spoke out on the virtues of parochial schools or the moral dangers inherent in secular education, the suspicion that there was a treacherous Catholic plot underfoot to subvert the public schools hardened into an inflexible conviction. An ex-Catholic's warning that "the order has gone out from the Vatican, and a war upon the public school system has begun," was quoted with approval as indisputable proof that a conspiracy did in fact exist.[3]

The "Poughkeepsie Plan" arrangements between school authorities and Catholic parishes in various parts of the state, dating back to the 1870's in some cases, suddenly became the objects of wide-spread popular alarm. The details of the plan were publicized, and its merits and demerits vigorously debated. One defender of secular education exclaimed that "there is no compromise possible between the absolutely unsectarian, non-religious public school and the religious, parochial school." Catholics were mistaken if they saw in the "Poughkeepsie Plan" a preliminary step to outright public aid for their schools. "Under no circumstances can the demand for a division of the public money be allowed. That is not only forbidden by most of our State Constitutions, but it ought to be." The state must not assist religion in any way. This principle "is a matter no longer to be argued, however much ecclesiastics may bluster." [4]

School compromises within the towns of Faribault and Stillwater, Minnesota, in 1891, contributed to the uproar.

[3] Jay, p. 67.

[4] Editorial on the "School Question," *Independent*, Sept. 4, 1890, Putnam Collection; see "The Education of the People," *ibid.*, XLII (1890), 1221–33, for a discussion of the "Poughkeepsie Plan."

Similar to the "Poughkeepsie Plan" in New York, these accommodations received nationwide attention, because they occurred in the province of the controversial archbishop of St. Paul, John Ireland. The New York *Baptist Quarterly Review* described all such plans as "nothing more than an attempt on the part of the Roman hierarchy to take by a flank movement what they have failed to take by storm." Now was the time "for standing firm, for educating the public mind and conscience, for resisting the beginnings of what might easily be a great evil." [5]

Secularists saw in the heightened agitation for publicly supported sectarian education not only a threat to the secular public schools, but also a prelude to destructive religious strife in the body politic. Dr. Howard Crosby of New York City expressed this fear when he wrote that sectarian schooling encourages

> controversies that infiltrate our politics and prepare the way for the overthrow of all liberties. Religious contests form the fertile soil of tyrannies, and it is for us Americans to avoid carefully the beginnings of a false system that would intensify religious hatreds and strife. While the Government is neutral, all religions can grow according to their own vitality, and the truth will eventually triumph peacefully and satisfactorily to all.[6]

The *New York Sun*, observing that "the proposition has been made that the school fund be distributed among Catholics and Protestants," concluded that "the only way to escape discord is to keep the instruction purely secular, and it is the only course consistent with our theory of Government." [7]

While secularists attacked the Catholic church as a threat to the ideal of nonreligious public education, many Protestant organizations were launching assaults on the Roman church from another direction. The major Protestant sects could

[5] "A New Phase," p. 108.

[6] *Independent*, Sept. 4, 1890, Putnam Collection.

[7] *New York Sun*, Sept. 13, 1890, Putnam Collection.

agree with the New York *Christian Union* that there was little reason to "doubt that the Roman Catholic hierarchy is determined, if possible, to break up the public school system." [8] But many believed just as strongly that the secularist approach to public education, with its eschewal of any moral or religious training in the schools, was encouraging the Catholic crusade against the godless public schools. The Presbyterian Synod of New York launched a campaign to bring together all religious groups in the state "in emphasizing the distinction between sectarianism and religion, in excluding sectarianism in every form from the public schools, and in maintaining the necessity of having the State, for its own sake, instruct its wards in reverence for God as the basis of morals." [9] A convention of twenty-three Protestant denominations in New York City, in the fall of 1890, resolved that while "discountenancing any union of Church and State," they advocated the "necessity of having the truths of Christianity inculcated in the public schools." [10]

Protestants and secularists might be at odds over the question of moral instruction in the schools, but they were unanimous in their belief that a serious Catholic threat to the existing system of public education existed in New York. Few of them would argue with the analysis of a Methodist pastor in Syracuse. "We are contending," he said, "for the existence of the common schools. In the day when the State of New York shall decree the division of the school funds collected by taxation of all the citizens, giving to the Roman Catholics a portion for the support of parochial schools, that day her common school system perishes." [11]

The advocates of American church-state principles in New York did more than view with alarm. They were increasingly receptive to the urgings of the more militant among them that

[8] *Christian Union,* March 27, 1890, Putnam Collection. [9] *Ibid.*

[10] *New York Sun,* Nov. 19, 1890, Putnam Collection.

[11] *Catholic Review,* April 26, 1890, Putnam Collection.

they take "whatever legislative or judicial action may be required to maintain the supremacy of the State and the rights of its citizens" against the Catholic peril.[12] Rev. Henry Potter, bishop of the Protestant Episcopal diocese of New York, advised church censure for the practice of appropriating public money to sectarian institutions. We must, said Bishop Potter, "abhor it as a crime against honesty and good citizenship, and a thing to be everywhere reprobated as fraught only with evil and danger."[13] Official church bodies were pressed for declarations condemning sectarian appropriations. The General Assembly of the Presbyterian Church in the United States of America, at its meeting in Saratoga Springs in May of 1894, was persuaded to pass such a resolution to be forwarded to the state of New York. The measure attacked sectarian appropriations as "prejudicial to the national welfare" and as being "in conflict with the First Amendment to our National Constitution." All such grants for ecclesiastical uses were officially condemned, particularly "in view of the enormous and portentous grants of financial aid which are persistently bestowed by the Government upon the Romish Church."[14]

Public expressions of opposition to the Catholic church were bolstered by the lobbying and propaganda activities of well-organized pressure groups. The spearhead of the anti-Catholic thrust in New York was the National League for the Protection of American Institutions, the NLPAI. The NLPAI grew out of a convention of "patriotic men" held at Saratoga in 1889, and it was subsequently incorporated under the laws of New York. Its chief objects were "to secure constitutional and legislative safeguards for the protection of

[12] Jay, p. 66.

[13] Protestant Episcopal Church, *Journal . . . of the 107th Convention of the Diocese of New-York, 1890* (New York, 1890), p. 109.

[14] Presbyterian Church in the United States of America, *Minutes of the General Assembly, 1894* (Philadelphia, 1894), p. 167.

the common-school system and other American Institutions, and to promote public instruction in harmony with such institutions, and to prevent all sectarian or denominational appropriations of public funds." One means to these ends was to obtain passage of a sixteenth amendment to the federal Constitution prohibiting the states from extending money to "any church, religious denomination or religious society, or any institution, society, or undertaking, which is wholly, or in part, under sectarian or ecclesiastical control." [15]

The NLPAI purposely concentrated on winning the support of leading figures in politics, business, and the professions. The league was to be a prestige organization which would rely on the power and standing of its members to gain its desired objectives. John Jay, wealthy descendant of the John Jay of Revolutionary fame, was the league's first president. William Strong, former justice of the United States Supreme Court, was the original vice-president. Other members from across the nation were General Thomas J. Morgan, commissioner of Indian Affairs in the administration of President Benjamin Harrison; Henry Hitchcock, one-time president of the American Bar Association; the historian Francis Parkman; the presidents of the University of North Dakota, Stanford University, and Northwestern University; and many other lesser-known jurists, lawyers, educators, and public officials.[16]

While active nationally, the NLPAI always maintained its headquarters in New York City, from which it exerted considerable influence in New York politics in the early 1890's. A great many of its chief supporters resided in the metropolis. These included such lawyers as William Allen Butler and

[15] J. M. King, *Facing the Twentieth Century, Our Country: Its Power and Peril* (New York, 1899), p. 520.

[16] *Ibid.*, p. 519; "Separation of Church and State," *Independent*, XLIV (1892), 37–40; D. L. Kinzer, *An Episode in Anti-Catholicism: The American Protective Association* (Seattle, Wash., 1964), pp. 56–57.

Dorman B. Eaton, who represented the league before public bodies; wealthy backers such as J. P. Morgan, John D. Rockefeller, Russell Sage, Cyrus W. Field, Abram S. Hewit, and Cornelius Vanderbilt provided the funds and lent the authority of their names to the cause. James M. King, pastor of the Union Methodist Episcopal Church in New York City, was the league's general secretary. It was largely through his dedicated efforts that the NLPAI became the force in New York which it did.[17]

The NLPAI's activities were diverse and many. For the benefit of voters, it kept up a running interrogation of candidates for public office in New York to elicit their views on the school question and on sectarian appropriations. The league fought the passage of the so-called "Freedom of Worship" law in New York, supported by the Catholic church, which permitted Catholic chaplains access to penal institutions on the same terms as Protestants. Large sums were spent for printed materials mailed out by the thousands to opinion leaders all over the country to arouse public interest in the league's proposed sixteenth amendment. Congress was similarly deluged with literature, and its members buttonholed by league lobbyists. The NLPAI claimed to have influenced the passage of constitutional prohibitions on sectarian appropriations in Kentucky, Mississippi, Montana, North and South Dakota, Idaho, Wyoming, and Washington. One of the league's major ambitions was to secure a similar provision in the constitution of New York. As it prepared for this, and awaited its opportunity, the NLPAI kept up a steady attack upon the Catholic church in New York.[18]

The anti-Catholic movement in New York in the 1890's was due more to fertile non-Catholic imaginations than to any

[17] *Ibid.*, p. 101; *New York World*, May 16, 1890, Putnam Collection.

[18] King, pp. 521–22, 524–32.

real Catholic threat. Even the emotional campaign to defend the public schools against Roman inroads was directed largely at appearances instead of realities. This misunderstanding stemmed from years of vicious anti-Catholic propaganda, from a willingness to believe the worst about Catholicism, and from a consequent failure to see beneath the seemingly monolithic exterior of the Catholic church in America. While partisans screamed of Romish intrigues, attributing to the church a totalitarian unanimity of views on all public issues which has seldom been the case, the American hierarchy was being rocked within by the tremors of a great debate.

This debate, which began in the European church, dealt with church attitudes toward the rapidly changing world of the nineteenth century.[19] How was the church to fit its ancient mission into a brave new world increasingly dominated by the forces of secularism, materialism, and nationalism? On one side conservative European Catholics advocated a militant opposition to all change. The conservatives looked upon non-Catholic society as their greatest enemy. They exalted orthodoxy and authority, favored increased centralization of power in the person of the pope, and fought every tendency which savored of accommodation between the church and the modern age. Opposed to the conservatives were those among the clergy and laity who were liberal in the sense that they wished to understand the changes taking place in Western society and to bring their church into some more realistic relationship with modern tendencies. Their object was the spreading of Catholicism through the peaceful conversion of non-Catholic society, rather than centering their efforts on strengthening the Church from within, as conservatives desired, to prepare for an expected anti-Catholic onslaught. To do this would

[19] R. D. Cross, *The Emergence of Liberal Catholicism in America* (Cambridge, Mass., 1958), is the best study of this subject. For the European phase, see his ch. i.

require a friendlier and more sympathetic approach to the world outside the church than the conservatives were willing to countenance.

The European debate carried over into the American church. Conservative American clerics firmly believed themselves to be surrounded by a heathen and inimical American society which was always threatening to crush the church. The reaction to anti-Catholic prejudice and the conservatism of the large immigrant element in the church produced a strong hostility toward American ideals and institutions. An uneasy coexistence with its Protestant and secular enemies, by which the church would maintain its internal purity and discipline by avoiding all contact with the paganism encircling it, was the most conservatives ever hoped for from America. The German Catholic clergy, the Jesuits, and Irish clerics such as Michael Corrigan, archbishop of New York, and his friend Bernard McQuaid, bishop of Rochester, were among the leading spokesmen for the conservative point of view in the American church.

On the other hand, there was an influential liberal element in both the hierarchy and the laity which did not consider all non-Catholic Americans to be enemies. The liberals were inclined to accept the facts of religious diversity in America, a free competition in religious ideas, and the neutrality of the state in such matters. Here was a society which offered the church a freedom of action unknown in many European states with their formal and often restrictive working agreements between church and state. It was in the church's interest to attune its appeal to this pragmatic and libertarian nation. The liberals found their support among foreign groups who had already made the difficult transition from their European cultures to American culture and who thought of themselves as Americans, and among native-born Catholics. Their leaders were such vigorous and outspoken men as Archbishop John

Ireland of St. Paul, Father Isaac Hecker, founder of the Paulist order, and—in New York—Fathers Sylvester Malone of Brooklyn and Louis Lambert of Waterloo.[20]

On no issue was there greater difference of opinion between liberals and conservatives than on the school question. This was as true of the New York church as of the church in other parts of the country. Both liberals and conservatives supported improved educational opportunities for Catholic children. In theory they were also agreed on the paramount efficacy of parochial schooling. But on the question of Catholic policy toward the public schools the two groups were poles apart. In the last decades of the nineteenth century, Catholics were faced with the problem of too few schools and too little money to provide each Catholic child with a parochial education. While accepting the need of public assistance for parochial schooling in the long run, liberals believed that it was futile to hope for such a program in the near future. They were so desirous of seeing Catholic youths receive an adequate education that they were willing to encourage their attendance at public schools. Religious instruction in the home and in the parish church would make up for the spiritual failings of the secular public schools. Where possible, the liberals favored arrangements between parish schools and local school authorities such as the "Poughkeepsie Plan" compromises in New York. Through these amicable accommodations liberals felt they were preparing a suitably friendly environment for eventual non-Catholic acceptance of public support for parochial schools.

Conservative Catholics such as Corrigan and McQuaid were alarmed by the liberal position.[21] To them the public

[20] *Ibid.*, ch. ii.

[21] For the liberal-conservative differences over education and the public schools, see *ibid.*, pp. 130–41; "Pacificus," "The Public School Question by a Roman Catholic," *Christian Union*, XLVII (1893),

schools were either godless or else dominated by Protestant interests. Encouraging Catholic children to attend such schools meant exposing them to the corrupting influences of a secular and anti-Catholic society. Education unpermeated by Catholic doctrine was meaningless and dangerous. If the state insisted on taxing for the support of education, it was only right and fair that it assist schools which Catholics could attend without violating their consciences. According to the ideal plan suggested by the New York *Catholic Review*, "The State simply allows each denomination to teach its own views of religion to its own children, and pays according to results in secular studies of which it takes cognizance, or, according to the average number of children taught" in sectarian schools.[22]

Believing such an arrangement would never be acceptable to non-Catholics, conservatives preached the necessity of greater sacrifices on the part of their parishioners to improve and expand the parochial system. In the meantime, McQuaid and others continued to demand public support for their schools as a matter of right. The responsibility for an equitable settlement was left entirely to non-Catholics. In the words of the Rochester *Catholic Journal:* "It would seem as though our non-Catholic friends, being the aggressors, should make the overtures. They are using us unjustly and from them should come all offers of a compromise." Meanwhile Catholics would support parochial schools at their own expense while continuing to protest "against the present state school system, as it is now conducted, and the injustice done Catholics in taking their money to aid in maintaining schools

215–17. Also, see the interesting recent article by W. E. Akin, "The War of the Bishops: Catholic Controversy on the School Question in . . . 1894," *New-York Historical Society Quarterly*, L (1966), 41–61.

[22] *Catholic Review*, Oct. 5, 1890, Putnam Collection.

to which, as a matter of conscience, they cannot send their children." [23]

The "Poughkeepsie Plan" was particularly objectionable to the conservatives. It implied that Catholics were willing to settle for considerably less than their full rights. But when conservatives attacked compromise arrangements, liberals were quick to answer their charges. A German Catholic Congress, held at Buffalo in 1891, officially condemned the Poughkeepsie compromise as unwise and dangerous. The pastor of St. Peter's parish in Poughkeepsie retorted through the press that the

> plan has worked admirably for eighteen years. . . . It satisfies all intelligent people. But those who do not understand it condemn it. It is safe to say that not one of those foreign priests ever visited our schools. Some of them cannot comprehend the lessons in the first English reader. Their condemnation is a eulogy.[24]

The willingness of conservatives and liberals to fight out their differences in public in the early 1890's only added to the confusion. Liberal arguments for compromise arrangements and conservative demands for public aid seemed to anti-Catholics, habituated to the idea of a monolithic church, to be related phases of the same massive Catholic assault on the public schools rather than opposing positions in an internal church dispute. When Pope Leo XIII sent Archbishop Francesco Satolli to America in 1892 to end the public show of disunity among the hierarchy on the school question, outsiders claimed that the pope was planning, through Satolli, to assume personal command of the attack on public education.[25]

Vehement Catholic countercharges to the equally vehe-

[23] [Rochester] *Catholic Journal,* May 24, 1890, Putnam Collection.

[24] *New York World,* Sept. 25, 1891, Putnam Collection; see also Cross, p. 139.

[25] *Ibid.,* pp. 141–45; F. J. Zwierlein, *Letters of Archbishop Corrigan to Bishop McQuaid* (Rochester, 1946), pp. 142–43, 146–47.

ment attacks of anti-Catholics did little to disabuse the public of its beliefs in the malign intentions of the Catholic church. Catholic writers delighted in equating the movement against sectarian appropriations in New York with the American Protective Association, the most recent of a long line of nativist and anti-Catholic organizations which had sprung up in the Midwest and was spreading its tentacles into the East in 1893 and 1894. One Catholic, with typical gusto, asked, "Don't you see, standing out there on the field, and a little too close too, that Pharisaical hypocrite—the 'National League for the Protection of American Institutions'?" Then, with a characteristic twist, the writer continued: "And cannot you see lurking behind him the League's secret, masked auxiliary, 'The American Protective Association,' with hands already 'damned for forgery and dripping with deceit,' fumbling in his breast for the stiletto, and eager to rush out and stab us in the back?" [26] The Catholic press accused the NLPAI of introducing the APA into New York to assist it in its nefarious activities; identified the NLPAI as an adjunct of the APA, or "American Pagan Association"; claimed that the two organizations shared the same national headquarters in New York City and were led by the same group of prominent New York men.[27] Catholic publicists also connected the anti-Catholic movement with the Republican party. One charged that "the Republican party first of all acted as godmother to this anti-Catholic crusade, has since nursed and fostered it, and is to be held responsible for the power that it has been able to wield at the polls." [28]

The American Protective Association had gained the repu-

[26] Alfred Young, "The Coming Contest," *Catholic World*, LVIII (1893–94), 458–59.

[27] *Catholic Review*, Dec. 10, 1893, and May 12, 1894, Putnam Collection; "An American," *A.P.A., An Inquiry into the Objects and Purposes of the So-Called "American Protective Association"* (n.p., n.d.), p. 1.

[28] Young, p. 702.

tation by 1894 of being the leading anti-Catholic society in the nation. In the same year the APA appeared in New York, claiming no less than fifty thousand members in the state. It operated four newspapers in Brooklyn, Albany, Buffalo, and Lansingburg, and it professed to hold the balance of power in the Republican party. The *New York Times* was among the newspapers which helped to create a popular image of APA strength—which the APA of course did not dispute—by their sensational treatment of the society. But there is no sound evidence for supposing that the APA ever had any significant part in the fight on sectarian appropriations in New York. Instead, it was given credit for the work of the National League for the Protection of American Institutions. This undeserved distinction resulted from the efforts of the Catholic press to lump all anti-Catholic groups under the name of the most notorious of them and from the uncritical acceptance of the myth of APA invincibility by political newspapers solely on the basis of APA and Catholic claims. The manufacture of an APA monster which had little relationship to the truth only added to the bitterness attending the church-state controversy in the 1890's.[29]

Virtually the only concrete result of the false reputation enjoyed by the APA in New York was to frighten the Republican party into a noncommittal position regarding it. This was understandable, for the APA was most active in traditionally Republican upstate areas; the Democratic party in New York was too closely identified with the Catholic vote to be receptive to APA advances. As it developed, New York Republicans need not have straddled the APA issue, but until the fall elections of 1894 they were impressed by the as yet untested claims of the association. The Republican stand lent plausibility to the charges of a secret Republican-APA al-

[29] Kinzer, ch. iv and nn., especially pp. 95–100, 101, 122, 124–25, 127, 128–29, 134–35 for New York.

liance and convinced Catholics all the more of the enormity of the anti-Catholic crusade.[30]

By early 1894, with a constitutional convention scheduled to meet in the spring, Catholics and anti-Catholics were preparing to do battle in defense of their respective positions. Both sides correctly foresaw that church-state issues would be among the leading topics of interest at the upcoming convention. The National League for the Protection of American Institutions took charge of the preparations to present the anti-Catholic case to the convention. In January 1894, the NLPAI formulated a draft amendment, prohibiting sectarian appropriations, to be placed before the constitutional assembly. The support of prominent lawyers and other leading citizens was secured for the NLPAI draft, and explanatory literature was distributed across the state to excite public opinion in its favor. Statistics on parochial schools and on public grants to sectarian institutions were laboriously compiled for the convention's use. NLPAI petitions were sent out for signatures. Local groups were encouraged to prepare similar memorials and forward them to the convention through the headquarters of the league. NLPAI representatives approached the ruling bodies of the leading Protestant denominations to solicit resolutions supporting the NLPAI amendment.[31]

The activities of the NLPAI stimulated Catholic organizational efforts in their own defense. A Committee on Catholic Interests, made up of seventeen prominent laymen, was formed to counteract the NLPAI campaign and to dissuade the constitutional convention from adopting any sweeping anti-Catholic measures. The committee, with the full co-operation of Archbishop Corrigan, sought the active assistance of every bishop in the archdiocese in organizing local Catholic

[30] *New York Times,* May 23, 24, 25, 27, 1894.
[31] King, pp. 531–33.

groups to influence the views of convention delegates. At the state level subcommittees were formed to seek out support from sympathetic non-Catholic interests, to collect statistics favorable to the existing system of public aid to sectarian charities, and to raise funds to pay for the committee's heavy expenses. From the beginning, the committee and the hierarchy seem to have judged that the charities question offered them the likeliest opening; their side of the raging school controversy was purposely played down. They also tried to avoid any appearance of belligerency lest it further excite anti-Catholic emotions.[32]

The Constitutional Convention of 1894 met at one of those points in time when a political change is in the wind. The politicians, however, were still uncertain about its real significance and its ultimate direction. Scheduled to convene in the late 1880's, the convention had been postponed from year to year until the Democrats, who were in possession of the state executive departments but not of the legislature, believed that they could control the selection of delegates. The Democratic sweep in the state legislative elections of 1892 convinced the party's leadership that the time for a convention had come. An election of delegates was called for the fall of 1893. The Republican organization was so convinced of a Democratic victory that it nominated a ticket headed by such notables as Joseph Choate and Elihu Root rather than by the usual party hacks associated with the machine of Boss Tom Platt. The Republicans hoped by this means to salvage all they could from an already unpromising situation.[33]

Much to the surprise and delight of the Republicans, their party won a smashing victory in winning 103 convention

[32] E. M. Connors, *Church-State Relationships in Education in the State of New York* (Washington, D.C., 1951), 131–32.

[33] Elihu Root, *Men and Policies: Addresses* (Cambridge, Mass., 1924), pp. 33–34; Philip Jessup, *Elihu Root* (New York, 1938), I, 173–74; *New York Times*, May 7, 1894.

seats, including all the delegates-at-large, to only 66 for the Democrats. The Republican triumph was a portent of the imminent breakup of the David B. Hill–Tammany machine which had presided over the state for several years. Republican leaders were well aware of how important their party's conduct of the constitutional convention would be for their chances to recapture the governorship from the Democrats in the fall of 1894. The convention was an opportunity to build a winning combination looking toward the November balloting. By associating themselves with the right issues, that is those with the greatest voter appeal, and avoiding the wrong ones, the GOP constitution-makers were in a position to strengthen their own party and to contribute to the fragmentation of the Democratic majority. In the spring of 1894 it seemed that these ambitions would dictate a course favoring the popular NLPAI campaign to protect the public schools and end sectarian appropriations. The NLPAI, with its many leading Republican backers, had always found a friendlier reception for its program in the GOP ranks. The Catholics, on the other hand, had little cause to rejoice. They appeared to be tied to a defeated Democratic party, which would be in the minority at the convention, by the traditional alliance of the two institutions in New York politics.[34]

The opening session of the constitutional convention was held in Albany at the state capitol on May 8. As expected, the Republican majority controlled the organization of the convention. Joseph H. Choate, the respected constitutional lawyer from New York City, was elected presiding officer. Elihu Root, then on the threshold of a remarkable career in the

[34] Jessup, I, 174; H. F. Gosnell, *Boss Platt and His New York Machine* (Chicago, 1924), ch. iii; letter, Frederick W. Holls, New York City, to Hon. John I. Gilbert, Jan. 29, 1894, Holls Papers, Columbia University. Another view of the entanglement of religion in politics in 1894 is afforded by the sharp fight to elect a Catholic to the New York Regents; Akin, pp. 49–61.

service of his party and the nation, was named floor leader by the Republican caucus. To these two men would fall the major responsibility for directing the work of the convention and for making the key political decisions. They quickly made clear their intention to provide such leadership.[35]

In his opening address to the delegates, President Choate made it quite explicit that church-state questions would occupy a leading place in the deliberations of the assembly. One of the most important issues before the convention, he said, related to "the protection, the fostering and permanent establishment of our common schools, and the discussion and perhaps the decision of that other delicate and difficult question, whether its due protection requires, and how far it requires the retention of all public moneys from all rival sectarian institutions of learning." [36]

After the opening-day ceremonies and the election of officers, the convention marked time while Choate and Root went into the country to consider the distribution of committee seats. Choate wrote to his wife, "Now I have a pretty perplexing task before me in the arrangement of the Committees on which the successful accomplishment of the real work of the Convention depends." [37] The National League for the Protection of American Institutions was equally impressed with the importance of this task. The league's chief representative at the convention, Frederick W. Holls, delegate-at-large from Westchester, was already busily at work seeking to influence the convention's leaders. Holls, a successful lawyer and a veteran party worker and campaign speaker, enjoyed the confidence of both Choate and Root. He planned to use this

[35] New York [State], *Revised Record of the Constitutional Convention of . . . 1894* (Albany, 1900), I, 7–9; *New York Tribune,* May 9, 1894; Jessup, I, 174–75.

[36] *Rev. Record,* I, 6.

[37] Letter, Joseph H. Choate, Albany, to his wife, May 10, 1894, Choate Papers, MSS. Division, Library of Congress.

advantage to secure key committee posts for the friends of the NLPAI.[38]

Through the intercession of Melvil Dewey, state librarian and devisor of the famous Dewey decimal system, Holls obtained the backing of prominent public figures for his own appointment as chairman of the Committee on Education. Professor Nicholas Murray Butler and President Seth Low of Columbia, President Jacob G. Schurman of Cornell, President James M. Taylor of Vassar, and Chauncey Depew, GOP orator and good-humor man, permitted the use of their names in Holls' behalf. In view of this support, Choate gave Holls the coveted first place on the committee that would deal with the school question.[39]

The other important assignment in which the NLPAI was interested was the chairmanship of the Committee on Charities. Holls recommended the name of Edward Lauterbach for this post to Choate. Lauterbach was a wealthy leader of the New York City Jewish community as well as a distinguished party leader in city, state, and national Republican circles. As Holls shrewdly observed to Choate, working from the assumption that the passage of an antisectarian amendment was a foregone conclusion:

> the anti-sectarian amendment will probably have to be discussed by the Committees on Education and Charities in joint session, and the Hebrews are even more largely interested than the Protestants as they get a larger proportion of public money. Mr. Lauterbach is very strongly in favor of the amendment, notwithstanding the injury it will be to the Hebrew Orphan Asylum and other Hebrew charities. His being the Chairman of one of the Committees having this matter in charge will tend to allay much of the hostility which the Hebrews might otherwise feel towards

[38] *National Cyclopedia of American Biography* (New York, 1893–1952), XI, 38.

[39] Letters, Holls, New York City, to Dewey, May 17, 1894; and Choate, Stockbridge, Mass., to Holls, May 19, 1894, Holls Papers.

the Constitution. I think, too, that the Hebrews . . . would consider it a very graceful compliment to have a permanent representative of their race at the head of that Committee.[40]

Lauterbach was given the charities assignment, but he would later prove to be a disappointing ally to Holls.

Soon after the organization of committees had been completed, the NLPAI's campaign to shape the thinking of the convention went into high gear. Early in the convention Holls had submitted the proposed amendment drafted by the NLPAI "to protect the free common schools and to prohibit all sectarian appropriations." Choate, as anticipated, referred it back to Holls and his committee for consideration. No less than eight antisectarian amendments were formally presented from the floor. They were evenly divided between those intended to protect the public schools and those proposed as a blanket prohibition on any form of public grant to sectarian institutions, whether schools or charities.[41]

The convention was inundated with petitions calling for an end to sectarian appropriations and for the preservation of the public school system. Many of these appeals were the direct results of the NLPAI's massive educational campaign throughout the state. The majority of the memorials originated with Protestant organizations. They came from the Baptists, Quakers, Congregationalists, Presbyterians, and Methodists. Petitions from citizens of New York City and Brooklyn, headed by such names as John D. and William Rockefeller, and Lyman Abbott, poured in. The faculties of Syracuse, Cornell, and Colgate Universities added their me-

[40] Letter, Holls, New York City, to Choate, May 18, 1894, Holls Papers. On Lauterbach, see also *Nat. Cyclopedia Amer. Biog.*, XXVI, 227–28; and Moses Rischin, *The Promised City: New York's Jews, 1870–1914* (Cambridge, Mass., 1962), p. 221. For the growing importance of the city Jewish vote in this period, see Rischin, ch. xi; Republican cultivation of this vote beginning in the 1890's is mentioned in *ibid.*, p. 228.

[41] *Rev. Record*, I, 25, and *passim*.

morials to the growing list. A few were the work of openly nativistic societies, like those from the state council of the American Protective Association and the American Patriotic League. Then, of course, there was the huge NLPAI petition with forty thousand signatures. It is always difficult to determine the precise effect of petition campaigns upon the thinking of elected officials; however, the great number of petitions from respectable organizations, all on one side of the question, must have suggested to the delegates that a sizable body of opinion favored the separation of church and state in the areas of public education and charitable aid.[42]

The high point in the church-state debate at the convention occurred in the joint public hearings conducted by the Committees on Education, Charities, Taxation, and Legislative Powers. Until this time the NLPAI had the field to itself, and sweeping antisectarian action by the convention seemed a near certainty. The hearings were directed to the antisectarian amendment offered by the NLPAI.[43]

The opening speaker for the amendment was Rev. James M. King, general secretary of the NLPAI.[44] King, employing the usual lobbying techniques prescribed for such situations, suggested that the league had the backing of many prominent public figures as well as "hundreds of thousands" of ordinary, public-spirited citizens. "Propriety dictates," he continued, "that I should not name any of the numerous members of the Convention who are approvers of the principles and purposes of the League."[45] After this attempt to awe the committees with a display of political strength, King launched into his argument.

[42] *Ibid.*, I, 326–29 and *passim;* King, p. 533.

[43] Stenographic reports of the joint hearings appear in Committee on Catholic Interests, *Catholic Charities and the Constitutional Convention of 1894* (New York, n.d.).

[44] *Ibid.*, arguments of June 6, pp. 3–12.

[45] *Ibid.*, p. 4.

King asserted that the hallowed principle of church-state separation was being seriously threatened by "the introduction of sectarian interests in the matter of public support of schools and charities." [46] By little stretch of the imagination it was evident that King believed the Catholic church to be the source of this threat. The NLPAI was part of a great and noble national movement to erect constitutional barriers against this most recent sectarian invasion of educational and charitable affairs. Twenty-three states now had antisectarian provisions in their constitutions, but New York, one of the first states to have proclaimed the principle of separation a century ago, had grown lax and unmindful of the danger.

"We have reached the critical and crucial period in the history of our Republic," King charged, "so far as the integrity and very existence of our free school system, the safe relation of ecclesiasticism to our civil government, and the separation of Church and State are concerned." "Cowardly compromising" and "time-serving" politicians would deny the urgent need for the antisectarian amendment, but the political threats of its opponents—again the Roman church was meant here—were proof enough of its necessity. King concluded that the citizen who objected to the NLPAI-sponsored amendment may "impeach his own patriotism." [47]

King was followed by a succession of NLPAI witnesses, all seconding the first speaker's remarks on the imminent danger to traditional church-state principles unless the antisectarian amendment was adopted, and all sounding the tocsin against the unprincipled influence of the church of Rome. Attorney William Allen Butler stated: "If the divorce of Church and State is real, let it be understood not only as a sentiment embodied . . . in a written constitution, but as a practical rule in the administration of the affairs of society." [48] William Croswell Doane, Protestant Episcopal bishop of Albany, con-

[46] *Ibid.* [47] *Ibid.*, pp. 7–9. [48] *Ibid.*, p. 14.

tended that the principle at stake "is the utter and entire separation of Church and State; and it can be done in no other way but by such a positive cleavage as now proposed." Doane believed that "it is always better to take the bull by the horns —even if it happens to be a Papal bull." [49] The burden of the day's testimony was clear. The NLPAI was taking its stand on the principle of church-state separation, following the nineteenth-century secular view that the state should cut itself off entirely from all contacts with organized religion. The various speakers had also conveyed their belief that the Catholic church was the major enemy of this patriotic ideal.

Rebuttal arguments were presented to the joint committees on June 20. A representative of Jewish charities in New York City warned against the injection of religion into politics and attacked those "who, in their pretended desire to separate Church and State, stir up the terrible fire of religious hatred." [50] He believed that the state had a responsibility for poor children which it was meeting in the best possible manner by supporting the activities of private charities. Private institutions afforded a warm and personal atmosphere that public institutions could not provide. All that was asked for was the continuation of per capita grants to cover the costs of physical care for the inmates of private asylums. Public funds never had been and never would be used for the sectarian purposes of private institutions.

The next speaker was Frederic R. Coudert, a leading New York City lawyer and Catholic layman noted for his wit and his oratorical abilities. Though a Democrat, Coudert had never been closely linked with the notoriously pro-Catholic Tammany machine in the city. No better choice could have been made to represent the Catholic point of view. Coudert rose to address a packed hall that included President Choate among the interested spectators. The calm reasonableness of

[49] *Ibid.*, p. 24. [50] *Ibid.*, arguments of Meyer Stern, June 20, p. 5.

his remarks was quite unexpected and, according to one report, left a very good impression with the politicians present.[51]

Coudert commented on the strange tendency of his opponents to range themselves in defense of the principle of church-state separation while accusing Catholics of being inimical to this ideal. No one, least of all the Catholic church, any longer disputed the correctness of this principle. Coudert then turned to the school provision in the proposed antisectarian amendment: "Let it be understood . . . that this [public school] system shall remain intact, that it shall continue nonsectarian, that public opinion will not tolerate the diversion of any public moneys from their lawful object to encourage denominational instruction. Put it, if you are so inclined, into our Constitution." The Catholics of New York would go on carrying the double burden of paying taxes for the public schools while maintaining their own parochial schools. They would do this willingly rather than "resist public opinion, and public opinion, our common master, will not permit any such distribution as has been asked for by Catholics." [52]

Coudert made it very clear that neither he nor the speaker who would follow him "is intrusted with the duty of opposing this amendment, so far as it relates to the common schools, and the arguments . . . of our friends on the other side shall not be answered by us." The church in New York had not given up its thirty-year-old view of what was right, but had decided that "Justice must sometimes wait." [53] Here was implicit evidence that Coudert spoke with the blessing of the Catholic hierarchy; only Archbishop Corrigan and his clergy were capable of making such a decision on behalf of the church.

[51] *Nat. Cyclopedia Amer. Biog.*, VI, 59–60; *New York Tribune*, June 21, 1894.

[52] Comm. on Cath. Interests, arguments of Frederic Coudert, June 20, pp. 5–6.

[53] *Ibid.*, pp. 6–7.

Coudert's fellow witness was George Bliss, Jr. Bliss, the scion of an old New England Yankee family, had been educated at Harvard and had since pursued a creditable career in the law and in the service of his country. He was a lifelong Republican. In 1884 Bliss became a convert to Catholicism and subsequently served as legal adviser to Archbishop Corrigan. His interest in honest government had recently brought him into close association with Joseph Choate and Elihu Root in a joint effort to clean up corruption in the New York County Republican organization. Bliss came before the joint committees as a tried and true Republican, speaking not to strangers but to many who were his personal friends.[54]

Bliss devoted the greater part of his remarks to the charities issue. By way of preface he stated that the seventy to eighty thousand Catholics in New York who voted Republican were preponderantly in favor of what he had to say. He also read a letter from an unnamed party, identified only as one of the highest Catholic dignitaries in the New York church, most probably Corrigan, supporting Coudert's offer on the school question. The author of the letter emphasized that since the Catholics would never compromise on anything less than full public support for their schools, and this was an unlikely development, "this disturbing element of the parochial and public schools can be eliminated from this question for to-day, if not for this generation." [55]

Bliss went on to say that "no money is taken from the State Treasury or City Treasury in aid of any denominational or ecclesiastical body . . . [or] for the dissemination of tenets of any religious body." Public aid to sectarian charities went for services actually performed, and for nothing else. "The

[54] *American Catholic Who's Who* (St. Louis, 1911), p. 39; *Lamb's Biographical Dictionary of the United States* (Boston, 1899–1903), I, 329–30; Jessup, I, 172.

[55] Comm. on Cath. Interests, arguments of George Bliss, June 20, pp. 1, 2.

money appropriated is certainly, so far as Catholic institutions are concerned, appropriated for the support of those who are in them and whom the State would have to support, if not in those institutions, then elsewhere." The system of public aid, originally begun to assist Protestant orphan asylums in 1849, was now widely accepted as humane and necessary and should not be overturned for transient reasons. "In an economical point of view it helps the State by throwing upon private benevolence a portion of the expense which otherwise would fall wholly upon the State." Bliss returned to this economy argument again and again. He also stressed the humanitarian theme: the present system of charitable grants "gives to the wards of the State the advantage of the private care—of the personal interest—which cannot be got in an institution managed by officers of the State." [56]

Taken together, the statements of Coudert and Bliss amounted to an offer of an accommodation. This was encouraging in itself, for it suggested that the conservative-dominated New York hierarchy, for whom Coudert and Bliss had been authorized to speak, was willing to submit its case to the workings of the American political process. At its best, this process supposes a mutual give and take, not a perpetual war of antithetically opposed ideologies. Here was a significant concession for a man like Corrigan, supposedly convinced of the utter antagonism between the American compromise spirit and the moral purity of a church which could admit of no compromise with a non-Catholic society.[57]

The Catholics were saying that, while in theory they could not budge from their convictions regarding the justice of state support, in practice they were prepared to accept a constitutional prohibition on any future public monetary aid to parochial schools. True, Corrigan was actually not giving

[56] *Ibid.*, pp. 4–6.

[57] See Cross, pp. 26–27, for the view of Corrigan as an uncompromising conservative.

up as much as it may have seemed. Shrewd man that he was, he probably realized that outright state aid was unthinkable under present conditions. The only recent agreements that had been possible between Catholics and non-Catholics were local school compromises like that in Poughkeepsie. But conservatives such as Corrigan and McQuaid were absolutely opposed to this liberal Catholic solution to the school question. By acquiescing in a constitutional prohibition, Corrigan was excluding the likelihood of future "Poughkeepsie Plan" arrangements in New York. In return for submitting quietly and temperately to the demands of non-Catholics on the school question, the church sought their agreement to a retention of the existing system of public aid to sectarian charities.[58]

At the final day of hearings on the antisectarian amendment, held July 11, Rev. James M. King returned to answer the testimony of Coudert and Bliss. King admitted that the compromise offer posed "a very delicate political question," but the NLPAI could not violate its principles by surrendering to any continuation of aid to sectarian charities. He appealed to the delegates to rise above mere politics and, "regardless of party considerations," adopt the antisectarian amendment.[59]

King was in reality very disturbed by the turn in events. He now informed Holls that Joseph Choate had changed his mind on "the amendment." Choate seems to have been sufficiently impressed by the arguments of Coudert and Bliss that he now believed the "other side was right" on the charities question, though he still "admitted that the schools must be protected" chiefly "because the other side were willing." King complained to Holls that Choate "does not seem to have the slightest intelligent grasp of the principles involved." Elihu Root also was having second thoughts about the NLPAI

[58] Zwierlein, pp. 147–64 *passim*, and 183.

[59] Comm. on Cath. Interests, arguments of Rev. James M. King, July 11, p. 20.

amendment. According to King, Root "stuck on the meaning of sectarian and seemed to think that the Protestants were trying to take advantage of the Catholics." [60]

What King was witnessing was the beginning of a compromise on the sectarian issues before the convention, an experience always quite disappointing and disgusting to the doctrinaire. By July 18, King was forced to acknowledge that the prospects of favorable action on the antisectarian amendment by Lauterbach's charities committee were growing dimmer with each passing day. He even feared that the convention might take no stand at all on church-state issues. King reported to Holls, "A liberal Roman Catholic priest said to me in my office yesterday that Archbishop Corrigan and his constituency (which means Tammany Hall) were already rejoicing that they had scared the Republicans and defeated the amendment." [61]

All was not lost, however. Holls' Committee on Education reported out a strong school amendment:

> Neither the state nor any sub-division thereof, shall use its property or credit or any public money, or authorize or permit either to be used, directly or indirectly, in aid or maintenance, other than for examination or inspection, of any school or institution of learning wholly or in part under the control or direction of any religious denomination or in which any denominational tenet or doctrine is taught.[62]

A second paragraph had been added by the slim majority of one in committee, and over the strongest objections from Holls, stating that the foregoing section "shall not apply to

[60] Note marked "confidential," to Holls from J.M.K., n.d., Holls Papers.

[61] Letter from J. M. King, New York City, to Holls, July 18 ,1894, Holls Papers.

[62] *Rev. Record*, V, 693; this amendment was finally adopted as sec. 4 of art. 9, Constitution of 1894. See also the letter from Holls, Albany, to King, July 23, and the reply of King, July 24, 1894, Holls Papers.

schools in institutions subject to the visitation and inspection of the State Board of Charities." The supporters of this clause did not wish the prohibition to extend to the long-standing policy of public aid to sectarian orphanages for the secular instruction of their inmates.

The final report of the education committee explained that the strict amendment proposed by the committee was the direct result of "unmistakable, widespread and urgent" demands from the people. These demands dictated that the public schools of New York "be forever protected by constitutional safeguards from all sectarian influence or interference, and that public money shall not be used, directly or indirectly, to propagate denominational tenets or doctrines." [63]

But if the NLPAI and its friends succeeded in winning their point on the school question, they lost the battle to cut off public aid to sectarian charitable institutions. The amendment presented by the Lauterbach committee proposed the continuation of existing policy:

> Nothing in this Constitution contained shall prevent the Legislature from making such provision for the education and support of the blind, the deaf and dumb, and juvenile delinquents, as to it may seem proper; or prevent any county, city, town, or village from providing for the care, support, maintenance and secular education, of inmates of orphan asylums, homes for dependent children or correctional institutions, whether under public or private control. Payments by counties, cities, towns and villages to charitable, eleemosynary, correctional and reformatory institutions, wholly or partly under private control, for care, support and maintenance, may be authorized, but shall not be required by the Legislature.[64]

The unanimous report of the charities committee gave the arrangements for public aid to private charities, first formulated by the Constitutional Commission of 1872–73, the full protection of constitutional guarantees. The committee ob-

[63] *Rev. Record*, V, 705.

[64] *Ibid.*, p. 770; later adopted as sec. 14, art. 8, Constitution of 1894.

served that, despite insistent public demands made upon it, its investigations had led to the conclusion that it would not be in the best interests of the state to apply the principle of church-state separation to charities. Charitable institutions differed from the public schools in that education was only incidental to their main function of providing shelter and care for the various dependent classes. Private, including sectarian, institutions performed a valuable and humanitarian service to society, a conclusion confirmed by committee inspections of several private asylums. They also provided facilities at greater economy to the state and local governments than would be true if the public established and maintained its own institutions. In other words, economic and human welfare considerations had prevailed over the church-state separation principle within the committee.[65]

Thus the education and charities amendments together embodied the results of an important compromise. The education amendment was the answer to widespread agitation for constitutional restrictions on any future Catholic attempts to divert public funds to parochial schools. The Catholic church went along with this. In return the convention's leaders refused to cut off the sectarian charitable institutions of the state from public grants in aid. Choate referred to the compromise as "an implied understanding before this Convention when the discussions on the subject took place in our public hearings." Elihu Root denied charges that there had been a deal; he preferred to think of it as "an honorable understanding which linked the two amendments together." [66]

The reasons for the compromise of the sectarian contro-

[65] *Rev. Record,* II, 948–55.

[66] Joseph H. Choate, *Arguments and Addresses,* ed. by F. C. Hicks (St. Paul, 1926), p. 682; Root's comment is in the *New York Tribune,* Sept. 16, 1894; also of interest is Choate's analysis of the school and charities amendments appearing in *ibid.,* Oct. 31, 1894. E. M. Connors, pp. 133, 136–37, supports the compromise view from the Catholic side; Connors' book is in part based upon a study of materials in the New York Archdiocesan Archives.

versy are readily apparent. The success of the Republican party in the fall elections was to an important measure dependent upon its having an acceptable constitution to take to the voters and which could be associated with the party's fortunes. But the dispute over church-state issues threatened to disrupt the work of the convention. If the Republican majority temporized on this question, it took the chance of estranging Protestant, anti-Catholic votes marshaled by the NLPAI. If, on the other hand, it met all the demands of the advocates of sweeping church-state separation, there was the possibility that the Catholic church would take to the field against the party in the fall. As George Bliss had pointedly reminded the delegates, there were over seventy thousand Republican Catholic votes at stake. Moreover, the votes of Jewish Republicans, whose views Edward Lauterbach represented, had to be considered. At one point midway through the convention, sectarian animosities seemed on the verge of bringing the convention to a standstill. Choate and Root referred to this as the "crisis" of the convention, and as "one of the most dangerous wounds to which a majority in a deliberative body is exposed." [67]

When the Catholics indicated that they were agreeable to a compromise, a way out of the quandary was opened up. The resulting accommodation enabled the Republicans to heal their differences. It did not please extremists, but it won the support of a majority of the GOP delegates, and ultimately of many Democrats in the convention. A settlement that placed the explosive sectarian issue beyond the reach of partisan contention was now possible.

The education and charities amendments were brought to a final vote on the last day of the convention. During the

[67] See the highly interesting letter from Holls to Melvil Dewey, Sept. 1, 1894, Holls Papers. Holls explains that once the accommodation had been reached, Choate and Root shut off further attempts to change it from the Republican side by imposing party discipline on the subject. Though not satisfied, Holls had little choice, loyal party man that he was, but to submit.

debates in the committee of the whole, the proviso clause in the education article, excluding schools in sectarian asylums from the prohibition on public aid to private schools, was deleted. The proviso was treated as an underhanded attempt to upset the understanding that had been reached on the education and charities amendments.[68] The final vote for the education article, 108 to 37, cut across party lines. The convention then turned to the charities amendment. The preceding day Choate had thrown his powerful support behind the measure in a major speech. He admitted that early in the proceedings there had been "a very decided raid made upon the Convention with the intention of preventing the payment of any public money to any sectarian institutions whatever." If the allegations made at that time were correct, the convention would have been justified in ending public aid to such institutions. But Choate had since come to the conclusion that the antisectarian campaign "was largely inspired by a sentiment with which I have no sympathy whatever, and I do not believe this Convention has—namely, a fear, a hatred for the Roman Catholic church as a religious body." [69] On the day of the voting it was understood by the delegates that the education and charities amendments were considered by the leadership to be companion measures. A move to adjourn following the adoption of the education article was shouted down, and the life of the convention was prolonged beyond the hour appointed for its adjournment to permit the passage of the charities article, through a bipartisan vote of 114 to 16 with a considerable number of abstentions. The compromise had succeeded.[70]

[68] See the forceful speeches by Choate and Root opposing the proviso clause: Choate, *Arguments*, pp. 682–86; Elihu Root, *Addresses on Government and Citizenship* (Cambridge, Mass., 1916), pp. 137–40.

[69] Comm. on Cath. Interests, quoting Choate's speech on the charities question, p. 1.

[70] *Rev. Record*, IV, 881–87; *New York Tribune*, Sept. 16, 1894.

PART FOUR

In Our Time

FROM the Constitutional Convention of 1894 to the early 1960's, church-state issues have come to be regarded by the political leadership of New York as vital matters of policy. It is seen that such issues relate to the sources of political power in the Empire State. They are in a very real sense political questions, affecting "the fashioning of coalitions of influence in an attempt to determine what values will be authoritatively implemented by government." [1] As political questions, church-state problems oblige politicians, whose fortunes are directly bound up with the resolution of these problems, to apply the delicate techniques of accommodation as an alternative to disruptive controversy.

The basically political function of seeking out, issue by

[1] Stephen K. Bailey and others, *Schoolmen and Politics: A Study of State Aid to Education in the Northeast*, Economics and Politics of Public Education Series, no. 1 (Syracuse, 1962), p. vii.

issue, some mean between the extremely practical principle of church-state separation and the equally compelling religious sentiments of a great many New Yorkers has had a stabilizing influence upon the relations of church and state in New York's recent past. It has enabled New York to move beyond the threatening phase of religious-political infighting attending the nineteenth century. And it has contributed to the settlement of church-state issues in a manner faithful to the principles and needs of a complex community short of the vicious, emotional disputation that had shaken that community in the century of Seward, Tweed, and the National League for the Protection of American Institutions.

But the early 1960's have seen the culmination of a series of developments, the effect of which has been to bring the federal government directly into the realm of church-state relations at the local and state levels to a degree never before anticipated by most Americans. The evolution of the Supreme Court of the United States as the final arbiter of church-state questions and the umpire of the electoral system, as well as the acceptance by the national executive and legislative branches of responsibilities for the education of American youths, have had, and in all likelihood will continue to have, determinative roles in the future conduct of church-state relations in New York.

X

A Working Principle

THE Constitutional Convention of 1894 represents a turning point in the relations of church and state in New York. A way to avoid the disruptive contentions of Protestants and Catholics—of strict separationists and those to whom the wall metaphor was unacceptable—became discernible in the work of that convention. It is evident in the agreement among the warring factions at the convention to submit their differences to the peaceful give and take of the political process.[1]

The compromise spirit of 1894, of which the school and

[1] For the key debates on the school and charities questions, see New York [State], *Revised Record of the Constitutional Convention of . . . 1894* (Albany, 1900), IV, 857–87. Throughout the floor debate there are numerous references to the understanding reached on the church-state problem. Edward Lauterbach, chairman of the convention Committee on Charities, said "that there has been a general understanding throughout the whole discussion that the educational article and the charities article should follow each other" (*ibid.*, p. 873). Later, he speaks of the "moral understanding" in the convention to link the two matters together (*ibid.*, pp. 876–77). Another delegate said he would not "discuss church and state, nor the educational or the charities articles, because it has been substantially agreed here that those two measures shall become laws" (*ibid.*, p. 870). The lengthy remarks of a delegate opposed to the church-state accommodation made clear his unhappiness with a "political" compromise aimed to appease "bigots" on both sides (*ibid.*, pp. 867–69).

charities amendments were the surface manifestations, was shaped almost entirely by immediate considerations. The Republican party of New York, aware that its fortunes were on the upswing, was eager to heal old partisan wounds. Its leaders in the convention, searching for winning electoral combinations, finally concluded that it would be unwise to perpetuate their party's anti-Catholic image. The continuing movement of Catholics to upstate Republican areas and the rise of the New York City Jewish community, accompanied by growing Republican support from both elements, suggested the wisdom of new approaches less antagonistic to either faith. On the other side, the Democrats were concerned over their party's reputation outside New York City as the "state church" and "Catholic" party. Confronted by gloomy prospects in the upcoming fall elections of 1894, the Democratic leadership was disposed to remove one cause of its current difficulties. As for the Catholic hierarchy in New York, content in earlier years to repose its fortunes in the friendly hands of Tammany, there was the awakening produced by the sweeping defeat of Democratic candidates for seats in the convention of 1894. If the church had not been prepared to come to some understanding with the Republican convention majority, there was a strong possibility that the organized anti-Catholic element, in and out of the convention, would have succeeded in forcing through amendments intolerable to Catholics.[2]

Sometimes political understandings tailored for a present need have a way of becoming institutionalized as passing time reveals their usefulness in dealing with recurrent and difficult situations. This has been the case with the church-state settlement hammered out in 1894 to weaken the force of sectarian animosities in the fall elections of that year. In the diverse and cosmopolitan setting of New York, it required no great in-

[2] On these points, see the treatment of the 1894 constitutional convention in Chapter 9 and nn., particularly nn. 40, 55.

sight to be aware of the continuing interplay of religious issues and the political process. At every turning there have been questions relating to education, welfare policies, marriage and divorce, where opposing points of view arising from differing sectarian beliefs came into contact and frequently into conflict.

The political leadership in the 1894 convention had sought some means of resolving differences short of the emotional religious strife of the nineteenth century. No strict application of a "wall of separation" would do, for its sweeping affirmation by anti-Catholic groups had only further embittered New York political life. This was not to say that the idea of separation had lost its usefulness as a guideline for a society of such great religious diversity as New York's. It would amount to political suicide for a political party, temporarily in control of state government, to underwrite one or a few sects where none of the three great faiths, Protestant, Catholic, and Jewish, could command a majority. On the other hand, it was difficult to deny that a large portion of New York's people believed in the continuing relevance of religion to the life of their community. They believed this so strongly that the various religious organizations with which they were affiliated were moved from time to time to claim some recognition of this relevance from government.

Given these two not very compatible but nonetheless demonstrable facts—an acceptance of the efficacy of some degree of separation between church and state as well as the existence of strong religious sentiments—a way to deal with them presented itself to the political leadership of the late 1890's. Where the major faiths felt strongly enough about a course of action and could agree on a common approach, then the state might co-operate with them as long as it was not drawn into the thicket of establishing or supporting particular denominational tenets. The path to such co-operation would be smoothed if the policy proposed could be maintained on grounds other than, or in addition to, strictly sectarian ones. In 1894 the policy of public aid to sectarian charities was justified on the grounds that these charities were meeting a public need that would exist irrespective of sectarian considerations, and thus sectarian charitable institutions were performing a vital public service. But where there was no basis for agreement among the churches, as well as considerable opposition from nonreligious groups, as there was with the issue of state support for parochial schools, the only wise and expedient recourse was to apply a strict standard of separation.

Through all this ran the implicit assumption that when a co-operative arrangement between the state and religious bodies had been worked out, there was to be no coercion of nonparticipating individuals. That would run counter to long-established ideals of religious freedom and to the reality that a considerable minority of New Yorkers was opposed to any form of church-state accommodation. Here was an instance where commitment to principle and to expediency reinforced each other to produce a generally viable result.

Working in the light of a policy at once fluid but still guided by principle and good sense, New York's leaders proceeded to apply the constitutional settlement agreed upon in 1894. The state superintendent of public instruction, employing his quasijudicial authority to resolve disputes arising in the state's school system, ordered an end to the "Poughkeepsie Plan" arrangements between school districts and Catholic parishes that had so exercised opinion in the 1880's and early 1890's. In a series of decisions from 1896 to 1902, the superintendent voided four "Poughkeepsie Plan" experiments, relying greatly upon the new section 4, article 9, of the revised Constitution of 1894 banning public support of sectarian educational institutions. A lead decision issued by State Superintendent Skinner in 1896, affecting the West Troy school district, after citing article 9, section 4, noted:

This amendment . . . has but recently been adopted by an overwhelming majority. It indicates very clearly an unmistakable and earnest desire on the part of our citizens to permanently establish and maintain a public school system that shall be entirely nonsectarian. . . . The public school system has achieved its greatest measure of success where this has been insisted upon. It is my duty, as it is the duty of the public schools in the several districts of the State, to see that the provisions of the Constitution above cited are neither directly nor indirectly violated.[3]

In striking down the public lease of a parochial school and the employment of nuns as public teachers in the city that gave the "Poughkeepsie Plan" its name, Skinner judged this arrangement to be unwise as a matter of policy as well as a "violation of the letter and spirit of the Constitution." "Our public school system," the superintendent continued, "must be conducted in such a broad and catholic spirit that Jew, and Protestant, and Catholic alike shall find therein absolutely no cause for complaint as to the exercise, directly or indirectly, of any denominational influence."[4]

When Superintendent Skinner's ruling against the use of a Catholic parish hall in Lima, New York, as a public school was taken to the state courts, the Court of Appeals in 1906 outspokenly approved the constitutionality of the 1894 prohibition on public educational ties with sectarian schools.[5] In affirming Skinner's 1902 decision in the Lima case against appellant's claim of necessity, the unanimous court held that in section 4, article 9, of the 1894 state constitution "we have

[3] T. E. Finegan, ed., *Judicial Decisions of the State Superintendent of Common Schools . . . from 1822 to 1913* (Albany, 1914), p. 552. The series of decisions referred to in the text appears at *ibid.*, pp. 538–74. In those "Poughkeepsie Plan" districts whose arrangements never came to an open test, the rule laid down by the superintendent was binding, forcing their dissolution.

[4] *Ibid.*, pp. 563–64, 567. See also E. M. Connors, *Church-State Relationships in Education in the State of New York* (Washington, D.C., 1951), pp. 118–23, and 119 n.

[5] Finegan, pp. 572–74; *O'Connor* v. *Hendrick*, 184 N.Y. 421 (1906).

the plainest possible declaration of the public policy of the state as opposed to the prevalence of sectarian influences in the public schools."[6]

Evidence of public support for the state's official efforts to enforce the 1894 prohibition on public assistance to religious schools is apparent from an incident occurring in 1901. A revised charter for the city of New York passed the legislature with a section giving the city Board of Education discretion to allot public school funds to certain "private schools" on the same terms as to the city's public schools. A public outcry followed, it being assumed that the section was meant to sneak subsidies for Catholic parochial schools into the board's budget. Members of the Charter Revision Commission, the city superintendent of schools, the mayor, the press, and the Board of Education itself all protested this attempt to subvert the clear meaning of the 1894 constitution. New York Mayor Robert A. Van Wyck used his power to veto the entire charter largely because of the offending section. The state senator who, it developed later, was responsible for inserting the provision during the legislature's review of the Charter Commission's report, found it necessary to defend his actions as an innocent desire to help struggling private charitable institutions required by law to maintain schools for their school-age inmates. This defense, of course, conveniently overlooked the fact that aid for such institutional schools was provided for elsewhere in the 1894 constitution. The legislature subsequently repassed the charter over Mayor Van Wyck's veto after having quickly and with some embarrassment amended the disputed passage to bring it into line with the state constitution and the rulings of the state's education officials.[7]

[6] 184 N.Y. 421, at 428.

[7] This episode can be followed in Connors, pp. 140–41; and in the *New York Times*, April 7–9, 14–17, 19, 23, 1901. Also see New York [State], *Laws, 1901*, ch. 466, secs. 1151, 1152.

That the principle prohibiting state aid to denominational schools had become virtually unassailable can be seen in the perfunctory manner delegate Alfred E. Smith, at the 1915 state constitutional convention, introduced an amendment from unnamed Catholic parties to repeal section 4, article 9. In an equally perfunctory fashion, without debate, the convention proceeded to bury the proposal in committee "where, by common consent, it remained buried."[8] The convention's official report to the people of the state emphasized its decision to "leave unchanged the provisions in the present Constitution" forbidding either direct or indirect public support of schools under sectarian control.[9]

Roman Catholic interests had been prepared in 1894 to give up for the time being their claims to public aid for parochial education. But their acquiescence was dependent upon a concession to them that no similar prohibitions on grants to sectarian charitable institutions would appear in the revised constitution of that year. This concession appeared as section 14, article 8, in the 1894 constitution.[10]

To be sure, the same section specified that while local subvention of private charitable institutions could be authorized by the legislature, it could not be mandated.[11] However,

[8] Connors, p. 145; New York [State], *Journal of the Constitutional Convention . . . 1915* (Albany, 1915), p. 188.

[9] *Ibid.*, p. 755. Also, New York [State], Constitutional Convention Committee, 1938, *Problems Relating to the Bill of Rights and General Welfare* (Albany, 1938), pp. 263–65; Connors, p. 145 n. Alfred Smith, later as governor, became a strong exponent of improved public education and "continually goaded the legislature into increasing the appropriations for the state's local school systems." D. M. Ellis and others, *A Short History of New York State* (Ithaca, N.Y., 1957), pp. 402–03. The same authors say of Smith: "A product of a Catholic church school on the Lower East Side of Manhattan, Smith did as much for upstate public schools as did any governor in the history of the state" (*ibid.*, p. 403). Smith's career illustrates the institutionalizing of the 1894 commitment to promote only public education.

[10] Constitution of 1894, art. 8, sec. 14. [11] *Loc. cit.*

the net effect of this last clause was to permit a continuation of the local option which most localities outside of New York City had been in possession of since at least the mid-1870's. By a statute of May 1895, the legislature overwhelmingly recorded itself in favor of the former policy by authorizing local governments to make payments to "charitable, eleemosynary, correctional and reformatory institutions" under private management.[12]

One possible hitch lay in the activities of the state Board of Charities created by the 1894 constitution. It was charged with inspecting both public and private institutions and setting minimum standards for their operation. Conceivably the board, in the hands of anti-Catholics or strict separationists, could be employed to curb sectarian charities despite the understanding of 1894. For this reason, both clerical and lay Catholic leaders were keenly interested in the composition and policies of the new body. The Catholic bishops of New York quietly proposed reliable candidates for the office of state commissioner of charities, executive head of the newly constituted organization presided over by the state Board of Charities. The bishops were particularly attentive to the political connections of their choices. Archbishop Corrigan commented to Bishop McQuaid of Rochester that "when the names are all in, some prominent layman will see Governor Morton." [13] Later, Corrigan would write to McQuaid:

> Next Tuesday there will be a meeting . . . of the State Board of Charities, when an opportunity will be given various Institutions, through their representatives, to make observations on the new rules devised for the reception and maintenance . . . of the inmates in such institutions. Mr. Gerry [director of the New York Society for the Prevention of Cruelty to Children] sent me word this morning of such meeting—suggesting that Mr. Coudert, on

[12] *Laws, 1895*, ch. 754.

[13] F. J. Zwierlein, *Letters of Archbishop Corrigan to Bishop McQuaid* (Rochester, 1946), p. 186.

account of his many good qualities and his freedom of affiliation from Tammany, would be a good representative for us. I will ask him to act for us accordingly.[14]

Mr. Coudert, of course, was the same Frederic Coudert who had presented the Catholic case to the 1894 Constitutional Convention on the school and charities questions and who had been a leading figure in the accommodation of these issues that was reached in the convention.[15]

Catholics need not have been concerned over the implementation of the 1894 charities compromise. Under the direction of the state Board of Charities, local grants to private, including sectarian, agencies were not only continued but also extensively enlarged. Under the so-called "New York system," several classes of public charges, the largest of which was dependent children, were placed in the care of private institutions, the latter being compensated from local public funds through a per capita arrangement. This, together with the legal requirement that child charges be placed where possible with agencies of the same religious faith as the parents, greatly encouraged, in the words of the historians of this subject, "the growth of sectarian institutions." [16] In 1899, the state Board of Charities could report that over four hundred private institutions and agencies were receiving public money. By 1914, New York City was appropriating funds at a rate of five million dollars annually to private welfare sources. By far the largest single category of private recipients of public charity grants were institutions conducted by one or another of the three major religious faiths. A check of thirty-eight such agencies in the city of New York on the eve of World War I revealed that twenty were operated by Catholics, fifteen were

[14] *Ibid.*, pp. 186–87.

[15] For Coudert's part in the 1894 convention, see Chapter 9 above.

[16] D. M. Schneider and Albert Deutsch, *The History of Public Welfare in New York State* (Chicago, 1938–41), II, 160; *Laws, 1875*, ch. 173, and *Laws, 1878*, ch. 404.

under Protestant management, and three were run by Jewish organizations.[17]

Attempts were made in this period to upset the policy of public support for private charities, but they were turned aside as the courts joined with other public bodies in upholding the church-state settlement that grew out of the Constitutional Convention of 1894. When the city of Brooklyn interpreted section 14 of article 8 as ending their obligations under past state laws to make payments to private welfare institutions, the Court of Appeals without a dissent ordered the city to turn over the moneys due.[18] The opinion of the court, after a masterfully concise summary of welfare developments in New York State, concluded that "it is not reasonable to suppose that the Constitution, dealing with the great subject of charities, intended to cut off the means of support upon which institutions had relied, and leave them helpless until new legislation in accordance with the new principle [of art. 8, sec. 14] should be enacted." [19]

A challenge of a different order confronted the Court of Appeals in the 1904 case of *Sargent* v. *Board of Education of Rochester*.[20] Sargent, a taxpayer, brought suit to prevent the Rochester school board from paying money to four nuns of St. Mary's Boys' Orphan Asylum. The nuns were engaged in teaching secular school subjects to the youthful inmates during regular daytime hours, while imparting religious instruction in the evenings. Counsel for the appellant argued that these payments violated article 9, section 4, of the state consti-

[17] Schneider and Deutsch, II, 133, 135, 144, 146–48, and 147 n.

[18] *People ex rel. Inebriates' Home* v. *Comptroller of Brooklyn*, 152 N.Y. 399 (1897).

[19] 152 N.Y. 399, at 408–09. The historical summary appears at 405–08. As the conclusion of the opinion makes clear, 152 N.Y. 410, in this case the court was showing great solicitude for the "aid to private charities" policy due in part to its study of the policy's history including the events of the 1894 constitutional convention.

[20] 177 N.Y. 317 (1904).

tution prohibiting aids to schools under the direction of religious organizations. A unanimous Court of Appeals refused relief to Sargent, deciding that an asylum was not a school within the terms of article 9, section 4. The orphanage, as a charitable institution, was instead subject to article 8, section 14, which plainly stated that local aids for secular education in such places could not be prohibited by the state on constitutional grounds. The court accepted the local board's contention that the nuns were being paid only for teaching secular subjects. Turning then to the convention of 1894, the state's highest appeals court observed that

> when we look into the debates on this subject in the Constitutional convention when the provisions of the Constitution already quoted were the subject of debate, it is clearly apparent that the members of that body understood that instruction in the case of orphan children detained in an asylum was neither practicable nor possible elsewhere than in the institution itself.[21]

With this decision, the charities provision of the 1894 church-state compromise was successfully upheld.

This compromise, observed and maintained by the state legislature, the Board of Charities, local authorities, and the state courts, has continued in the present century. And through it a close working relationship has grown up between public welfare officials and religious charitable organizations. Public administrators are solicitous of the views of these special clients and careful to avoid any indication of favoritism to one or another of the several denominations. When disputes develop in this field, as happened in New York City between reform Mayor John Purroy Mitchel and the state Board of Charities in 1914, both sides actively cultivate an image of interdenominational support, appealing to the sentiments and interests of Catholic, Jewish, and Protestant agencies alike.[22]

[21] 177 N.Y. 317, at 326–27.
[22] Schneider and Deutsch, II, 144–48.

When changes are sought in the welfare laws, the large associations of sectarian charitable institutions are among the first to be consulted.[23] The new public welfare law of 1929 set forth as a basic policy that "every public welfare official shall . . . cooperate whenever possible with any private agency whose object is the relief and care of persons in need or the improvement of social conditions." [24]

With the passing years, both Catholics and non-Catholics have observed the spirit of the 1894 settlement of the school and charities questions. The former, while they could not admit to any retreat from basic church doctrine concerning the primacy of religious education, have in fact made no serious effort to turn aside the constitutional prohibition of direct public aid to parochial schools. The latter, for their part, have given up any serious objections to public aid for sectarian welfare agencies.[25]

[23] See the interesting sectarian sidelights of the campaign of welfare organizations to revise the state's old poor law and replace it with a new public welfare law between 1925 and 1929; B. Zeller, *Pressure Politics in New York* (New York, 1937), pp. 144, 146, 149–50. For example, the secretary of a special welfare law revision committee of the influential state Charities Aid Association, in drawing up her plan of attack in late 1925, set down as point two of the plan: "To call together a group of persons . . . including representatives of the larger private charities, such as . . . Catholic Charities of the Archdiocese of New York, the United Hebrew Charities, and the Federation of Institutions for Protestant Children" (*ibid.*, p. 146).

[24] *Laws, 1929,* ch. 565.

[25] The most recent opportunity for a broad re-examination of the 1894 prohibition on aid to sectarian education occurred at the convention to revise the state constitution in 1938. At that time, Catholic interest in so-called "welfare" benefits for parochial children, such as bus transportation, health and welfare services, and the purchase of secular textbooks, was evident. But there was no support from church spokesmen for rescinding the 1894 prohibition. Charles J. Tobin, representing the New York State Catholic Welfare Committee and the dioceses of the state, disclaimed any desire for changes "at present in the Constitutional prohibition against State aid to denominational schools" (*New York Times,* May 19, 1938). True, the disclaimer was qualified by "at present." But to expect no qualification would be like

Not only has the policy of selective church-state accommodation been useful in carrying out the provisions of the 1894 compromise, it has also been found helpful in dealing with new problems of church and state arising in this century. Three of the more significant of these problems, all related to the education of the young, illustrate the workings of a process apparent in most areas of church-state concern in New York in our time. The three problems are the released time question, the public busing of children attending private sectarian schools, and the matter of religious observances in the public schools. Each of these offers a case study in the political methods by which a diverse, but politically sophisticated community has come to grips with some of the most difficult and potentially unsettling of contemporary church-state issues.

By World War I—and perhaps the coincidence is significant—some Americans were experiencing second thoughts about the prevailing policies of nonsectarian education in the states. Concern was being expressed over what was described as a woeful lack of religious or moral training in the public schools. It is conceivable that this concern reflected misgivings over the sweep of the latter-nineteenth-century drive to protect the public schools from the alleged menace of Catholicism.[26]

In New York, this concern about moral training led to

---

expecting the post-Stalinist Russian regime to deny the doctrine of class struggle, although its actual behavior increasingly belies that doctrine.

At the same 1938 convention, the state felt free to reauthorize public financial aid by the state to private institutions caring for dependent children, and even to underwrite health services for parochial school children. The explanation for this seems to have been that objections to direct state grants were no longer determinative. This generalization about the decline of resistance to the 1894 charitable aids policy rests in part on negative evidence: the issue simply drops out of contention. Schneider and Deutsch, II, 364–65.

[26] A. P. Stokes, *Church and State in the United States* (New York, 1950), II, 488–572, offers abundant evidence on this.

unique experiments with interfaith co-operation to cope with the problem. Co-operation was in fact facilitated by a new spirit of tolerance following the church-state understandings of 1894. In 1923 the *New York Times* found newsworthy a joint Protestant, Catholic, Jewish public appeal to the citizens of New York City urging that all the city's children be allowed the "priceless boon of religious education." While the account is incorrect in denying past instances of interdenominational co-operation, what is interesting is the sense of surprise in the *Times* reporter's comment that this was "the first time that these three faiths have ever united in a religious enterprise" in the city.[27]

If the spirit of co-operation evinced in 1923 was surprising to those out of touch with recent religious developments, the interest shown in promoting religious instruction should not have been. At the 1894 constitutional convention, the same committee reporting the amendment to prohibit sectarianism in the public school system and the expenditure of public funds to "propagate denominational tenets" assured the delegates that it was not intended thereby to "interefere with the reading of the Bible in public schools." [28] During the floor debate of the amendment, before its adoption, one of the delegates summed up what seems to have been the prevailing opinion when he said the amendment meant that "religion as a principle can be taught, not as a denominational doctrine, but as a great, broad principle that is believed by nearly all the people of the land." [29] This reflects a conviction which, despite all the difficulties it presents, would seem to be held by a large number of New Yorkers in this century as well as in the last. It reveals the root of the dilemma over religion and the public schools, what Canon Anson Phelps Stokes referred to

[27] *New York Times*, Dec. 31, 1923.

[28] New York [State] Constitutional Convention of 1894, *Documents*, doc. no. 62 (Albany, 1894), pp. 15–16.

[29] *Rev. Record, 1894*, IV, 861.

as the dual concern of Americans "that sectarianism in every form shall be kept out of our public schools; and that the schools shall not be dominated by secularism or irreligion, which would be out of keeping with the best American tradition." [30]

During the 1920's several local school districts, in response to urgings from a number of interests, began to experiment with programs to provide religious instruction for public school children in New York. Most of these involved some form of what had become known as the "released time" plan. This was the practice of releasing public school children, with parental consent, from their regular classes during one period a week to receive instruction in religion, either on or off school property, from teachers of their respective faiths. In 1927, the version entailing instruction off school grounds gained favor over other versions when it was given the unanimous approval of the New York Court of Appeals. The court saw no constitutional objection to accommodating a portion of school time to religious purposes as long as no public funds were used and the religious instruction was kept apart from the public school program.[31]

However, other variations, continuing in use in some school districts, were of questionable legality in view of the constitutional prohibition on direct or indirect public support for the teaching of sectarian doctrines. Specifically, grave doubts were raised over the admissibility of released time programs conducted in public schoolrooms.[32] It was partly to meet these objections that, in the 1930's, the state education authorities began to consider plans that would afford uniformity of practice throughout the state.

There were other inducements for a review of the problem

[30] Stokes, II, 497.

[31] *People ex rel. Lewis* v. *Graves*, 245 N.Y. 195 (1927). For a general account of released time in the United States, see Stokes, II, 525–30.

[32] *Ibid.*, pp. 498–99.

at the state level besides the question of constitutionality. In recent years religious organizations had been calling publicly for co-operation between the public schools and the churches in working out an arrangement for religious education on a state-wide basis.[33] And since 1934 "backbenchers" in the state legislature, without apparent urging from any church, had been regularly introducing bills to provide either for state aid to denominational schools or religious education through the public schools.[34] Early in 1938, as a new convention to revise the constitution prepared to meet, the activity in the legislature led educational and other civic groups to warn that there might be a renewal of the old Catholic drive to gain aid for parochial schools and that steps were required to forestall it.[35]

When a New York City delegate to the 1938 constitutional convention introduced an amendment to legalize public grants in support of parochial education, and rumors circulated of possible Republican interest in the proposal,[36] it seemed in several quarters that countersteps were necessary to protect the delicately balanced structure of amicable church-state relations in New York. Spokesmen for the Roman Catholic hierarchy proceeded to reaffirm the church's commitment to the 1894 constitutional prohibition on public support of religious schools. One of these, however, a prominent Republican and recent candidate for governor, stated that "the church believes that religious instructions for pupils should be permitted in the public schools, such instructions to be given by instructors of the same faith as the pupils instructed." [37] Public announcements such as this, and informal consultations

[33] For example, see *New York Times*, Dec. 7, 1936.

[34] Constitutional Convention Committee, 1938, *Problems*, pp. 265 and nn. 30–32, 279.

[35] *New York Times*, April 4, 1938.

[36] *Ibid.*, May 4, 1938.

[37] *Ibid.*, May 19, 1938. The quote is from William F. Bleakley, Westchester Republican, 1936 candidate for governor, and vice-chairman of the 1938 convention. The other spokesman mentioned was Charles J. Tobin (see n. 25 above).

among church and party leaders at the convention,[38] pointed to a significant demand for some type of released time program. Yet it was also clear that Catholic leaders did not desire, and non-Catholic spokesmen would not countenance, any state financing of such a program.

As various sectarian bodies moved toward an agreement on the released time form of religious instruction and indicated their willingness to work together for it, state authorities felt it possible to take part in the efforts to construct an acceptable policy. The Board of Regents, governing body of the state's educational system, became the forum for these efforts aimed at building a common platform of agreement.

It is no secret that the Regents are a political body, owing their selection to the interaction of the legislative process with educational and other interests in the state. Moreover, "it is one of the political realities of the mid-twentieth century that a balance of various religious sects and denominations is always represented in the membership of the Board of Regents." [39] With its deep commitment to maintaining a consensus of support for public education in New York, and its sensitivity to the great variety of sectarian and other viewpoints respecting public education policy, the board was well suited to decide whether or not to extend the area of church-state accommodation to encompass released time.

In the summer of 1938, the Regents received a request from the State Council of Churches, the association of the major Protestant sects in New York, and from the State Council of Catholic School Superintendents asking them to "recognize the right of all children of the state to receive religious and

[38] *New York Times,* July 24, 1938. The "representatives of the Catholic Church" mentioned, are not named; but the political leaders, all Catholics, were: William J. Wallin, regent and chairman of the convention's Committee on Education; Al Smith; and Bleakley.

[39] Stephen K. Bailey and others, *Schoolmen and Politics: A Study of State Aid to Education in the Northeast,* Economics and Politics of Public Education Series, no. 1 (Syracuse, 1962), p. 8.

moral instruction during the hours of the regular school day." The communication also called on the Regents to "require" local school districts to set up released time programs for the children of parents desiring it. Although the places where the instruction was to be given were not spelled out, the implication was that in-school instruction was preferable.[40]

This latest expression of interest in released time, from organizations representing a substantial number of the state's people, led the Regents to establish a subcommittee to study the question under the chairmanship of a distinguished board member, Owen D. Young. Even at this early stage, however, the Regents displayed their customary solicitude for those likely to be opposed to or undecided about such a program. The full board instructed its subcommittee "to report upon what further provision should be made to give this instruction, not at public expense and not within school buildings or grounds and to be given only with the consent of the parent or guardian of a child."[41]

After canvassing public thinking on the religious education proposal, a process requiring considerable time and careful attention, the Young subcommittee returned a favorable report to the Regents with the general observation that "parents had requested it." In May of 1939, the Regents "proposed" to the state commissioner of education that he draw up rules to regulate the administration of released time in local school districts. By this time it was becoming clear that the institution of released time in communities where a balance of interests opposed it would not be required. As with the Young committee, the Board of Regents set down important limits that were to guide the commissioner in formulating rules. Parents' permission was to be required, classes were to be held

[40] *New York Times*, Aug. 3, 1938.

[41] *Ibid.;* the other members of the Young subcommittee were Richard B. Woodward and Susan Brandeis, suggesting some attention to religious balance in the selection.

off school grounds, religious bodies sponsoring instruction had to be "duly constituted," and the program was not to interfere with the regular functions of the public schools.[42]

The commissioner of education, in the year between the Regents' proposal to him and the promulgation of a set of rules, appears to have consulted carefully with political leaders in Albany, religious groups, and other interested parties. One result of this further process of testing public response was the decision to obtain statutory authorization. During March 1940, the state legislature passed a bill amending the education law to allow excusing of school children from classes "for religious observance and education"; the bill was passed with remarkable speed and wide agreement among the legislators. Introduced jointly by a Republican and a Democrat, the statute was adopted by huge bipartisan majorities in both houses.[43] In signing the bill, Governor Herbert Lehman commented that the measure created nothing new in New York; it merely recognized the right of school boards to excuse students from classes if they chose to do so. Lehman also noted that a major purpose of the bill was to "assure some uniformity and permanency" to already operating released time plans, an indication that this was a matter too important to be left solely to the unguided judgments of local school officials.[44]

With this statutory backing, but only after the Regents had reviewed and approved them, the commissioner handed down

[42] *Ibid.*, May 20, 1939.

[43] *Ibid.*, March 27, 1940; such bipartisan majorities normally do not occur in the legislature unless there has been an agreement among the leaders of both party contingents, usually in concert with the governor's office. See also *ibid.*, March 28, 1940.

[44] *Ibid.*, April 10, 1940; *Laws, 1940*, ch. 305, sec. 2. Governor Lehman was under some pressure from New York City teacher and parent groups to refuse his signature; that such pressure had to be applied at this stage indicates the lack of strength of these groups at the legislative stage. See *New York Times*, March 30, 1940.

rules to govern released time in July 1940. The rules specified parental consent, sponsorship by regular religious organizations, and registration by pupils to be filed with the schools. Attendance reports of released time classes were also to go to the schools. Local school authorities were given discretion when to permit their pupils to take their released time hour each week.[45]

Some religious leaders were not entirely pleased with these rules. The State Council of Churches felt that by excluding the use of public schoolrooms, as the rules explicitly required, released time would not be practicable for large districts with scattered populations. But generally the response of sectarian and other groups was favorable, and interfaith efforts to implement the program commenced over the state.[46]

The major opposition to released time came from New York City. Here were important interests that objected, both on religious and ideological grounds, to the plan in general and to the prospect of its adoption by the city. Jewish organizations, acting with parent and teacher groups as well as other

[45] The rules appear *ibid.*, July 5, 1940; also Stokes, II, 542. The rules read as follows: "1. Absence of a pupil from school during school hours for religious observance and education to be had outside the school building and grounds will be excused upon the request in writing signed by the parent or guardian. . . . 2. The course in religious observance and education must be maintained and operated by or under the control of a duly constituted religious body or . . . bodies. 3. Pupils must be registered for the courses and a copy of the registration filed with the local public school authorities. 4. Reports of attendance of pupils . . . shall be filed with the principal or teacher at the end of each week. 5. Such absence of pupils shall not be for more than one hour each week at the close of a session at a time to be fixed by the local school authorities. 6. In the event that more than one school for religious observance and education is maintained in any district, the hour for absence . . . shall be the same for all such religious schools."

[46] Stokes, II, 542, 543–44; *New York Times*, May 15, 24, 1940.

civic organizations, protested that the plan was an infringement of the principle of church-state separation. Ranged against these critics, the principal group laboring for released time was the Greater New York Interfaith Committee, a coordinating body for Protestant, Jewish, and Catholic organizations.[47] The proponents made every effort to assure their opponents that, in the words of a spokesman for the Jewish Education Committee, "the public schools can encourage religious education without jeopardizing in any way the precious principle of separation between Church and State." [48]

Once again, as had been the case at the state level, the decision to allow released time in the city was reached only after a lengthy process of consultation and public hearings to assess the division of opinion and attempt to reduce the areas of disagreement. While the final decision of the New York City Board of Education went against the opponents of the program, the cautious sifting, weighing, and balancing by school officials and board members did result in further elaboration of the safeguards for nonparticipating children.

The rules adopted for the city schools were tailored to the requirements of the most diverse city in the state, resulting in a set of regulations which authorities believed the large majority could accept. The chief departures from the state commissioner's rules were procedures that left a good deal more of the initiative for released time and the keeping of records in the hands of sponsoring religious groups. The hour for released time instruction was set as the last hour of each Wednesday's school session; pupils receiving such instruction were to be dismissed with no responsibility by the schools other than to allow their dismissal. Administrators and public school

[47] *Ibid.*, Sept. 6, Oct. 10, 24, Nov. 14, 1940.

[48] *Ibid.*, Nov. 10, 1940; here and in the other items cited in n. 47 above the reader gets an enlightening view of the process of accommodation at work.

teachers were specifically forbidden to comment on any pupil's participation or nonparticipation in the plan.[49] Released time instruction went into operation in New York City in early 1941. With minor readjustments and with fluctuations in enrollments over the years, the program has continued to operate.[50]

From at least as early as the 1920's, New York Catholics had shared with Protestant and Jewish groups the concern over a lack of moral fiber in the public school curriculum. It had been this mutual sharing of both apprehensions and a determination to do something about them that had figured so prominently in the adoption of the released time program. But if released time was regarded by most of the state's churches as a means of keeping touch with the youthful thousands of their communicants in the public schools, the Church of Rome was also faced with additional concerns for the many Catholics attending parochial schools.

[49] The New York City regulations appear in the *New York Times*, Oct. 24, 1940. The significant modifications of the state commissioner's rules were: "1. A program for religious instruction may be initiated by any religious organization, in cooperation with the parents of the pupils concerned. There will be no announcement of any kind in the public schools relative to the program. . . . 3. Religious organizations, in cooperation with the parents, will assume full responsibility for attendance at the religious center. . . . 5. Pupils released for religious instruction will be dismissed from school in the usual way and the school authorities have no responsibility beyond that assumed in regular dismissals. 6. There shall be no comment by any principal or teacher on the attendance or non-attendance of any pupil upon religious instruction."

[50] On interfaith planning for the New York City program, see *ibid.*, Oct. 26, Nov. 18, 28, Dec. 16, 19, 1940. For the early operation of released time in New York, see *ibid.*, Feb. 5, 6, 1941; also Stokes, II, 542–43. A potentially explosive incident occurring on the first day of the New York City program, viewed by critics as a use of school property to proselytize, was handled with care and good sense, to the satisfaction of the parties involved, by the city school superintendent (*New York Times*, Feb. 6, 7, 8, 1941).

Supporting a system of denominational schools had always been difficult for Catholics ever since their first efforts to do so in the last century. Yet the basic teachings of their church commanded them to provide religious schools wherever humanly possible. Predominantly an immigrant's church in the nineteenth and early twentieth centuries, and all too often the poorer immigrants, the New York church had nonetheless struggled on since the mid-nineteenth century supporting and enlarging the parochial schools where it could. It had been not only church doctrine but also acute financial pressures that had led many Catholics to seek a way out of their quandary through requests for public subsidies after the Civil War.

Yet this expedient to which they were brought by the tenets of their church and their lowly economic condition had only served once again to stir up anti-Catholic hatreds in the community. Confronted with the dilemma of real needs leading not to relief but to an unjust and frightening anti-Catholic hysteria, the leaders of the church had come reluctantly to the decision in 1894 to give up, temporarily at least, their claims to public subvention. Better that, than to dwell in the midst of constant frictions and harassments because of their beliefs. But the 1894 acceptance of a ban upon state support for sectarian (meaning Catholic) schools did not bring escape from the money burdens, only from the gnawing, alienated uneasiness that was the lot of many American Catholics in the nineteenth century. If the relations of New York Catholics with their fellow Americans were generally easier after 1894, the necessity of carrying their own schools in addition to helping pay for the public schools in a growing society was as unsettling as ever.

On top of this came the disastrous Great Depression after 1929. Hitting the poorer classes more heavily than others, it was also bound to affect the churches of the poor. In New York State this meant the Catholic church particularly. This added plight helps to explain the renewal of demands among some of the laity in the early 1930's for the repeal of the constitutional prohibition on public aids to denominational schools.[51] This could not be the solution, however, for the majority of lay and clerical leaders who spoke for the church; they were committed to living by the agreement their predecessors had been a party to in 1894. But perhaps some alternative, acceptable to non-Catholics, might be worked out to help lighten Catholic burdens. At first tentatively, and then with more firmness, proposals were offered that government supply textbooks to parochial children, or that school bus transportation be furnished them, or that public school health and welfare services be provided to parochial school children as well.

With the advent of the New Deal and its concern for social justice and equal treatment, welfare concepts were "in the air," so to speak. Assistance to private school pupils could be, and increasingly was, justified as welfare benefits to children in need rather than as state underwriting of religion.

Of the various school proposals, those that succeeded in the 1930's were the busing of private school children at public expense and the provision for making those health services already available to public schools similarly available to children in nonpublic schools. The latter was virtually uncontroverted, being widely conceded as a humane and sensible act.[52] But busing was very controversial, at least in the beginning. The initiative for it came almost entirely from Catholics, since they alone had a major private school system, and for a time it divided them from others along old and familiar, if undesirable lines. Here was an issue seemingly quite clear-cut to non-Catholics. Standing out in front of public opinion on

[51] Constitutional Convention Committee, 1938, *Problems*, p. 265 and nn. 31–32.

[52] New York [State] Constitutional Convention, 1938, *Journal and Documents* (Albany, 1938), doc. no. 16, pp. 84–85, 91; Connors, pp. 160–61.

the school bus question, Catholics were visible in a community where such visibility could still draw fire.

Yet the Catholic position was substantial and impressive to a political system increasingly attuned since 1894 to heeding sectarian discontents before they precipitated open political warfare. Moreover, the Democratic party held the important state executive offices throughout the 1930's, and its leaders shaped the programs acted on in the legislature. As a party with a large Catholic following, it had an added incentive for listening with careful attention to the Catholic bus suggestions. Republicans, a majority in the legislature much of the time, could not be outshone, given the operational nature of gubernatorial politics in New York. They, too, contributed support to the Catholic cause. In 1935, the Senate and Assembly passed by wide margins a bill mandating busing for private school children in districts where school buses were provided for public school children.[53]

Governor Herbert Lehman proceeded to veto the 1935 measure, which was soon being referred to as the "Catholic bus" bill. Lehman contended that the bill was contrary to "the public policy of the State," since it ordered the spending of public funds to benefit students attending private, more particularly sectarian, schools.[54] The veto immediately drew fire from Catholic groups. The *Tablet*, weekly organ of the diocese of Brooklyn, complained of the governor's arbitrary disposal of a measure which had broad support in the legislature. Later, the Supreme Council of the Knights of Columbus, meeting in annual convention in New York City, unanimously resolved that the Lehman veto had been "unwise, unfair, unjust," in view of the hardships encountered by Catholic children attending church schools.[55]

[53] The political system and its relation to church-state matters is dealt with at length below. For the 1935 bus bill, see *New York Times*, May 7, 1935.

[54] *Ibid.*, May 7, 12, 1935.

[55] *Ibid.*, May 12, Aug. 23, 1935.

In the 1936 session of the legislature, against a continuing drumfire of criticism leveled at the Lehman veto, the "Catholic bus" bill was resurrected. This time, it was modified to avoid the appearance of a direct order by specifying referenda on the proposition in local school districts. Obviously, this method would mean in practice that districts with significant Catholic populations would probably accept busing, while those with fewer Catholics would not. In the process, parochial schools with the more acute busing problems would likely be taken care of first. As in the previous session, the new bus bill passed easily with bipartisan support. In the Senate, before adoption of the measure without dissent, Republicans sought to make political capital in an election year by heaping abuse on Lehman for his earlier bus veto. Of doubtful utility as tactics, the Republican performance still reveals just how broad the support from both the major parties was for the bus measure. Shortly after, Governor Lehman changed his mind and signed the 1936 bus bill into law.[56]

Initiated in the fall of 1936, the busing of private school children operated until the spring of 1938. At that time, a suit which had been working its way up through the courts was finally decided by the Court of Appeals in a narrow four-to-three holding. The court majority voided the 1936 bus law as a violation of the ban in article 9, section 4, of the state constitution against direct or indirect public aid to denominational schools. This ruling, however, was destined to be short-lived. At the time the bus decision was handed down, the 1938 convention to review and revise the state constitution had convened in Albany. A move began in the convention to write authorization for the busing of private school children into the constitution itself. Rumors spread that Chief Judge Frederick E. Crane of the Court of Appeals, author of the dissenting opinion in the bus case, intended to use his influ-

[56] *Ibid.*, April 24, 29, May 14, 1936; *Laws, 1936*, ch. 541.

ence as presiding officer of the convention to undo the injustice that he believed resulted from the court's ruling.[57]

The Constitutional Convention of 1938 ultimately did amend the constitution to allow busing of private school children. Its vote exemplifies the ability of an aggrieved interest, with a substantial claim, to achieve a favorable access to decision-making centers on a church-state matter in this century. Convention delegates, fearing a revival of Catholic demands for outright aid to parochial schools as such and the conflict and bitterness that would surely follow, seemed inclined to accept the lesser and potentially more practicable request for busing. This held true for Catholic and non-Catholic delegates alike, for leaders from as disparate backgrounds as Chief Judge Crane of the Court of Appeals and Al Smith; they were prepared to consider and to grant relief where it could possibly strengthen rather than upset working church-state principles. On the day after the Court of Appeals decision voiding the 1936 bus law, school bus amendments were sponsored by State Attorney General John J. Bennett, Jr.; New York City Democratic Assembly leader Irwin Steingut; and state Supreme Court Judge Charles Poletti. Considerable backing from outside the convention was given by the New York Council of the Knights of Columbus, the National Catholic Alumni Federation, the New York State Catholic Welfare Committee, and disinterested citizens alarmed by the prospect of Catholic school children walking alone and untended on the highways of rural and suburban areas. Opposition to the amendment, led by the Protestant State Council of Churches and the State School Boards Association, never successfully marshaled itself in the convention.[58]

[57] *Judd* v. *Board of Education*, 278 N.Y. 200 (1938); *New York Times*, May 25, 1938.

[58] *Ibid.*, May 26, July 24, 1938; V. A. O'Rourke and D. W. Campbell, *Constitution-Making in a Democracy: Theory and Practice in New York State* (Baltimore, 1943), pp. 157–59, 161–62 and 162 n. 6,

A month later, the amendment was favorably reported from the Committee on Education chaired by William J. Wallin, vice-chancellor of the New York State Board of Regents and a prominent Catholic layman. The measure would add to the 1894 provision prohibiting public aid to religion, now to become section 4 of article 11, a closing phrase stating that "the legislature may provide for the transportation of children to and from any school or institution of learning." [59] Delegate Wallin assured the convention that the amendment in no way would affect the constitutional prohibition on grants to schools under the control of religious denominations. It would merely exclude bus transportation for children attending private schools from the general prohibition, as the opinion of the executive and legislative branches had been shown to favor. The proposal was then passed to a third reading with no objection from the floor. A week later, the assembled delegates formally approved the bus amendment by a vote of 135 to 9 to the satisfaction of leaders from both the major parties.[60] The prediction of a newspaper reporter that passage would put an end to a lengthy controversy "which has agitated members of the Legislature, figured in a recent political campaign, and was the cause of litigation through the Court of Appeals" seemed to have been borne out in the vote.[61]

The constitutional convention's adoption of the school bus amendment signaled the opening of a spirited contest among

---

pp. 189–90. The reference to humanitarian support for the bus amendment is based upon conversations with Prof. Arthur E. Sutherland, Jr., of Harvard Law School; as a young upstate lawyer, Sutherland sat as a delegate in the 1938 convention and headed a drafting group to frame proposals.

[59] *New York Times*, June 29, 1938; Constitution of 1938, art. 11, sec. 4 (after Nov. 6, 1962, this became art. 11, sec. 3).

[60] New York [State] Constitutional Convention, 1938, *Revised Record* (Albany, 1938), II, 1055–56, 1597–98; *New York Times*, July 28, 1938.

[61] *Ibid.*, July 19, 1938.

interested groups in the state. Since the convention proposal would go into effect only if approved by the voters in the fall elections of 1938, vigorous campaigns were launched to persuade the electorate to favor or to turn back the bus measure. Joining the Catholic organizations active since before the 1938 convention, were clergymen whose voices were heard for the first time urging adoption of the proposal. Monsignor J. Francis A. McIntyre, chancellor of the archdiocese of New York, asked Catholics to support Proposition One carrying the bus provision. He remarked that he felt justified in advising the public on a controversial political matter solely for "educational" purposes. A letter from Bishop Stephen J. Donahue, administrator of the New York archdiocese, recommending passage of the proposition containing the bus amendment along with several other propositions, was read in the Catholic churches of the archdiocese and of the diocese of Brooklyn on the Sunday before election day. Monsignor McIntyre reported that he believed similar efforts to inform Catholics were being made elsewhere in the state.[62]

Opposing the bus provision as a violation of the principle of church-state separation was a series of groups none of which seem to have been very active during the convention. They appear to have waited too long to register their views, or else to have concluded from the start that they had little chance of prevailing with the convention delegates. Included among them were organizations of Evangelical Lutheran ministers and of Baptist clergymen. Bishop William Manning registered opposition as a spokesman for Episcopalians, while the American Civil Liberties Union appealed to civil libertarians to vote the proposition down. Of interest for their absence from among the opposition or for their silence in public were the majority of the major Protestant faiths forming the influential State Council of Churches; by then the council seems to have lost much of the zeal of its earlier resistance to the bus amend-

[62] *Ibid.*, Oct. 13, Nov. 7, 1938.

ment. Also, leading Jewish religious associations were relatively quiet; many of these, however, conducted religious schools whose students would receive public bus transportation if the amendment was successful.[63]

The school bus provision had the advantage of appearing on the ballot as part of Proposition One. This was an omnibus proposition containing many of the major revisions submitted to the people by the convention of 1938. A vote against the school bus provision would therefore be a vote against the entire proposition. For this reason, but also because of a commitment to moderation on church-state issues, Proposition One had the backing of both gubernatorial candidates in 1938, Lehman and Thomas E. Dewey, and of both major parties. Dewey specifically urged support of free transportation for private school children.[64]

On election day, Proposition One was approved by a margin of over 200,000 votes in a total vote on the proposition of approximately 2,700,000. In New York City, the majority for it was 184,000; upstaters gave it an edge of 34,000. While it is impossible to state that Catholic support for busing carried the proposition, it is also impossible to conclude that it did not. The narrow but favorable upstate margin is of interest, since the amendment's supporters had feared a great outpouring of negative votes there that would very likely have overcome the anticipated margin of approval in heavily Catholic New York City. The upstate counties most strongly in favor of Proposition One were either urban counties with large Catholic populations such as Erie, Monroe, Onondaga, and Albany, or rural counties of the northern tier such as Franklin and Essex with their French Canadian voters.[65]

[63] *Ibid.*, Oct. 11, 12, Nov. 3, 1938; O'Rourke and Campbell, pp. 225–26.

[64] *Ibid.; New York Times*, Nov. 6, 1938.

[65] *Ibid.*, Nov. 10, 11, 13, 1938; O'Rourke and Campbell, pp. 245–46, and charts, pp. 243 and 241.

In the 1939 session of the state legislature, on recommendation from Governor Lehman, the legislators proceeded to implement the new constitutional mandate. There was broad support from both major parties for a school bus bill; large majorities in each house, with very little dissent, passed the school bus measure in May 1939. Governor Lehman promptly signed it into law.[66]

The newly adopted statute authorized the state commissioner of education to require districts to pay the cost of busing nonpublic school children if it could be shown either that there was great "remoteness of the school to the pupil or for the promotion of the best interests of such children." The choice of providing busing for such children lay first with the boards or voters of local school districts. But there were also procedures by which parents or taxpayers could appeal from adverse local votes to the state commissioner. The commissioner issued the definitive ruling on the bus law in August 1939. Acting Commissioner Ernest Cole ruled that the statute made performance by local school authorities obligatory "notwithstanding that undue hardship, financial or otherwise, results to the district." [67] The state Education Department has not departed from this basic position since then. After the Supreme Court of the United States approved a similar bus law in the Everson case, a decision applying to the busing of parochial students in New Jersey, public transportation of private school pupils became a fixture in New York. There is still sporadic resistance from school districts, but significant opposition has declined considerably. In fact, the matter has become a kind of routine where non-Catholic voters at annual

[66] *New York Times,* Jan. 5, 25, 26, Feb. 13, April 27, May 3, 4, 17, 1939.

[67] *Laws, 1939,* ch. 465; for the commissioner's ruling in an appeal affecting a request by Catholic parents for busing of their children, denied by a school district vote in the town of Southampton, Suffolk County, see *New York Times,* Aug. 29, 1939.

school budget meetings have the satisfaction of voting down their boards' proposals to finance bus transportation for parochial students, only to have the results of the vote reversed by what is a virtually automatic order from the state education commissioner in Albany.[68]

The case of the Regents Prayer was somewhat different in its origins than the released time or school busing questions. Initiative for the prayer came not from religious groups, but from the New York State Board of Regents. Only after its issuance did the process of accommodation actively come into play. And once that process had worked its way, the results were rather meager to justify the problems that had arisen. For this involved a prayer, a religious exercise to be performed in public school classrooms. From the beginning it aroused old fears and suspicions of using the schools to indoctrinate children.

On November 30, 1951, the Board of Regents, composed of Protestant, Catholic, and Jewish members, unanimously recommended that the school day be opened with a "brief non-denominational prayer." In an accompanying policy statement, the Regents suggested that the prayer be linked with school programs "stressing the moral and spiritual heritage which is America's." As the statement explained:

> We believe that thus constantly confronted with the basic truth of their existence and inspired by the example of their ancestors, our children will find all their studies brought into focus and accord, respect for lawful authority and obedience to law will be the natural concomitant of their growth, and each of

[68] *Everson* v. *Board of Education,* 330 U.S. 1 (1947); for an instance of how busing has become so institutionalized that it is extended by virtually automatic action of the legislature, see the story of the 1960 bus amendment in *New York Times,* Feb. 6, Mar. 5, 10, 21, 23, 24, May 2, 1960. Also see *ibid.,* July 15, 1961, for a court dismissal of a suit to enjoin implementation of the amendment; and *Laws, 1960,* ch. 1074.

them will be properly prepared to follow the faith of his or her father, as he or she receives the same at mother's knee, by father's side, and as such faith is expounded and strengthened for them by his or her religious leaders.

The prayer itself, to be recited at the start of each school day in conjunction with the pledge of allegiance to the flag, was short and general: "Almighty God, we acknowledge our dependence upon Thee, and we beg Thy blessings upon us, our parents, our teachers and our Country." [69]

The sources of the Regents decision lay both in a general, long-term concern and in a set of more immediate circumstances. Generally, the prayer must be viewed as another in the series of responses to the long-standing belief of some that the schools should be doing more to inculcate reverence and morality; the released time program had been another similar response over a decade earlier. But there were also immediate considerations involved, as the evidence of the Regents policy statement itself suggests. The year 1951 found America engaged in a bitter cold war with the Soviet bloc and in a grim hot war with Red China in Korea. It was the beginning of the McCarthy era, a time when loyalties were no longer taken for granted but were being questioned, a day when Americans were being asked to reaffirm their faith. From all sides came appeals for action to strengthen the nation's moral armor against the anticipated lengthy struggle ahead with a menacing, atheistic communism. The Regents stated:

We are convinced that this fundamental belief and dependence of the American—always a religious—people is the best security against the dangers of these difficult days. In our opinion, the securing of the peace and safety of our country and our state against such dangers points to the essentiality of teaching our children . . . that Almighty God is their Creator, and that by

[69] Quotations from the Regents statement are from the text in the *New York Times*, Dec. 1, 1951.

Him they have been endowed with their inalienable rights to life, liberty and the pursuit of happiness.[70]

Beset by foreign perils, the United States of the early 1950's seemed also to be weakening within. There were the espionage cases and loyalty investigations, the "Truman scandals," lurid revelations of errors in high places, and rising crime rates. Some were discovering what should have been obvious to them for a long time, that the American family was no longer the cohesive basic unit of social control that it once had been. The schools along with other institutions were coming in for their share of blame for permitting these shameful developments. The Regents proclaimed that through their recommended program of training in American values the public school would once more be fulfilling "its high function of supplementing the training of the home, ever intensifying in the child that love for God, for parents, for home which is the mark of true character training and the sure guarantee of a country's welfare." [71]

But despite the sense of compelling need that lay behind the prayer statement, the customary restraints operating in the realm of church-state relations were evident in the announced scope of the Regents proposal. The *New York Times* referred to the comment of an official in the state Education Department that the Regents "recommendation in no way could be considered a mandate upon the schools" and to his emphasis on the point that "individual school boards would make the final decision." This was clearly to be a case of local option. As the *Times* noted, "The statement of policy is expected to cause repercussions from some groups who op-

[70] The quotation in this paragraph is from *ibid.*

[71] See n. 69 above; Eric Goldman's light, popular account, *The Crucial Decade: America, 1945–1955* (New York, 1956), succeeds in recapturing the moods, confusions, and alarms of that upset time. It suggests the tense environment within which the Regents acted.

pose formal prayers in the schools."[72] Of this, the Regents were certainly among the first to be aware. Conceivably the prayer itself was an effort to ward off the witch hunting of superpatriots from the New York schools, while necessarily pitching the prayer program in as low a key as possible to escape the wrath of advocates of a strict separation between church and state.

The public reaction to the Regents Prayer was pronounced and divided. It reveals what was becoming a characteristic grouping of interests on church-state issues in New York. Generally, groups and individuals that would probably be classed in the parlance of our day as "establishment" interests approved the Regents statement. Opposed were organizations and individuals representing minority or liberal points of view. In the first category were political leaders, school administrators, and prominent clergymen of well-established sects or churches. In the second, were parents from areas of heterogeneous ethnic and religious composition, spokesmen for Jewish groups invariably suspicious of policies that might excite religious differences, ministers of liberal congregations, all voicing their disapproval of the prayer.

Governor Thomas E. Dewey praised the prayer, viewing it as a positive step in the international East-West struggle for men's minds. The Protestant Episcopal bishop of western New York endorsed the prayer as significant for "the times." Maximilian Moss, president of the New York City Board of Education, called the prayer a "refreshing answer" to charges that the public schools were ungodly. Norman Vincent Peale expressed his approval in a statement urging that letters of support be sent to the governor and to New York City school officials. Dr. Clarence W. Hall, editor of *The Christian Herald*, upheld the prayer in a speech to the annual meeting of the Manhattan division, Protestant Council of New York City. In

[72] *New York Times*, Dec. 1, 1951.

a formal public announcement, Monsignor John S. Middleton, a secretary for education of the New York archdiocese, endorsed the Regents Prayer. The State Association of Secondary School Principals and the Directors of the New York State School Boards Association adopted resolutions of approval, the latter advising their member boards to adopt the prayer.[73]

Favorable in principle, but questioning the form in which the prayer was presented, was a resolution from the Association of Reformed Rabbis in New York City. The substance of the prayer was acceptable to the association, but serious questions were raised by the fact that its content was "specified." Rabbi Julius Marks, senior rabbi of Temple Emanu-El in the city, stated that no Protestant, Catholic, or Jew could possibly object to the prayer, but he asked that the governor appoint a three-member interfaith committee to pass on any future school prayers.[74]

Highly vocal disapproval of the Regents Prayer came from the United Parents Association, a New York City organization claiming to speak for 235,000 parents of city school children. Nine hundred delegates of the UPA voted with but one dissenting voice against the prayer as injecting sectarian differences into a public school system marked by great religious diversity. The UPA president, Mrs. Ruth Farbman, said that prayers should not be recited by youthful pupils who "do not even understand the words." The Liberal Ministers Club of New York City objected to the prayer, stating that the home and the church were the proper places for such observances. An organization representing orthodox, conservative, and reform Jewish opinion, the New York Board of Rabbis, expressed fears that the prayer would introduce sectarianism into the public schools. Both the American Civil Liberties Union and its New York chapter opposed the school prayer

[73] *Ibid.*, Dec. 1, 3, 4, 12, 14, 1951; Jan. 7, 1952.
[74] *Ibid.*, Dec. 9, 15, 1951.

as falling under the ban on establishments in the First Amendment to the Constitution of the United States.[75]

As local school systems had time to react, it became clear that only a minority of them chose to adopt the Regents Prayer. Mainly, these were districts in smaller upstate communities where Protestant, occasionally aligned with Catholic, interests exerted some influence. Larger districts in urban areas were often chary of the consequences and tended to avoid having to make any decision about it. A newspaper survey in the autumn of 1952 found that "many education board members and school superintendents . . . throughout the state regard the prayer as a 'hot potato' and have steered clear of the issue, because of vigorous opposition from some segments of the community." Dr. James E. Allen, then deputy state commissioner of education, reported that while exact statistics were unavailable since the prayer had only been recommended and not mandated, he believed that about three hundred of the state's three thousand school districts were using it. Many of these were in rural areas.[76]

New York City, where opposition to adopting the prayer was very strong, demonstrates the process of give and take at work in an extremely divided setting. The city Board of Education was confronted on one side with demands that the prayer be adopted. Others argued for some more acceptable alternative. On other sides were groups adamantly averse either to the prayer alone, or to any kind of religious exercise. Rather than rush precipitately into a hasty and perhaps unwise decision, the board postponed action for several weeks while it investigated the situation. Given the spread of views on the issue, a way out eventually presented itself. Arthur Levitt, at that time a member of the Board of Education from Brooklyn, proposed what in time became the basis for the final settlement. He suggested that city school children begin

[75] *Ibid.*, Dec. 3, 10, 12, 1951; Jan. 9, 1952. [76] *Ibid.*, Oct. 12, 1952.

the day by reciting the familiar first stanza of the popular song "America," and the fourth stanza which reads:

> Our father's God! to Thee,
> Author of liberty,
> To Thee we sing:
> Long may our land be bright
> With freedom's holy light;
> Protect us by Thy might,
> Great God, our King!

Levitt believed that this substitution would end the "simmering" dispute over the Regents Prayer, while still not compromising the objectives for which the Regents had recommended the prayer.[77]

An interfaith committee formed to look into the matter, including representatives from the Catholic archdiocese, the Board of Rabbis, and the Protestant Council, was brought around to accept the Levitt substitute. It was during this stage that the Board of Education's Committee on Instructional Affairs came up with a further modification of the Levitt proposal that eventually would figure decisively in the final determination of the controversy. The committee suggested that the stanzas of "America" be sung instead of recited.

At an excited public hearing conducted by the Board of Education in late November 1952, two hours of testimony revealed that the only possible consensus on religious observance—and that a narrow one—lay with the modified Levitt formula. Groups as far apart as the Catholic Lay Organizations of the Archdiocese of New York and the United Parents Association were able to find some common ground here. The former said that it preferred the Regents Prayer but that use of the fourth stanza of "America" was an acceptable substitute. A spokesman for the UPA agreed to the substitute, although insisting that the exercise not be made mandatory. In

[77] *Ibid.*, Oct. 22, 27, 31, Nov. 3, 1952.

early 1953, the New York Board of Education after careful deliberation finally and unanimously voted to order the singing of the fourth stanza of "America" in the city schools "as an act of reverence intended to help strengthen moral and spiritual values." The board explained that it was not including the first stanza in its directive because it amounted to a mere "patriotic" duplication of what was already served by the flag pledge.[78] In this fashion, the prayer issue was resolved in New York City through the construction of a formula that could be lived with both by many of those who desired religious exercises in the schools, and by many others to whom the original Regents recommendation had been completely unacceptable.[79]

The process of maintaining a continuously functioning balance in the relations of church and state, observable in recent New York history, is sufficiently important to attempt a summary of its most prominent normative features. As the term balance implies, the task is one of striking a mean between two equally compelling principles: the conviction that the peace of the state and the freedom of private religious and other groups are best served by some degree of separation

[78] *Ibid.*, Oct. 25, Nov. 21, Dec. 19, 1952; Jan. 16, 1953.

[79] New York City's experience should be contrasted with that of the Herricks School District of New Hyde Park, Long Island. The school board there, with apparently little effort to weigh the possible repercussions, adopted the Regents Prayer in July 1958. Even before the prayer was recited, elements in the district had contacted the American Civil Liberties Union to initiate a test case, this in itself suggesting the rather poor relations between the board and certain groups in the community during the process of deciding to adopt the prayer. The suit ultimately reached the Supreme Court of the United States in the landmark case of *Engel* v. *Vitale*, 370 U.S. 421 (1962), which struck down the Regents Prayer as violating the disestablishment clause of the First Amendment. The background of *Engel* was vividly presented in CBS Television's March 13, 1963, program, "Storm Over The Supreme Court, Part II: The School Prayer Case," tape and transcript on file, CBS News, New York City.

between the primary functions of the state and of the churches; and the belief that religious faith is so private a matter to the individual that it is best for all that the state guarantee it from interference by itself or by others. But what is not often adequately appreciated is that these principles have a way of overlapping in practice so that what may seem to some an acceptable degree of separation is regarded by others as an infringement upon their free exercise of religion. It is at these points, where conflict may develop, that church-state questions become problems for the politician.[80]

When the politician is in a position to affect the balance on specific issues, he often finds himself under pressure to do so. This is particularly the case where, as one student has put it, "the diversified and cosmopolitan character of the population of New York not only makes for more varieties of viewpoint, but has led to a sensitivity among the various religious, racial, and ethnic groups to the way in which public policy . . . affects their interests." [81]

Suffice it to say that the politician is not a free agent in this job of striking balances; his efforts are circumscribed by certain more or less clear principles. Yet neither do principles free him from having to use the arts of compromise. New Yorkers who hold strong convictions about the relations of church and state are also likely to be voters. And as voters, their choices may be influenced by how closely they judge political performance to conform to their convictions. This would pose few problems for the politician if an overwhelming majority of his constituency favored either a very close

[80] When I use the word "politician," I intend it in the broad sense of the term "politics" for which a working definition was offered in the introduction to Part Four above, drawn from Bailey and others, p. vii. In this sense, a politician may be a party functionary or elected official —as the term usually denotes—or a school administrator; in short, a person engaged in constructing "coalitions of influence . . . to determine" public policy (*ibid.*).

[81] L. K. Caldwell, *The Government and Administration of New York* (New York, 1954), p. 335.

alliance of the state with religion or no contact whatsoever. But this has never been the case in New York; both extremes are in practice closed to him. Instead, he is confronted with a broad spectrum of opinions ranging between these extremes but never quite forsaking either. Given this situation, and the contemporary tendency to prefer amity over enmity in church-state relations, the politician is obliged to strive for accommodations among competing views of policy. It is his fate to play the broker's role in a society where most accept the relevance both of the separation ideal and of religious tradition and sentiment [82] to public life, and yet continue to believe that the two are not incompatible.

How then does the politician perform the feat of making compatible what many logical men think is incompatible? There are no hard and fast rules. Yet by the lessons of New York's past, he has learned the wisdom of leaving the overtures for accommodation to private groups. This immediately excludes a wide range of problems, because there are issues about which even sectarians of good will cannot possibly agree.[83] These can be consigned to the reach of the separation principle. Conversely, there are practices deemed so harmless or useful to most as not to occasion much controversy at all.[84]

[82] By "religious sentiment" is meant religion in the broad "God of our Fathers," or "nondenominational" sense. Whether one agrees or disagrees with this sentiment, a great many New Yorkers would seem to be convinced that religion has not been and is not a negative force in public life, and that—by reciting the Regents Prayer or the words "under God" in the flag pledge—they are reaffirming their faith much as the flag pledge reaffirms faith in the nation. To fail to appreciate this, to confuse it with a narrow, misdirected religiosity or dismiss it as delusion, is to lose sight of a crucial influence in shaping contemporary attitudes on church-state relations.

[83] Examples would be government subsidies for church operating funds or for sectarian school budgets.

[84] Such practices as tax exemption of church property and the provision at public expense of chaplains for penal institutions and legislative chambers would fit this category.

It is the problems arising in between that create so much difficulty. And in this century so many of them seem to center around the education of the young. As the accounts of released time and school busing suggest, once a strongly expressed desire for some *modus vivendi* between government and religion is made known to the politician, normal caution requires him to sound out possible sources of opposition. If anticipated opposition does not appear to be strong enough to veto any such proposal outright, the next step is to formulate a tentative statement of policy in concert with the involved groups. At this point soundings of opinion are again taken. If called for, further modifications are made in the proposed policy and it is determined whether it will operate statewide or through local option, whether as a mandate or merely as a recommendation. The diversity of New York between upstate and downstate, and even between community and community in the same region, is so great that normally the choice is for local option and voluntary compliance by individuals, but with oversight and control of appeals retained by the state. Along each step of the way, special efforts are made to detect and remove any implication of coercion and any possible source of embarrassment to objecting minorities, for the situation in New York is such that offended religious minorities can frequently punish the heedless politician at the polls.[85]

By such means as these, by the give and take of the democratic process, viable relationships on church-state issues have been achieved. It is of course true that at times certain of the steps in this process have been slighted or deliberately evaded; the origination of the Regents Prayer was one such instance. The Regents reacted before there had been any clear expression of interest from the community, before possible consequences had been fully assessed. The checks in the system,

[85] Warren Moscow, *Politics in the Empire State* (New York, 1948), p. 22.

however, have been effective in preventing most such mistakes from getting by.

Repeated allusions have been made to the shaping influence of New York politics upon the treatment of church-state issues in this century. It is this political framework, a product of history, habit, and diversity, which at once gives rise to demands upon government for recognition of religious sentiments and to pressures for settling clashes of principle and opinion in a peaceable fashion. Because this framework is so determinative, it requires special consideration.

A basic fact of New York political life into the 1960's was the practical impossibility of the Democratic party electing a majority in the state legislature save for those rare occasions when a major contest over personalities or policies, usually generated at the national level, upset established voting habits. This situation dated back to an apportionment scheme written into the state constitution by the Republicans in 1894 and maintained in its essentials until the intervention of the federal courts brought about reapportionment in the middle 1960's.[86]

This fact of legislative politics determined that meaningful interparty competition could only be achieved through contests for statewide office, particularly for the office of governor.[87] Such competition has been keen because New York voters have tended to identify themselves more closely with the two major parties than have the people of other states, and because the total votes cast in general state elections have often been narrowly divided between the two parties.

The importance of what could be called gubernatorial politics in New York[88] has also been conditioned by the power of

[86] O'Rourke and Campbell, p. 66; F. J. Munger and R. A. Straetz, *New York Politics* (New York, 1960), p. 61. On reapportionment in New York, see R. B. McKay, *Reapportionment: The Law and Politics of Equal Representation* (New York, 1965), pp. 380–90.

[87] Munger and Straetz, p. 61.

[88] Moscow, p. 12; Munger and Straetz, p. 58.

the governor in the state and nation. The chief officer of the Empire State is in a position to wield tremendous personal influence inside the state, while the population and party regularity of New York have qualified him for a major role in the presidential politics of his party nationally. The Democratic party in New York has had an added incentive to control the governorship. While normally it could not hope to win majorities in the legislature, the 1894 apportionment system did virtually guarantee it a large minority representation in each house. This minority bloc, given the comparatively tight party discipline in the legislature, has been sufficient to render the Republican majority powerless to override opposition gubernatorial vetoes. The enhanced status of a Democratic governor, through the constant implied threat of the veto, has been an important counterweight to the legislative position of the Republicans. Some of the best government in the last half century has occurred with Democrats in the governor's office, since this required serious interparty negotiation if anything at all was to be accomplished.[89]

Another feature of New York politics in this period must be grasped if there is to be any comprehension of the pressures on the two parties to provide responsive and responsible government. This has turned on a geographical polarization of party voting strength. The Democrats have had a substantial majority in New York City, while upstate—meaning areas outside of the city—normally has given an edge to the Republicans. Because populations upstate and down were roughly comparable, "save in the rarest of rare occasions, the election outcome . . . [was] determined by which margin . . . [was] the larger."[90] What this meant in statewide elections was that each party not only had to be attentive to the needs of the voters in their home base, but had also to reduce the margins of its opponent in that party's home base. Republi-

[89] Moscow, pp. 168–69.
[90] Munger and Straetz, p. 39.

cans have had to keep the electorate upstate reasonably satisfied, but not at the cost of alienating New York City support in any broad fashion. On the other hand, the Democrats have had not only to maintain their wide electoral edge in New York City, but also try to win more votes upstate.[91] As one astute journalist described this phenomenon: "Both parties have developed a sense of state-wide responsibility. They know they have to run their candidates [for state executive office] in Yonkers as well as Penn Yan, in Syracuse as well as Canarsie." This same observer of the New York political scene concluded that "the result is a democracy calculated to do the most good for and secure the most votes of the greatest number of people." [92]

It may be asked legitimately at this point just what all this has to do with church-state relations in New York. The answer is implicit in the size and distribution of the major religious denominations across the state. While Catholics are found throughout New York, perhaps half of them reside in New York City. Protestants, although a goodly minority in the metropolis, have had their greatest strength outside its limits. New York Jews have been concentrated in large numbers in New York City. Well-organized as religious groups, vocal in pursuit of the felt needs of their respective faiths, and fiercely protective of what each has deemed its vital interests, the three major denominations have constituted a political factor that had to be dealt with.[93]

[91] *Ibid.*, pp. 7, 39, 60–63. [92] Moscow, p. 12.

[93] Zeller, *Pressure Politics*, p. 5 and n. 12; Munger and Straetz, pp. 37–38, 48–49, table on p. 37. On the interesting institution in New York of the religiously and ethnically "balanced ticket," see Caldwell, pp. 36–37; Moscow, pp. 15, 19–20, 44–45, 84–85. Ticket balancing typifies one side of the approach to church-state politics in New York.

Another illustration can be seen in an exchange on the floor of the state Senate, March 21, 1960, during debate on a bill to amend the bus transportation law covering nonpublic school children. One opponent of the change saw it as upsetting "a delicate balance we have reached

But while organized religious groups have exerted pressures on government, these frequently have been contrary pressures. The major parties cannot afford to turn their backs either on sectarian demands for change or on pressures for maintaining the *status quo*. For example, large numbers of Protestants and Roman Catholics, and some Jews, have been unhappy with the lack of religious training in the public schools, while some groups speaking for the Jewish community have been quite content with the situation. As members of the smallest of the three main denominations in New York, many Jews feel that religious exercises in the schools will be insensitive and possibly dangerous to their minority beliefs. But the advocates of religious instruction were persistent. The political machinery of New York, attuned to respond when wide-spread sentiment appears to have coalesced, began to move in the direction of providing some form of religious education. Yet the requirements of statewide politics, which have given to the New York City Jewish minority great weight in the calculations of both major parties, induced the political leadership in Albany and in the city to write careful minority safeguards into their plans. The result, as we have seen, was the released time program. And because each sect, as well as most other interested parties in this area, are minorities, there has been wide agreement among politicians that this in general is the most realistic way of dealing with church-state questions that arise inevitably from the very nature of our society.

These, then, have been the political realities of contemporary church-state relations in New York. With the national

---

between conflicting points of view." Another said the bill "may substitute something unworkable for something workable" (*New York Times*, Mar. 22, 1960). The rhetoric is significant, coming as it does from opponents of this particular measure. It is the language of balancing and accommodation. Behind it lies much of the spirit that gives rise to the New York style for confronting and resolving the difficult problems of church and state in our time.

penchant for clothing such plain facts in the garb of high principle—a tendency it might be added which has often been a salutary and uplifting one in our history—New Yorkers have attributed the "nay saying" decisions of this political process to the operation of the principle of church-state separation. On the other hand, results of the process which have led to a conformance of governmental functions to the demands of religious sentiment, people have preferred to characterize as beneficent recognition of the free exercise of religion—unless they could justify these results in terms of motives other than religious, as bus transportation for parochial students has been justified as a child welfare benefit.

Epilogue

THE era in our history when church-state questions were primarily the concern of state and local governments is now drawing to a close. Increasingly, church-state matters are becoming federal questions as the three branches of the national government involve themselves in problems which historically have been the spawning grounds of church-state controversies. One of the most obvious contemporary instances of this is the expanded activity of the federal government in the field of education. With passing time, Americans can anticipate that as concerns of this kind, once regarded to be purely local in nature, become objects of attention from the federal government, the focus of attention in church and state will also be drawn to the national level.

There have been three major recent developments heralding this greater involvement of the federal government in problems pregnant with meaning for the relations of church and state. To New Yorkers, probably the most apparent of these developments has been the evolution of the United States Supreme Court as the ultimate authority on proper church-state relations across the country. Having somewhat less immediate consequences for local church-state arrangements, but destined to pose far-reaching challenges to these arrangements, is the policy embodied in the federal Elementary and Secondary Education Act of 1965. Finally, reapportionment of state legislatures, as ordered and enforced by the federal courts, promises over the near future to reshape the political context which in the recent past has had so determinative an influence upon the treatment of church-state issues in New York.

In 1940 the Supreme Court ruled explicitly that the First Amendment clauses of the Bill of Rights proscribing federal actions "respecting an establishment of religion, or prohibiting the free exercise thereof," applied equally to state actions through the provisions of the Fourteenth Amendment.[1] In a series of landmark decisions since then, the Court has proceeded to spell out in broad fashion what the First Amendment restrictions on state action mean in detail.[2] The attitude of the Court toward the establishment clause of the First Amendment has particular relevance for New York, for it has been through this clause that Supreme Court rulings have had their greatest impact upon the Empire State. The position of a majority of the Court has tended to follow the large view,

[1] *Cantwell* v. *Connecticut*, 310 U.S. 296 (1940).

[2] The free exercise of religion clause in the First Amendment received considerable attention from the Court in the so-called "Jehovah's Witnesses" cases beginning with *Cantwell*. Others in this line of cases were *Minersville School District* v. *Gobitis*, 310 U.S. 586 (1940); *West Virginia State Board of Education* v. *Barnette*, 319 U.S. 624 (1943); the two decisions in *Jones* v. *City of Opelika*, 316 U.S. 584 (1942), and 319 U.S. 105 (1943); *Murdock* v. *Commonwealth of Pennsylvania*, 319 U.S. 105; *Douglas* v. *City of Jeannette*, 319 U.S. 157 (1943); and *Prince* v. *Commonwealth of Massachusetts*, 321 U.S. 158 (1944). Also see *United States* v. *Ballard*, 322 U.S. 78 (1944); and *Girouard* v. *United States*, 328 U.S. 61 (1946). The foregoing cases, and most of those listed below are conveniently collected for the layman in Joseph Tussman, ed., *The Supreme Court on Church and State* (New York, 1962).

The First Amendment's establishment clause has been interpreted in another series of cases over this same general time span. See: *Everson* v. *Board of Education*, 330 U.S. 1 (1947); *Illinois ex rel. McCollum* v. *Board of Education*, 333 U.S. 203 (1948); *Zorach* v. *Clausen*, 343 U.S. 306 (1952); *Engel* v. *Vitale*, 370 U.S. 421 (1962); *Abington Township* v. *Schempp*, and *Murray* v. *Curlett*, 374 U.S. 203 (1963).

sometimes called the absolute view, of Justice Hugo Black, first stated in the Everson case, the New Jersey school busing decision of 1947:

> Neither a state nor the Federal Government can set up a church. Neither can pass laws which aid one religion, aid all religions, or prefer one religion over another. Neither can force nor influence a person to go to or to remain away from church against his will or force him to profess a belief or disbelief in any religion. No person can be punished for entertaining or professing religious beliefs or disbeliefs, for church attendance or non-attendance. No tax in any amount, large or small, can be levied to support any religious activities or institutions, whatever they may be called, or whatever form they may adopt to teach or practice religion. Neither a state nor the Federal Government can, openly or secretly, participate in the affairs of any religious organizations or groups and *vice versa.* In the words of Jefferson, the clause against establishment of religion by law was intended to erect "a wall of separation between church and State." [3]

Actually, New York has not fared so badly at the hands of a Court attuned to church-state issues. The Everson decision had the effect of validating the New York law permitting the public transportation of nonpublic school children. In 1952, the Supreme Court upheld New York's released time program of religious instruction for public school children in the case of *Zorach* v. *Clausen.*[4] Only in the instance of the Regents Prayer, struck down by the Court in the 1962 case of *Engel* v. *Vitale,*[5] has a New York church-state arrangement failed of acceptance on appeal to the Supreme Court of the United States.

But the real significance for New York in the Court's new role does not arise from rulings in specific cases. Rather, it lies in the fact that the resolution of church-state conflicts no longer turns on the operation of the political system in New

[3] *Everson* v. *Board of Education,* 330 U.S. 1, at 15–16.

[4] 343 U.S. 306. [5] 370 U.S. 421.

York alone; the Supreme Court is now a decisive influence which must be taken into account. The Court, with its considerable power to allow or disallow church-state accommodations reached in New York, has become the key element in the process. Minority interests in the state that were obliged formerly to commit themselves on church-state issues to the give and take of local politics, no longer have a similar incentive to do so. Policies arrived at through this process, deemed unfavorable by such interests, may now be appealed to the federal courts with the great likelihood that the Supreme Court will grant redress where the complaining interests—as is often the case—are opposed to any form of church-state accommodation. The seemingly absolute view of the First Amendment religious clauses held by a current majority of the Court [6] has in turn encouraged those elements in the state who embrace the absolute "wall of separation" idea. The legal strategy of the plaintiffs and their counsel in the Regents Prayer case, *Engel* v. *Vitale*, is an illustration of this development.[7]

The federal Elementary and Secondary Education Act of 1965 represents a milestone in the evolution of federal-state relationships in public education. For the first time, the Congress and the president have fully committed the national government to a major program of direct support for elementary and secondary education. Growing demands for federal aid to education had been put off by Congress for several years in large measure because of Roman Catholic resistance

[6] I refer to the "seemingly absolute" view of the Court, for in the establishment cases at least, rather than following a thoroughly consistent line, the rulings of the majority have been far from consistent. *McCollum, Zorach,* and *Engel,* with *Everson* thrown in for good measure, considered together are important more for the range of interpretative tools and the reach which they give to the Court in establishment cases, than as being representative of an "absolute" view of the First Amendment.

[7] See Chapter 10, n. 79 above.

to grants for public school construction and teacher salaries where compensating assistance to parochial schools was not included. Recently, church spokesmen have acquired a harried and aggrieved tone as Catholic educators, like their public counterparts, have encountered imposing burdens on the parochial system arising from growing enrollments, inadequate space, and understaffed teaching faculties. Francis Cardinal Spellman of New York, perennial advocate of public support for parochial education, reflected this increased concern of American Catholics in a draft amendment presented to the Ecumenical Council at Rome in November 1964:

> Parents should be free to choose the schools they wish for their children. They should not in consequence of their choice be subject to unjust economic burdens which would infringe upon this freedom of choice. Since it is the function of the state to facilitate civil freedoms, justice and equity demand that a due measure of public aid be available to parents in support of the schools they select for their children.
>
> Moreover, if these schools serve the public purpose of popular education, the fact that they may be religious in their orientation should not exclude them from a rightful measure of public support.[8]

The new education law was devised to overcome Catholic opposition to federal aid for public schools while offering as narrow a front as possible for the attack from strict separationists that is anticipated in view of the law's inclusion of parochial school children. The act, as constructed by President Lyndon Johnson and his advisers, in the words of one observer was "carefully tailored to skirt the church-state issue."[9] Abandoning the general school aid approach, Title I of

[8] *New York Times,* Nov. 18, 1964. Also see the sympathetic review of the Catholic school position in Carl N. Degler, "Aid for Parochial Schools—A Question of Education, Not Religion," *New York Times Magazine,* Jan. 31, 1965, p. 11.

[9] The observation was made by *Times* reporter Marjorie Hunter in *New York Times,* Jan. 2, 1965.

the act creates an extensive grant program to enrich the education of disadvantaged children both in public and parochial schools. Title III provides for shared-time arrangements under which public and parochial school children will share the facilities of federally financed centers for training in special subjects. In Title II, library services to parochial students will be supported by federal moneys.[10] Obviously, these provisions of the act are intended to relieve some of the financial pressures on Catholic parents and yet avoid the prohibitions of the First Amendment establishment clause. The law extends aid not to institutions but to individual school children with need being defined as the criterion for such help. Presumably a program of federal aid to education so constructed was meant to pass the test of constitutionality in the courts on the church-state issue by relying on the currently acceptable "child benefit" concept.[11]

While it is still too early to tell, the Elementary and Secondary Education Act of 1965 may very well reopen controversy between Catholics and non-Catholics in New York. The availability of federal grants offers to New York Catholics a means of circumventing the prohibition in the state constitution on state or local appropriations to schools under denominational control dating back to 1894. Given the presence of growing economic pressures on Catholic parents obliged to support two school systems, the public and parochial, there will be compelling reasons for Catholics to turn away from the church-state settlement worked out in New York since the 1890's. Catholic acceptance of this compromise, as far as it encompassed the prohibition on public subsidies for parochial education, has never been, and by the very nature of the Catholic position could not have been, an acceptance in principle. Instead it has reflected a pragmatic

[10] The act, Public Law 89–10, is at 79 *U.S. Statutes at Large*, 27; see also *New York Times*, Jan. 13, 1965.

[11] *Ibid.*; see also in *ibid.* items of Feb. 3, March 25 and 26, and April 10, 1965 dealing with the aid to education act.

realization of the impossibility of securing such aid. Thus New York may be confronted with weakening Catholic attachments to the existing process for working out church-state problems at the state level as the church turns to a more accessible federal government for assistance long foreclosed to it by the state constitution.

That this is a by no means fanciful prospect, there is the evidence of a recent opinion from the state Education Department commenting on the provisions of the Elementary and Secondary Education Act applying to shared-time arrangements. It was the considered opinion of the department's chief counsel that school districts in receipt of funds under the federal program could avoid the proscriptions of the state constitution on expenditures for private school children by keeping those funds strictly separate from state and local moneys. School boards would then employ only federal money to finance shared time. "The teachers thus employed," the counsel stated, "could be assigned to teach anywhere in the school district, including sectarian schools." [12] Should this actually occur, the "school question" supposedly settled in 1894 may well be reopened to the great detriment of the amicable spirit in church-state relations developed over the intervening years.

Reapportionment of the New York State legislature, following from decisions of the United States Supreme Court and lower federal court orders compelling redistricting and advancing the "one man, one vote" principle, poses a challenge of a different kind for the relations of church and state in New York.[13]

Reapportionment of the New York legislature is still in

[12] "State Rules Schools May Use U.S. Funds for Parochial Aid," news story datelined Albany, *ibid.*, July 27, 1965.

[13] The controlling line of Supreme Court decisions here includes *Baker* v. *Carr*, 369 U.S. 186 (1962); *Reynolds* v. *Sims*, 377 U.S. 533 (1964); and the case in which the holding in the Reynolds case was specifically applied to New York: *WMCA, Inc.* v. *Lomenzo*, 377 U.S. 633 (1964).

process. But at this writing, the former system of 1894 has been swept away. Events are moving in the direction of an apportionment scheme devised to give the Democratic party a much better chance of winning legislative majorities in any given election.[14] What this will mean for the conduct of New York politics is still uncertain, but the guess may be hazarded that reapportionment will reduce the importance of statewide contests by restoring competition to elections for control of the legislature. In a setting where purely local factors will carry more weight than formerly, the governors of New York are likely to become the hapless victims of growing demands for services offset by bitter resistance to rising taxes, and of localistic legislative blocs. There are already signs of such a development.

It is not inconceivable that as local issues increasingly compete for attention with state issues at the vortex of the party struggle, the enlarged direction given to New York public life by the necessities of gubernatorial politics will be weakened by a particularism long present both upstate and in the metropolitan area. Hitherto, this particularism has been held in relative check by the imperatives of the contest for statewide political office. One effect of such a change could be to remove the present incentives for party leaders to keep Catholic and Jewish opinion, concentrated downstate, and Protestant opinion, centered upstate, in reasonable working harmony. The really important consideration here, however, is that the initiative for setting the future course of politics in the Empire State will henceforth be shared with federal courts operating from a different set of premises than those operative in New York politics since the turn of the century.

Whatever the precise nature of church-state relations in the future, there will be little use in bemoaning the fact of change,

[14] The New York reapportionment hassle can be followed at great length in the files of the *New York Times* for the months April to July 1965 and the opening months of 1966.

for indeed it is already upon us. An older order in which affairs of church and state were matters primarily for the attention of local and state governments is passing. A new order, in which the treatment of church-state problems is more and more dependent upon the interplay of interests and the operation of institutions at the national level, and—in the cases of issues like birth control—even upon international considerations, is taking the place of the old. That older order, evolving in reaction to the bitter clash of ideas and emotions in the nineteenth century, brought comparative peace and amity to the relations of church and state in New York. It did so because the people responsible for constructing it recognized that the principles of religious liberty and church-state separation are useful and necessary guides to decision, not ends in and of themselves. Experience taught them the risks lurking in too exclusive a regard for principle at the expense of a feeling for the problems which principle was intended to help resolve. By this is meant the knowledge that American concepts of separation and of religious liberty have derived not so much from the natural rights philosophy of the eighteenth-century American Enlightenment, as from a rather matter-of-fact discovery. This was the discovery that a society which, at once, had so much to promise and such great sectarian diversity could not hope to achieve the former if deflected by contention arising from the latter. Ideas of separation and of religious liberty were means to avoid such contention so destructive of a body politic.

Whether the federal government repeats past errors committed in the name of church-state separation, or instead profits from the more recent experience of states like New York in managing its church-state problems, nevertheless we can be sure that these difficult and vexing problems will continue to arise. They will do so as long as the vast majority of the nation's people continue their attachments both to religious sentiment and to the American dream of progress through unity. Alexander M. Bickel of the Yale Law School offers a very wise observation:

> No society, certainly not a large and heterogeneous one, can fail in time to explode if it is deprived of the arts of compromise, if it knows no way of muddling through. No good society can be unprincipled; and no viable society can be principle-ridden. But it is not true in our society that we are generally governed wholly by principle in some matters and indulge a rule of expediency exclusively in others. There is no such neat dividing line. . . . Most often . . . , and as often as not in matters of the widest and deepest concern . . . , both requirements exist most imperatively side by side: guiding principle and expedient compromise. The role of principle, when it cannot be the immutable governing rule, is to affect the tendency of policies of expediency.[15]

It has been neither an indication of ignorance and moral flabbiness, nor evidence of the decline of our constitutional liberties, that New York's leaders have assigned such a role to principle in church-state matters. Certainly, it is not an insignificant role. Life has never been so simple that even the most noble and unvarying principles could relieve us of the necessity for choice.

[15] A. M. Bickel, *The Least Dangerous Branch: The Supreme Court at the Bar of Politics* (Indianapolis, 1962), p. 64.

Bibliographical Note

THE most extensive body of materials used in this study are public documents published by, or under the auspices of, the state of New York. For the colonial period, there are important works like E. B. O'Callaghan and B. Fernow's *Documents Relating to the Colonial History of the State of New York*, 15 vols. (Albany, 1853–87); and E. T. Corwin, ed., *Ecclesiastical Records of the State of New York*, 7 vols. (Albany, 1901–16). Both sources have a great deal of information for the student of early church-state relations in New York.

In the statehood period, there are excellent printed series of legislative journals and documents, session laws, and court reports, each of which contains revealing data bearing on church-state controversies and accommodations. By far the most useful of the public documents are the published records of the periodic state constitutional conventions dating back to the first in 1777. Since the early nineteenth century, these conventions have been meeting every twenty to thirty years to revise the state's basic law. They have been major forums both for the airing of church-state problems and for working out solutions to them.

Editions of local public documents, local histories, and printed church records have helped me to fill out details of the story at key points. I have also gone to both manuscript and printed papers of public men when further information was needed to clarify important events, particularly political developments. Here, the results were somewhat mixed. The John Jay Papers and the De Witt Clinton Papers at Columbia University, for example, contain virtually nothing on the politics of church and state in which these men were involved. On the other hand, the Thurlow Weed Papers in the University of Rochester had several important items, while the Frederick W. Holls Papers, Columbia University, contained an unexpected treasure of "inside" information. Frederick J. Zwierlein's editions of the Corrigan and McQuaid letters were among the more useful printed collections that I consulted.

For the nineteenth century, there is a considerable body of pamphlet and periodical literature—both sectarian and political in origin—which throws much light on attitudes toward specific church-state issues. The New York Public Library has an especially good collection of these materials.

Both the secular and the religious press of the last century were very important sources. Journals such as the *Albany Argus* and the New York *Christian Advocate* offer much evidence of opinion among particular groups. Quite by chance, I came across an amazingly comprehensive collection of periodical material in the library of the Harvard Divinity School, the Elizabeth C. Putnam Collection. This consisted of a large box of clippings systematically gathered from most of the leading secular and religious journals across the country dealing with the school question in the early 1890's.

In this century, there is one newspaper that has been a major source for information on church-state developments, the *New York Times*. For a number of years now, the *Times* has had probably the best staff of state and metropolitan reporters in New York. Moreover, the obvious editorial interest of the *Times* in church-state questions has keyed its reporters to issues arising in this area. It truly fulfills its claim to be a newspaper of record in its church-state coverage.

Finally, there were the many monographs treating special aspects of the subject that were indispensable to my work of synthesis. There are too many of them to single out more than a few here; my footnotes, however, bear ample testimony to my great reliance upon them. Because of their special contribution to our understanding of church-state politics in New York, Edward M. Connors, *Church-State Relationships in Education in the State of New York* (Washington, D.C., 1951); David M. Schneider and Albert Deutsch, *History of Public Welfare in New York State*, 2 vols. (Chicago, 1938–41); and Charles Z. Lincoln, *Constitutional History of New York*, 5 vols. (Rochester, N.Y., 1906), all deserve special mention. Connors had the added value to me of having had access to archival materials of the Roman Catholic Archdiocese of New York while researching his book. His study presented material that I was able to examine in no other way.

Index